KU-022-911

Contents

Preface

IF newspapers – as Francis Williams so famously once said – 'indicate more plainly than anything else the climates of the societies to which they belong', then they should act as a perfect barometer for judging prevailing attitudes to homosexuality. By listening to what the newspapers are saying, we can hear what the Great British public thinks about lesbians and gay men. Or can we? If what is written about homosexuals in tabloid newspapers is a reflection of how gay people are regarded in modern Britain, then we are in big trouble. So extreme is the hatred, so intense the contempt that emanates from the pages of the popular press that it is sometimes frightening to behold. Are the British public really full of such seething disgust for homosexuals?

As the popular press's aggression has intensified, violence in the streets has increased. It could be argued, of course, that the violence might have been provoked by the success and unprecedented visibility of the gay community. The tabloids certainly like to justify their hostility with the cry that gays provoke homophobia by their 'hysterical' demands and by their 'flaunting'. When Peter Tatchell complained to the editor of *The People*, Richard Stott, about offensive anti-gay remarks made by one of his columnists, Mr Stott replied:

> Neither John Smith nor this newspaper objects to or criticises homosexuals for being homosexual. What is criticised – and is reasonably criticised – is the desire of certain homosexuals to make an unnecessary public statement about their sexual inclination.[1]

Lethal thoughts

We know there are elements in this country who would like to eradicate homosexuality if they could. They have said so. They are not just the far-right neo-Nazi activists, either, but respected religious people and politicians, statesmen and stateswomen as well as 'housewives'. One woman was quoted in *The Independent on Sunday* as saying that 'homosexuals should all be sent to an island and shot',[2] while another wrote to *The Daily Express* that: 'The homosexuals who have brought this plague [AIDS] upon us should be locked up. Burning is too good for them. Bury them in a pit and pour on quick lime.'[3] A headline in a 1987 edition of *The Chester Mail* read: 'Execute gays says pastor', while the press gleefully reported the leader of South Staffordshire council, a Councillor Bill Brownhill, opining of homosexuality that: 'It's disgusting and diabolical. As a cure I would put 90 per cent of them in the ruddy gas chambers. Are we going to continue letting these queers trade their filth up and down the country?'[4] These murderous thoughts perhaps represent only the extreme end of some people's feelings, but there is undoubtedly a deep and abiding level of homophobia in every stratum of British society. And yet, as the general approach to gay people slowly, but perceptibly, begins to soften, there is also a noticeable change in the attitudes of broadsheet newspapers (termed 'posh' by those who prefer the merry violence of the tabloids). The serious press can no longer take for granted that there is universal condemnation of homosexuality among its readers and has had to recognize that the routine abuse, calculated exclusion and high-minded dismissal that they previously applied to gay matters is no longer sufficient. Major General Bigot-Smythe is not any more the representative reader of *The Daily Telegraph*. If traditionally reactionary newspapers are to survive, they have to come to terms with a younger and better-informed audience. Younger people have gay friends whom they refuse to dismiss out of hand or see reviled by newspapers. The appearance of AIDS has had something to do with this change, too, but it was more than just a medical emergency that jolted the complacency; the serious press in Britain are reflecting a seismic shift in social attitudes among its readers. The traditional silence on homosexuality is no longer an option.

If it is accepted that newspapers reflect, rather than create, society's opinions then it could be argued that in this book I am 'shooting the messenger'. Are newspapers really to blame if they simply tell us what the person in the street is thinking – thoughts that might not be pleasant to hear? My years of observation lead me to believe that newspapers are not simply messengers, they are not merely the conduit for information and news; they are organs of dictated opinion.

However, the area in which the press have proved more than anywhere else that they are not simply messengers but malevolent creators of the message is that of HIV and AIDS. Since the pandemic began, the British popular press have made a conscious choice to sensationalize – and thereby trivialize – an enormous tragedy; the sickening use of a fatal and debilitating disease as a weapon to hit at those they disapprove of has been nothing less than disgraceful. It is unforgivable that people already afflicted by serious illness should be further pilloried for their sexuality, then blamed for their condition. This is not the message, it is a *version* of the message – a deliberately distorted, biased, and unfair version. The tabloid press – and sometimes the broadsheets, too – have originated material that had no purpose but to bring obloquy to homosexuals and thereby feed homo-hatred. They have done this persistently for all the time that I have been looking at the papers in detail. The amount of negative copy relating to homosexuality that the British press have originated is absolutely enormous and most of it could hardly be described as 'news' in the sense that it had any importance outside the lives of those directly concerned. How can the revelation of a completely private individual's sexuality be described as 'of public interest'? It may be 'of interest to the public', but that is a different matter entirely. Nor was it accidental that newspapers assembled a coterie of otherwise obscure back-bench MPs who would be on hand at all times to provide quotes supporting the anti-gay slant of the stories chosen by the tabloids. This is a symbiotic relationship: publicity-hungry minor parliamentarians get their name in mass-market tabloids, and the right-wing press have apparently authoritative support for their extremist agenda. The quotes are often conjured up in advance by the journalist in order to fit his story; he or she then calls the MP and asks: 'Do you think it is absolutely disgusting that public money is being squandered on a filthy and degenerate way of life?' The MP simply replies: 'Yes, I do'. The journalist has the quote, the MP has the publicity and the gay community has yet another insult to add to its collection. The name of these MPs are mentioned many times in this book, but without honour.

What you will read in the following pages represents only a tiny fraction of what the newspapers have written about homosexuality over the past decade. During that time some newspapers have begun to report the gay struggle, reporting it fairly and objectively. Other papers continue to pour hate, spite and abuse on the heads of gay people.

So has the messenger been unjustly blamed?

Notes

1. Letter to Peter Tatchell, 10 July 1990.
2. February 1994.
3. 13 December 1986.
4. December 1986.

Note on Terminology

IT would be misleading to talk about 'the press' as though all newspapers were alike, but to make the book easier to read, I have categorized some newspapers which I believe have common characteristics. For clarity, I have defined these terms here.

By 'tabloid' or 'popular' or 'yellow press', I mean: *The Sun*; *The Daily Star*; *The Daily* and *Sunday Express*; *Daily Mail* and *The Mail on Sunday*; *Today*; *Daily* and *Sunday Mirror*; *The People*.

By 'quality' or 'broadsheet' or 'serious' press, I mean: *The Guardian*; *The Independent*; *The Independent on Sunday*; *The Daily* and *Sunday Telegraph*; *The Times* and *The Sunday Times*; *The Observer*.

By 'Conservative' or 'Tory' or 'right-wing press' I mean: *The Times* and *Sunday Times*, *The Daily Telegraph*, *The Sun*, *Daily Mail* and *The Mail on Sunday*; *Daily* and *The Sunday Express*.

By 'liberal press' I mean: *The Guardian*; *The Independent*; *The Independent on Sunday*; *The Observer*.

By 'non-Tory' press, I mean: *Daily Mirror*; *The Sunday Mirror*; *The People*; *The Independent*; *The Guardian*; *The Observer* and occasionally *Today*.

I have also used the term 'Fleet Street' to refer to the press as a whole. During the period that this book covers, all national newspapers have moved out of their traditional base in to more modern headquarters, many of them in the docklands area of London.

For more than twelve years I have been monitoring the British press's coverage of lesbian and gay issues in my *Mediawatch* column in *Gay Times*. Unfortunately, I did not apply dates to the quotations in the earlier columns. Where precise dates are not available for quotations cited in this book, I have tried, when practical, to indicate an approximate date.

Stop Press!

SINCE this book was completed, one of the most effective outing campaigns ever conducted by the British gay community was initiated by OutRage! (see Chapter 4). In November 1994, on the day of an important Anglican conference, members of OutRage! stood on the steps of Church House in London holding up placards naming ten Church of England Bishops as gay men. On 1 December *The Daily Telegraph* condemned the tactic as 'homosexual terrorism' and on the same day *The Guardian* said it was 'persecution by any other name' – even though *The Guardian* was one of only two newspapers to reproduce some of the names in its columns. The whole press erupted mightily once more over the legitimacy of outing, but their criticism, as before, seemed to centre almost entirely on the fact that power over who should be persecuted and who should be spared had suddenly slipped from their hands and into those of 'irresponsible' and 'cruel' gay activists.

There can be no doubt that these outings had a profound effect upon the hierarchy of the Church of England which promised that it would quickly reconsider its policy on homosexuality. However, church politicians said that behind-the-scenes negotiations would only take place on the understanding that there would be no more outing. *The Sunday Times* picked this up and reported (15 January 1995) that the Church was 'in peace talks with gays'.

The furore, however, was to re-emerge in March 1995 when the Bishop of London, David Hope, revealed that he had received a letter from OutRage! imploring him to come out – and do it with dignity. At a press conference the Bishop claimed that he had been pressurized by OutRage! into making a statement, and that his sexuality was 'a grey area'. Although the gentle and placatory letter that had been sent to the Bishop could hardly be interpreted as 'blackmail', that is how it was presented by an hysterical Fleet Street. The Bishop's claim that he was an innocent victim of intimidation prompted such massive coverage of the event that it finally gave outing a permanent place in the public consciousness.

The media coverage – which extended to many thousands of column inches and dozens of television features – aimed its fire almost entirely at Peter Tatchell and demonized him to the extent that his name seldom appeared without the addition of an insulting adjective ('odious', 'reptilian', 'disgusting' were just a few), with even *The Independent* and *The Guardian* joining in the hue and cry. Indeed, on this occasion outing became a broadsheet topic. The tabloids gave minimal coverage to events, while *The Times, Daily Telegraph, Daily Mail, Daily Express* as well as *The Independent* and *Guardian* devoted unprecedented coverage to the subject. Eventually, 156 Labour MPs signed an early day motion condemning OutRage!'s tactics, proving that the establishment was definitely discomfited.

Meanwhile, the tabloids' own outing agenda continues unabated. Commentators who are most vociferous in condemnation of the practice among gays seem blind to the activities of their fellow journalists. For the opinion formers, it is still a matter of tabloids can, but gays can't. The *News of the World*, for instance, carried a series of humiliating outings of clergymen during 1994 ('VICAR DUMPS WIFE FOR ROLLS WITH SANDWICH BOY'– 4 September; 'WE SNARE VICARS IN GAY VICE RING' – 30 October), while its sister paper, *The Sun*, continued outing gay people with AIDS ('PETER LILLEY NEPHEW IS DYING OF AIDS' – 19 January 1995). The panic-mongering over HIV also continued as more health workers were outed as having HIV or AIDS ('AIDS HUNT FOR 1,300 AFTER GAY DENTIST DIES' – *Daily Express*, 11 January 1995). In all cases, the sexuality of the person concerned became the central focus of the story. The underlying message was obvious: steer clear of gay health workers. (All this despite the fact that no-one has yet indisputably been shown to have been infected with HIV by a health worker.)

Terry Sanderson
March 1995

Chapter one

The Generations of Silence

To get into the news you have to be or do something newsworthy. To become feature material, your subject has to be worth talking or writing about at some length, photographed and recorded. If you meet these obligations, there is no reason at all nowadays why you should not get coverage, though, of course, there is no guarantee that the coverage you might get is precisely the sort of coverage you want. Such is journalism.

● *Gays in Media Bulletin, 1979*

FROM the beginning, some of the angriest campaigns in the gay struggle have been about the denial of media space to gay voices. In 1982, Andrew Lumsden – at the time the editor of *Gay News* – was complaining about the exclusion of directly expressed homosexual opinion from the press in Britain. In its tenth anniversary issue, *Gay News* carried an editorial which expressed his frustration felt at this carefully maintained exclusion.

A free press they say is the greatest defence against tyranny. There is no freedom of the press in this country for homosexuals. Apply a simple test: who can you think of who writes for the quality or popular press, whenever it would be relevant, as an out gay? If people cannot be open about their homosexual viewpoint to the same degree that heterosexual writers are about their viewpoint, then a significant section of opinion finds no expression in Britain's 'free press' and that press is not free.[1]

Although by 1982 homosexuality was far from being unmentionable in the press, serious representation was scattered and infrequent. Coverage tended to be polite to the point of patronization in the liberal papers and mostly hostile in the populars. Gay events and opinions were certainly being covered in the papers but they were overwhelmingly filtered through straight journalists. We were written *about* rather than being allowed to speak for ourselves. An example of this was *The Sunday Mirror*'s two-page feature article headed 'The gay explosion'.[2] Although gay people were interviewed (including Monty Python's Graham Chapman, and Roland Jeffrey, secretary of Friend) their words were only quoted and control of how this increasing gay visibility was ultimately presented remained with the journalists, editors and sub-editors. Meanwhile, in the conservative broadsheets, the word 'gay' had been appearing in headlines (often in quotation marks) since the mid-1970s.

There had been spurts of interest previously, of course, particularly at the time of the Wolfenden Report and during the passing of the Sexual Offences Act of 1967. But until Gay Liberation arrived, the Victorian opinion that homosexuality was not a topic for civilized debate was still as widespread in Fleet Street as it was throughout the whole of society. Indeed, during Parliamentary debates in the early nineteenth century, the words 'buggery' and 'sodomy' were considered too outrageous even to utter, and so the acts were referred to as those 'not named among Christians' (even this was rendered in Latin – *inter Christianos nondenominandum* – so that the masses would have even less idea of what was being referred to). At this point perhaps we should take an historical digression to find out why homosexuality was, for so many years, just about invisible in the British press.

The Labouchere Amendment

Late at night on 6 August 1885, Henry Labouchere MP managed to persuade a sparsely attended House of Commons to accept an amendment to the Criminal Law Amendment Bill, which provided that 'any male person who, in public or private, commits, or is party to the commission of, or procures or attempts to procure the commission by any male person of any act of gross indecency with another male person, shall be guilty of a misdemeanour, and being convicted thereof shall be liable at the discretion of the courts to be imprisoned for any term not exceeding two years with or without hard labour'. It was a law which would claim many victims ('monstrous martyrdoms' as Oscar Wilde called them).

Coincidentally, Labouchere was himself a newspaper editor.[3] Little can he have known that his amendment – originally introduced as a cynical attempt to discredit the law – would provide his journalistic successors with thousands of column inches of scandalous copy. Nor could he have known – or probably cared – about the misery his legislation would bring to thousands of otherwise blameless men over the eighty-two years it remained unchanged. One of these victims was Oscar Wilde, whose prosecution and conviction for sodomy scandalized the whole country. It brought forward a new kind of contempt for a class of people who had previously been considered exotic and rare – homosexuals. As Richard Davenport-Hines wrote in his book *Sex, Death and Punishment*:

> The emergence of the identity of the modern homosexual is as contradictory a story as might be expected from its component parts. On the face of it, Labouchere's facetious amendment, the baleful fears implicit in degenerationist psychiatry, the insecurity of the British empire at its apogee, the crisis of the Wilde trials all combined to produce an outburst of projective hatred.[4]

The newspapers had a field day. As *The News of the World* said on 26 May 1895:

4: Mediawatch

The Wilde case is over, and at last the curtain has fallen on the most horrible scandal which has disturbed social life in London for many years . . . Society is well rid of these ghouls and their hideous practices . . . It is at a terrible cost that society has purged itself of these loathsome importers of exotic vice.

The London *Evening Standard* proclaimed on the day of Wilde's conviction:

England has tolerated the man Wilde and others of his kind too long. Before he broke the law of the country and outraged human decency he was a social pest, a centre of intellectual corruption. He was one of the high priests of a school which attacks all the wholesome, manly, simple ideals of English life . . . We venture to hope that the conviction of Wilde for these abominable vices, which were the natural outcome of his diseased intellectual condition, will be a salutary warning to unhealthy boys who posed as sharers of his culture.

Most newspapers had doubled their circulations by recounting the trial in lurid detail. The sanctimonious tone of the reports, coupled with their slavering reportage, echoes a style that is familiar to readers of modern tabloids. At the time, though, it had a profound effect, for while readers may have been fascinated by these reports of rent boys and artistic decadence, the Establishment was worried. As the 'two penny press' revelled in the vicarious disgust generated by the Wilde events, *The St James Gazette*, a London evening newspaper, alone decided it would not report details of the trial. Its editor, Sir Sidney Low, claimed he found the evidence 'repulsive' and so spared his readers the pain of enduring it. This desire to 'look away' was indicative, too, of Government thinking. Soon after the Wilde trial, there were calls for all public mention of homosexuality to be banned. In 1896, Lord Halsbury introduced into Parliament the Publication of Indecent Evidence Bill, which was specifically aimed at suppressing the reporting of prosecutions brought under the Labouchere amendment. 'The evil only existed in *cause celebres,*' Halsbury said, 'and the difficulty, danger and mischief arose when those cases were being heard, as the most minute and disgusting details of every part of the evidence were brought forward.' The Prime Minister of the day, Lord Salisbury, supported him, telling the House of Lords: 'It is a well ascertained effect that publication of court cases of that kind has a horrible, though undoubtedly direct action in producing an imitation of the crime. It is especially important that such matters should not be discussed by the man in the street, not to mention the boy and girl in the street.' They were not even to be considered, he said, by the scholar in his library.

After pressure from newspaper publishers and editors, the Bill was abandoned, but it was an indication of the prevailing opinion: homosexuality was not a fit topic for public discussion. Mention of it in newspapers only provoked more people – who would otherwise never have thought of it for themselves – to try it. This is a familiar argument even today from opponents of honest sex education.

The philosophy of silence permeated the whole of society. Havelock Ellis's study *Sexual Inversion* was hidden from users of the British Museum Library by being excluded from the catalogue. Homosexuality had become a completely taboo subject, to be spoken about in only the most hushed and reluctant way. Newspapers continued to report trials and scandals, but only with severe disapproval and censure and employing an array of euphemisms penetrable only by the most worldly reader.

Such enforced silence about the existence of homosexuals had at least one positive effect: it prevented the criminalization of lesbianism. Proposed legislation to extend the Labouchere amendment to lesbians was brought forward in 1921 by a Scottish Tory MP, Frederick Macquisten. This was opposed, when it reached the House of Lords, by Lord Desart – who had been the Director of Public Prosecutions during the Wilde trial. He asked: 'How many people does one suppose are really so vile, so unbalanced, so neurotic, so decadent to do this?' He thought it would be a 'great mischief' to create an offence of 'gross indecency by females' because it would 'bring it to the notice of women who have never heard of it, never thought of it, never dreamed of it'. Lord Birkenhead, the Lord

Chancellor, said: 'I would be bold enough to say that of every thousand women, taken as a whole, 999 have never heard a whisper of these practices. Among all these, in the homes of this country . . . the taint of this noxious and horrible suspicion is to be imparted.' On this reasoning, the proposal was dropped.

And so 'the unspeakable crime', 'the love that dare not speak its name', 'the abominable vice', became totally unmentionable in any context other than abuse and condemnation. All attempts to break the taboo – such as the publication in 1928 of Radclyffe Hall's book *The Well of Loneliness* – were to end up in court or in public disgrace. Hall's book brought forth a positive orgy of self-righteousness from the press. *The Sunday Express* branded it 'an intolerable outrage' and in an editorial attack said: 'The English people are slow to rise in their wrath and strike down the armies of evil, but when they are aroused, they show no mercy.' Generations of homosexuals were doomed thereafter to see themselves portrayed in newspapers only as evil creatures to be despised and hated. Attempts at public self-expression were rare and, if they showed signs of succeeding, were crushed with all the might the Establishment – particularly the press establishment – could muster.

The if-we-don't-talk-about-it-they-won't-think-of-it theory held firm – with very few exceptions – until 1948 when, in America, the sex researcher Alfred Kinsey caused great consternation with the publication of his report suggesting that homosexuality was much more widespread than most people were prepared to concede. From interviews with twelve thousand people, he had concluded that as many as 4 per cent of them had mainly or exclusively homosexual preferences. His report had been preceded by much other medical and scientific research which had resulted in a 'medical model' of homosexuality. It was, by then, acceptable in some circumstances to describe homosexual people in pathological rather than moralistic terms. The explanation of homosexuality as a psychopathic condition made referring to it a little easier and reaction to it just a mite less fierce. This glimmer of a change in understanding was not, however, much reflected in newspapers. *The News of the World* was still scouring the country's Crown Courts for cases involving homosexuals, but these were reported with the use of coded terms such as 'improper behaviour' and 'unnatural practices' in order to justify using the stories and to avoid having to describe the sex acts involved. None the less, judging by the huge numbers of arrests that were taking place at the time, plenty of men were finding out about gay sex without the help of newspapers.

Police crackdowns on gay activities, and the attendant public humiliations, continued at a high level; but Kinsey had well and truly cracked the seemingly impenetrable edifice which prevented any serious discussion of homosexuality as a phenomenon beyond criminality. The editor of *The Thames Valley Times* recognized this shifting attitude, and was moved to write on 4 May 1949:

> It is a disease which cannot be easily eradicated, being driven deeper underground, perhaps when it becomes too blatant, but generally the efforts of the police can only result in a certain number of prosecutions driving more offenders to other places . . . The Victorian policy of pretending that unpleasant things do not exist is out of date and ineffective. They do exist, and are likely to become worse unless immediate action is taken.

The late 1940s and early 1950s brought not only a glut of 'importuning' ('cottaging') and indecency cases – gleefully and pruriently reported in the popular press – but also scandals involving homosexual murders and spy cases. By 1952, the editor of *The Daily Mirror*, Hugh Cudlipp, decided it was time to address the issue directly. He ran a series of articles under the heading 'Evil men' in the *Mirror*'s sister paper, *The Sunday Pictorial*:

> The natural British tendency to pass over anything unpleasant in scornful silence is providing a cover for an unnatural sex vice which is getting a dangerous grip in the country . . . a number of doctors believe that the problem would be best solved by making homosexuality legal between consenting adults. This solution would be intolerable – and ineffective. Because the chief danger of the perverts is the corrupting influence they have on youth. Most people know there are such things – 'pansies' – mincing, effeminate young men who call themselves queers. But simple decent folk regard them as

freaks and rarities . . . If homosexuality were tolerated here, Britain would rapidly become decadent.

In the same year, the paper also advised its readers on 'How to spot a homo' - implying such characteristics as 'dropped eyes', 'shifty glances', 'a fondness for the theatre' and a propensity for putting his hand on the shoulder of other men. The typical 'homo' was also, according to the article, likely to smoke a pipe and wear suede shoes.

Soon afterwards there were several widely reported indecency cases involving prominent people. Labour MP William Field was forced to resign his seat after being convicted of persistently importuning for immoral purposes. The author Rupert Croft-Brooke was found guilty of offences involving two young sailors. Then the actor Sir John Gielgud – only recently knighted – was fined for cottaging (his court appearance being reported on the front page of *The Daily Telegraph*). But the most sensational case was that of Lord Montagu of Beaulieu and the film director Kenneth Hume, who were charged with 'serious offences' involving boy scouts and, later, two airmen. In the light of such cases, it was becoming increasingly difficult to keep the topic of homosexuality out of sight. *The Sunday Times*, while generally contemptuous of 'inverts', managed to say about homosexuality, in an editorial prompted by the Montagu case: 'It is not, in the long term, a socially uncontrollable phenomenon. If, for some, perversion is an inherent and deep-rooted psychopathic state, for a greater number it is a tendency which can be resisted, sublimated or never awakened.'[5] *The News of the World*, on the same day, quoted judges as saying that the increasing number of cases of indecency between men was indicative of a trend towards 'moral decadence that is wholly regrettable'. *The Sunday Express*, meanwhile, declared that 'an emotional crusade' was developing 'to legalise perversion and even sanctify perverts'. The paper said:

STUFF AND NONSENSE. Perversion is very largely a practice of the too idle and the too rich. It does not flourish in lands where men work hard and brows sweat with honest

labour. It is a wicked mischief, destructive not only of men
but of nations.

As the Montagu case proceeded, the unfairness of much of the police
evidence, the means by which it had been obtained and the excessive
vilification of the men involved, was arousing sympathy and alarm,
rather than the intended revulsion. *The Sunday People* wrote that
the trial had: 'exposed the complete failure of our so-called
"civilisation" to find any remedy for sexual perverts to replace cruel
and barbaric punishment . . . society must realise that imprisonment
is no cure for abnormality'. This all led to calls in Parliament for
some kind of enquiry into the laws relating to homosexuality, and
eventually the Wolfenden Report was commissioned. When it was
published in 1957, the Victorian conspiracy of silence was broken
for ever. Suddenly the papers were discussing every aspect of the
Committee's findings – and on their front pages. Many of them
supported Wolfenden's call for a change in the law. *The Times* said:
'Adult sexual behaviour not involving minors, force, fraud or public
indecency belongs to the realms of private conduct and not of the
criminal law.' *The Daily Mirror* thought it a 'sensible and responsible report'. (In the fortnight after the report was published, the
Mirror devoted 963 column inches to the subject of homosexuality.
In the third week there were forty-three inches. After that, silence
reigned once more, proving that old habits die hard.) *The Manchester Guardian*, *The Observer* and *News Chronicle* were welcoming
of the report, with few reservations. Despite this, even the supportive papers agreed that the application of the proposed changes
would be difficult and would result in opposition.

That opposition came from all the predictable places:
'Homosexual vice – or weakness – is so abhorrent to normal minds
that public opinion will be slow to accept such a change' said *The
Daily Herald*, while *The Daily Express* thought that the Home
Secretary should tear the report up as it was 'his duty to see that
family life remains protected from these evils'. The paper considered
that the law needed 'stiffening' not relaxing. *The Daily Mail* judged
that 'the proposals to legalise degradation in our midst' would lead
to the fall of the Empire. The *Evening Standard* went further, when it
said: 'On no account must the Wolfenden recommendations be

implemented. They are bad, retrograde and utterly to be condemned.' *The Sunday Express* called the report 'the pansies'
charter', while *The News Chronicle* commissioned a Gallup poll
which indicated that 38 per cent of the population favoured change,
while 47 per cent did not.

It was to be another ten years before the law was reformed,
and when the time came, *The Daily Telegraph* said:

> It will end a law that is equally disreputable for being largely
> unenforceable and often cruel where enforced; it will shift a
> great fear from many people, no more sinful than most of
> their neighbours; it will cut the blackmailer's income; not
> least it will end a controversy that has become unseemly and
> disproportionate, and rob homosexuality of the false gla-
> mour which always attaches to persecuted minorities.[6]

Only *The Daily Express* was unremitting in its opposition ('it does
not represent the views of the great majority of people in Great
Britain. They would reject it given the opportunity'). But, of course,
even after the law was changed, public attitudes were not, and
neither was the approach of the tabloid press. The 'scandal' tag still
attached itself to everything that the newly liberated homosexuals
did. (After all, the law legalized sex only between consenting
civilians over the age of twenty-one in England and Wales.) Typical
of this approach was a story in *The Sunday People*, which was
reporting 'shocking practices' in a Midlands pub:

> The new law makes it quite clear that acts offending public
> decency will not be tolerated. It allows for stiff prison
> sentences for people who do not comply with it. But last
> week I witnessed conduct which I consider way beyond the
> bounds of decency. I saw men – dancing cheek to cheek to the
> sounds of a juke box. Kissing passionately on the dance floor
> and in secluded corners. Holding hands, petting and em-
> bracing unashamedly in the packed room . . . It's about time
> the authorities took some notice of the Crown and Anchor.
> It's about time, in fact, that the police put a stop to the odd
> goings on there.[7]

11: *The Generations of Silence*

All these developments had at last brought homosexuality out of the media closet, but even so, there remain even today editors and journalists who would prefer that the taboo had never been lifted. An editorial in *The Bucks Standard* on 1 March 1984 certainly gave the impression that a return to 'the good old days' would be welcome. After explaining that a 'very active homosexual lobby has been trying (not unsuccessfully) to persuade the general public to accept the relationship as a natural and public one' the editor went on to say:

> As a responsible and old established newspaper we know very well that homosexuals and homosexual activity exist in our area. We also know that the vast majority of our readership do not want to be subjected to the sort of propaganda we have mentioned. We say this because we have noticed that the letter pages and editorial columns of at least one of the free papers distributed locally are full of protests from the Milton Keynes homosexual community about the fairly well-proven connection between male homo-sexual activity and the killer disease AIDS. We do not question the right of any editor to open up his columns to the outcries of a minority (and frankly very frightened) group, but as far as this newspaper is concerned we propose to be selective in our comments and reporting of the more repellent activities which go on in the area that we cover.

In the spring of 1986, Max Hastings, editor of *The Daily Telegraph*, announced a redesign of the paper. In an editorial he reassured readers that although the look of the paper might be different, little else would change:

> *The Daily Telegraph*'s political commitment to the Conser-vatives as the only party currently fit to govern the country remains undiminished. So does the belief in traditional moral values. There will be no sudden discovery of enthusiasm for Gay Lib in the columns of the *Telegraph*.

And Paul Johnson began an article in *The Spectator* in February 1994 by saying: 'Nothing is more disagreeable than having to write about male homosexuality. The editor of the *Spectator* is not at all keen I should do so and I don't blame him.'

However, the passing of the 1967 Sexual Offences Act and the arrival of Gay Liberation from America in 1969 had shifted the focus significantly. Now that it was possible to acknowledge homosexuality in terms other than crime and degeneracy, gays did not want their lives to be presented completely through the eyes of straight journalists – who were at worst bigoted and at best uninformed: they wanted their own voices to be heard, telling their own stories without interpreters. The burgeoning gay community had already made a start on this ambition with the publication of an increasing number of books and pamphlets. This surge in gay publishing was explained by Alison Henegan (who was, at the time, literary editor of *Gay News*) in *The New Statesman*. She maintained that it had: 'sprung from one over-riding need: a hunger for truth after so many lies; and a determination that, having once found the truth, we would never again lose it to those with a vested interest in suppressing or controlling access to it'. To effect that change gays needed more direct access to the mass media. Andrew Lumsden's comments in *Gay News* indicated that, by the early 1980s, change was long overdue and its delay resented. He wrote again on the same topic in 1986:

> We have been put to a very particular servitude: 'we' lesbian and gay people, not lesbian and gay media employees, though the bulk of the latter are forcibly enslaved to passing as straight. We aren't regarded as existing in our own right. If we were there'd be 'out' reviewers, critics, interviewers and 'name' reporters scattered across the quality and popular media alike in rough proportion to the numbers of us in media employment. We are subject-matter, but are not, with the very rarest exceptions, permitted to be principals, writing or broadcasting in our own sexual persona. Journalistic objectivity is defined as the declared or taken-as-read hetero-sexual experience, 'Liberal' opinion, as in the *Guardian*, is that lesbians and gays should be spoken *for*; the fundamen-talist consensus, as in the *Spectator*, that lesbians and gays should be spoken *against*. There is so much speaking *against*

us and some speaking *for* us – arguments conducted entirely, across the spectrum of the media, as if between self-assured heterosexuals – that we are plainly useful for something.[8]

But gradually things began to change. Pressure was persistent from both without and within, and eventually the press became much more open to the opinions and happenings in the gay community. A special mention must be made here of Nicholas de Jongh, one of the first openly gay journalists to work on a national newspaper. His influence at *The Guardian* should not be underestimated.

However, the gay community's relationship with *The Guardian* has, over the years, been a stormy one. *The Guardian*'s offices have probably been picketed and occupied by gay protesters more often than any other paper in Fleet Street. One such demonstration was prompted by a major article by Rupert Haselden, a gay man living with AIDS, which was published on 7 September 1991. Haselden wrote that there is: 'an inbuilt fatalism to being gay. Biologically maladaptive, unable to reproduce, our futures are limited to individual existence and what the individual makes of it.' Haselden said that we waste our meaningless lives on a merry-go-round of promiscuous sex 'where AIDS dangles like flashing neon sign in the midst of the gay community becoming a metaphor for the self-destructiveness and self-indulgence that accompanies it'. The whole article was couched in this hopeless, passive style:

> All around friends, lovers and acquaintances are dying and we in turn prepare to make this supreme sacrifice. We are walking to the slaughter as stupidly as bullocks. Perhaps we have become fatalistic but there really isn't any choice. If there is, it's to sit at home and wait to die.

The publication of this article once more gave the opportunity for other papers to take up the anti-gay cudgels. *The Sunday Express* devoted a whole page to comment on the Haselden article, exhorting its readership to withdraw any residual sympathy it might have had for gay people on account of their apparently self-proclaimed irresponsibility.

Following the demonstration at the offices of *The Guardian*, the editor, Peter Preston, asked Nicholas de Jongh to suggest the names of some members of the gay community whom he could meet to listen to their complaints. The meeting was duly arranged and Preston took on board much of what was said by the protesters. Although he refused exhortations to send his journalists on gay awareness courses, he did admit in an interview in *The Sunday Telegraph* that he had made an error of judgement.

> Without being flip about it all, on the one hand it's being said that *The Guardian* has no readers left in the gay community because *The Independent* is now thought of as the gay community's newspaper. Others say that unless *The Guardian* thinks about these things more carefully then they will move on to *The Independent*.[9]

The threat was taken seriously and Preston made a conscious effort to improve *The Guardian*'s coverage of gay issues. The paper now frequently carries articles that would not disgrace the pages of a gay magazine. It commissions from openly gay writers – as do most of the other papers when the occasion demands it. For the most part, gay readers can buy *The Guardian* these days relatively safe in the knowledge that they will not be insulted by turning its pages.

However, the tabloid newspapers continue to blur the line consistently between fact and opinion. Denial of information, as well as its distortion, is an everyday tactic which many tabloid newspapers consider to be their 'right'. The democratic process – which newspapers claim themselves to be an essential element of – cannot be served unless all sides are given a fair hearing. Facts are sacred? In some tabloid newspapers they are a nuisance often dispensed with. Perhaps the reason for this was summed up by W. P. Hamilton who was a great believer in the freest of free markets. It was his opinion that newspapers have no 'duty' to society or anyone else. He wrote, in *The Wall Street Journal*: 'A newspaper is a private enterprise, owing nothing whatever to the public. It is therefore affected with no public interest. It is emphatically the property of the owner, who is selling a manufactured product at his own risk.' However Sir David Calcutt QC did not agree and observed in his second report on press self-regulation in 1993: 'All rights (including the right to manufacture and sell newspapers) carry responsibilities, especially when those exercising them have the potential to affect other people's lives.'[10] Despite the best efforts of newspapers to retard the development of the gay community, it is difficult to say whether they have succeeded. We will never know where that community might be now if the press has not been so implacable in its opposition.

Notes

1.   24 June 1982.
2.   27 March 1977.
3.   His paper was called *The Truth*.
4.   Fontana Books, 1990.
5.   1 November 1953.
6.   12 February 1967.
7.   24 March 1968.
8.   In an essay in *Bending Reality* (Pluto Press, 1986).
9.   22 September 1991.
10.   *Review of Press Self-Regulation*, Cm. 2135 (HMSO, London).

Chapter two

Loving Us and Loathing Us: TV Versus the Tabloids

THE first known British TV programme to tackle the subject of homosexuality directly was broadcast in 1954 when *In the News* included Lord Boothby discussing his demands for a Royal Commission to look at the laws relating to homosexuality. But it was not until 1957 that the first programme (*Homosexuality and the Law, a Prologue* produced by Granada) was entirely devoted to the subject. In 1964, the ITV current affairs programme *This Week* broadcast a documentary about the lifestyles of gay men but, because at the time homosexuality was still totally illegal, most of the participants were shown in silhouette. The broadcast caused a sensation, and the following year *This Week* followed it up with a programme about lesbians. *The Daily Express* – employing a tactic that was to become familiar over the years – feigned horror about this and forewarned its readers of the outrage to come. 'You still have time to keep this filth out of your living rooms!' it screamed on the day of the broadcast. The producers estimated that this display of tabloid righteousness provided the programme with an extra million viewers. It also caused columnists in *The Daily Mail*, *Evening Standard* and *Daily Mirror* to write pieces in support of law reform.

Throughout the 1970s, as sexual matters became generally more openly discussed, several other programmes addressed homosexuality directly. Little of this coverage was particularly positive (in fact, Caroline Spry, in her essay *Out of the Box*, describes it as 'bizarre and reactionary'), but it was important in that the long silence was being broken.

Gay activists, like everyone else, recognized TV's enormous power to influence change. And they knew that they would have to tap into it in order to counter effectively the widespread homophobia being exploited by the tabloids. Despite its many shortcomings, coverage of homosexuality on radio or TV has hardly ever been motivated by the hatred that seems to fuel that of mass circulation newspapers. Although there has been criticism of TV's portrayal of homosexuality – its stereotyping and 'arms length' approach – it has never displayed the level of sheer animosity that has been seen in the popular press. Sometimes TV's approach to gay subjects has been ill-judged and foolish, but hardly ever antagonistic and condemnatory. TV's speciality was, of course, exclusion. The fact that we had to wait until the mid-1950s before homosexuality was even mentioned on TV was indicative of the BBC's conservative values and the 'not to be talked about in polite company' policy. In the face of controversy, the broadcasting organizations in Britain have not always had the courage of their convictions. In early 1977, a Radio Four programme called *So You Think You've got Problems*, which tried to cover, in a balanced way, the topic of lesbianism, was arbitrarily banned by the station controller. Other programmes with gay themes that never saw the light of day included Thames Television's 1976 *Sex in Our Time: for Queer read Gay*; Southern Television's 1979/80 *Southern Report: Lesbians;* and a BBC 1986 *Horizon* programme on AIDS. However, as there is a great deal of wastage in TV production, we cannot automatically assume that dark motives were involved in the shelving of all of these programmes.

The Crezz, a Thames Television comedy-drama (1976), featured a gay couple in an episode unfortunately entitled *Bent Doubles*. Thames Television broadcast a dramatization of Quentin Crisp's autobiography *The Naked Civil Servant* on the network (1975) to general acclaim. In his exhaustive study of lesbian and gay broadcasting, Keith Howes described the showing of *The Naked Civil Servant* as 'a quantum leap'. He wrote: 'According to one survey by the Independent Television Authority, only 18 out of a sample of 475 viewers switched off because of the content. And 85 per cent said it was "not shocking".[1] In 1978 Thames Television showed *Gays: Speaking Up* – one of several documentaries in which gay people talked directly to camera about their lives. Homosexuals began to pop up in general programmes (such as *The London Weekend Show* – in which teenage gays talked about themselves. One of them was Tom Robinson, whose career was given a boost as a result). In 1980/81 London Weekend Television's London Minorities Unit produced a weekly late-night magazine series called *Gay Life* – which was the very first TV programme to be made especially for a gay audience in Britain. It went out at 11.30 on Sunday evening in the days before video recorders were generally available, ensuring that the audience never rose above 400,000. It was cancelled after two seasons.

There was some indirect and passing reference to homosexuality, much of it implicitly negative, and sitcoms such as *Are You Being Served?* still shamelessly peddled the image of effeminacy in gay men. But given the tens of thousands of hours of broadcasting, very little was actually given over to gay coverage of any kind. What coverage there was was generally unsatisfactory. The world was changing fast, and as James Baaden wrote in *High Risk Lives*:

> A new vision of lesbian and gay identity swept through the western world, replacing the pained terminology of penal law reform, abnormal psychology, mental illness, compassion, tolerance, isolation and anguish. Rights, liberty and equality came onto the agenda: lesbian and gay identity was celebrated; struggle and resistance replaced pleas for understanding.[2]

Gay Liberation was providing a new way of looking at homosexuality and gay people were anxious to see this 'new vision' on TV.

Pressure on broadcasters

Pressure was increasing on the broadcasting companies to improve their showing. In 1985 The Lesbian and Gay Broadcasting Project had monitored one week's output of the broadcasting media (except Radio Three) from 12 to 19 August to find out whether radio and television 'informs and educates about homosexuality in an impartial way'. The results were published in 1986 in a report entitled *Are We Being Served?* The researchers discovered that only a tiny amount of air time was given over to lesbian and gay representation. Out of eighty-eight hours of 'actuality broadcasting' (news and current affairs programmes) the 'total time of lesbian and gay representation as a percentage of total actuality broadcasting' was 1.85 per cent. The representation of lesbians during the monitoring period totalled 1 minute and 35 seconds. From these findings the report concluded:

> Whichever way you choose to look at it – and whichever way we present the information – it's clear that the proportion of lesbian/gay characters and issues (on television) is profoundly low. In entertainment broadcasting, eight and a half minutes out of 290 radio hours hardly registers as a significant statistic; it's 0.05%, which makes television's proportion, 4.5%, look massive. Both these figures can be used to illustrate the need for change. Measured against the true proportion of lesbians and gay men in society . . . even 4.5% is sadly lacking. And that was an exceptional week! Subtract the film *Victim* and 4.5% becomes 3.1%, or just over five and a half hours.
>
> Furthermore . . . only five representations (out of forty-five in total) were judged to be 'positive'. Our analysis confirms this by revealing that, on television at least, over 90% of characterisation amounts to two types: the criminal and the sissy.

This damning report was followed by a conference in London at which people prominent in the television industry were asked to explain the neglect of lesbian and gay lives. No representatives from the BBC attended, but Paul Bonner, then Channel 4's Programme Controller, said that he thought his channel's record on gay representation was good. He said that all programme makers were required to sign a contract with a non-discrimination clause, but this did not mean that they had to discriminate positively. Although other broadcasters were bound by law to ensure that there was 'balance' in programmes of a political or controversial nature, Channel 4 was required only to ensure that balance occurred over the whole output, not necessarily from programme to programme. Claire Mulholland of the Independent Broadcasting Authority said that the Authority was bound by statute to keep out of the schedules any programme which 'offended against good taste and decency' - and that charge often seemed to apply to programmes with gay relevance. She said that the IBA had done its own research into public attitudes as well as taking into account viewer reaction to programmes. This research indicated that there was still great resistance to portraying homosexuality as an ordinary aspect of life. She added that TV companies had been 'taken aback by the level of hostility' to the screening of an episode of *McMillan and Wife* as a tribute to Rock Hudson.

At the time of the conference, Winston Churchill MP was trying to introduce legislation into Parliament to amend the Obscene Publications Act so as to bring radio and TV within its scope – and using as justification the fact that Channel 4 had shown Derek Jarman's film *Sebastiane*. Even so, by the end of the conference, these broadcasting worthies were left in little doubt that the gay community felt neglected, marginalized and misrepresented on TV.

At about this time, the ethos of equal opportunities was beginning to permeate the BBC, as it was most large institutions, and more attention was being paid to the fairer representation of all sections of society. Channel 4, established in November 1982, had also shaken up the status quo. The Channel's remit was to ensure that its programmes 'contain a suitable proportion of matter calculated to appeal to tastes and interests not generally catered for by ITV'. The broadcasting bodies were also reminded of their obligations in a Government statement entitled *Broadcasting in Britain*:

Each authority provides its respective radio and television services as public services for the dissemination of information, education and entertainment. They must ensure that their programmes display, as far as possible, a proper balance and a wide range of subject matter, accuracy in news coverage, impartiality in matters of controversy, and also that programmes should not offend against good taste or decency, to be likely to encourage crime and disorder, or be offensive to public feeling.[3]

This statement is, of course, open to interpretation. The call for 'impartiality in matters of controversy' could well be seen as justification for more gay-oriented programmes, but equally, the demand that programmes should not 'be offensive to public feeling' gives a weapon to the tabloids and 'moral crusaders' in their assertion that homosexuality has no place 'in the living rooms of decent people' via their TV sets. For some people *any* mention of homosexuality – however fleeting – will represent a surfeit. Mary Kenny explained in *The Daily Mail* that she no longer watches television because she's afraid she'll catch sight of 'teenagers sprawled before the awesomely decadent, and wholly unfunny, Julian Clary, who seems like a character out of a movie about the decline of the Roman Empire, as interpreted by Fellini'.[4]

But despite this public reluctance, TV producers gradually accepted the validity of the complaints from gay people and responded with more and better air time. Gay characters appeared in most of the popular TV series (*Angels, Brookside, EastEnders, Casualty, The Bill, Medics* and *Emmerdale* – but not, significantly, in *Coronation Street* or *The Archers*). Then Channel 4 broke the mould completely by running a season of gay films (including *Mädchen in Uniform, Before Stonewall* and *The Life and Times of Harvey Milk*); it followed through by commissioning the first nationally networked lesbian and gay series, *Out on Tuesday*, from gay-run independent companies. The first edition went out on St Valentine's Day 1989 and since then several seasons of the show have been completed. A columnist in *The Worcester Evening News* greeted the programme with: 'What next? Can we look forward to special TV epics for paedophiles, necrophiliacs, pyromaniacs, sado-masochists, Satanists and sundry other freaks?'[5] The BBC, spurred into action, devoted six hours of one Saturday evening's BBC2 schedule to gay programming (*Saturday Night Out*).[6] Radio Four followed with a similar exercise (*Sunday Outing*),[7] about which Richard Ingrams in *The Observer* commented: 'There will be many regular Radio Four listeners whose inclination is thought to be tolerant and broad-minded, who will be irritated if not angered by what looks like a deliberate exercise in provocation.' In 1993 the BBC's Greater London Radio started a regular one-hour weekly magazine called *Lesbian and Gay London,* while in 1994 Radio Five broadcast a weekly half-hour news programme for the gay community – the run of which was extended after its initial season. In the face of this, the commentators in the straight press decided that making programmes especially for lesbians and gays was wrong for other reasons than 'morality'. When in February 1991 the BBC announced that it was to do some gay programming, it provoked Andrew Penman to write in *Today* that there would soon be 'a show for one-eyed Mexican dwarfs'. He mentioned *Brookside*'s and *EastEnders*' gay characters and said: 'Shows such as this portray gays as living in the same world as the rest of society, faced with many of the same problems – and a few more besides. This has to be better than dumping them in their own slot which everyone else can ignore.'

Despite these fears (and sometimes they seemed like the last, desperate throes of a defeated resistance), programmes of gay interest continued to pop up throughout the schedules, and there was certainly no indication that a gay broadcasting ghetto was being established. But the gay community is not complacent about this improvement in the range and frequency of gay-related programmes. There are still glaring omissions: homosexuality is still hardly ever mentioned in the major broadcast news programmes unless there is some major event which cannot be ignored, such as a change in the law. To point this up, the gay rights group OutRage! held a demonstration inside Broadcasting House to protest at – among other things – the BBC's poor record on reporting and representing gay life in current affairs programmes. The following day, OutRage member Peter Tatchell wrote to the head of publicity with a six-page list of complaints:

23: TV Versus the Tabloids

Your flagship current affairs programmes do not treat lesbian and gay rights as a serious human rights issue. They are constantly ignored. When did *Panorama* and *Newsnight* last do any substantial reports on the violations of lesbian and gay human rights? Why did the *Public Eye* programme have to pander to popular stereotypes by bringing in the totally irrelevant issues of cottaging and sex in the backrooms of Amsterdam bars? From 1986-90, at least 70 gay and bisexual men were murdered in Britain, many by queer-bashing gangs. Surveys show that 40 per cent of gay men and 25 per cent of lesbians have been victims of attacks motivated by anti-gay hatred . . . How many BBC programmes have their been about this monstrous scale of violence. Why did it take a mere 27 attacks on Jewish people in 1990 to (rightly) result in a series of programmes about anti-Semitic violence, yet dozens of murders of gay men have merited virtually nothing? Why did *Newsnight* scrap their programme about this subject in 1990 and never do anything about it since? . . . There have been dozens of imaginative, effective and news-worthy campaigns for lesbian and gay human rights over the last few years. Almost every one of them has been ignored by the BBC. Why?

Although the BBC did not accept these criticisms, it was notable that the next annual Lesbian and Gay Pride festival was, for the first time, extensively covered by all the major radio and television news and current affairs programmes. The main TV news bulletins and radio programmes such as *The World at One, Newsnight, The Nine O'Clock News* and *PM* all carried reports about the current issues facing the gay community: discrimination in the military, police liaison, adoption, fostering and agitation for law reform. (A less conventional way to get the gay community's views over on the BBC news is to invade the studios and shout it out. That is what happened in May 1988 when several lesbian women invaded *The Nine O'Clock News* during transmission and tried to protest about Clause 28. That incident has now gone down in broadcasting history.)

Age of consent

In 1994, on the eve of the Parliamentary vote to lower the age of homosexual consent, Radio Four's *The World This Weekend* carried a report by Carol West which angered many gay listeners with its insensitive and ill-informed approach. A member of the BBC's Lesbian and Gay Group, David Birt, wrote to the BBC's Head of News and Current Affairs with a withering critique of the broadcast, which he has given me permission to reproduce here:

> The programme contained a six minute item about the age of consent . . . It began by selectively quoting *The Sunday Times* NOP poll, without giving any details of how the poll was conducted, or the size of its sample. Of the unspecified 'only narrow' majority of the public said to support reducing the age of consent, an unspecified 'large majority' was said to be in favour of reducing it only to 18, not to 16. The quotations became more specific, and it was said that 25% of the population thought homosexuality should be made wholly illegal. That part of the NOP poll which states 'The big divide is between those who know homosexual men personally (just over a third of the sample) and those who do not. Of those who know gay men, a tiny 6% think homosexuality should be made illegal' was selectively not reported. That distinction between knowledge and myth is an important point.
>
> The programme then went on to say that the opponents of change argue that a change 'might render vulnerable' young men, uncertain of their sexuality, who 'ARE' seduced (as if of fact rather than opinion) into 'joining the gay community' (like joining a tennis club, as if sexual orientation was a matter of choice).
>
> It was then said that those in favour of change argue that the present law doesn't prevent gay teenagers having sex, merely creates 'THE SEEDY TWILIGHT WORLD in which they are forced to live.' This is a gross misrepresentation of the campaign for equality. Has Mrs Edwina Currie, or has Sir

Ian McKellen been speaking about 'the seedy twilight world'?

Then we were told that 'Carol West has been inside that world' of (?) – sound of disco music – leading into a replay of BBC news from last year reporting 'Scotland Yard say up to five men may have been murdered by a serial killer . . . ', a police representative saying 'it will certainly be a frightened community'. Back to Carol West who reminds us of the sado-masochistic nature of the murders, and takes the opportunity to use (yet again) the tabloid headline 'THE SEEDY TWI-LIGHT WORLD OF THE HOMOSEXUAL': not of some, or even a minority of homosexuals, but THE homosexual. She adds: opponents to change say that's the real picture of 'THE SLEAZY WORLD OF THE HOMOSEXUAL'. What exactly was the perceived relevance of the serial killer Colin Ireland to the debate on the age of consent?

We are now approaching 2 mins into the item and so far we have had only negativity. We have been told twice about the 'seedy twilight world of the homosexual'. The case for equality under the law has been seriously misrepresented, and it has been taken as read that the current law protects the young . . .

When the lawyer Angus Hamilton came on the pro-gramme, he pointed out the problem of public perception of what being gay involves which focuses on minorities and unfortunate incidents. BBC news and current affairs are a significant factor in shaping public perception and opinion, not to be taken lightly. It is evident that this programme thus far has entirely substantiated Angus Hamilton's identifica-tion of the problem of focusing on minorities (e.g. sado-masochism, which is also to be found in the 'heterosexual world') and unfortunate incidents (e.g. serial killers to whom heterosexuals also fall victim).

Now it's time for 'Seedy Clubs And Their Grubby Clientele' again, given an apparent authenticity by the owner of a coffee bar in Brighton, who adds the word 'disgusting'.

Only after this barrage of insult to the gay community, and innuendoes about predatory older men, do we get a short vignette about domestic life for Michael and Anthony, which is closer to reality, but which still funks the scale of the problem of violence to lesbians and gay men, and the attitude and position of the police in protecting them . . . The programme then went off at a tangent with a short tutorial on cottaging and the people who do it: married men with children, people who do not identify themselves as gay, who do not have confidence . . . etc. True though this undoubtedly is, what exactly was the perceived relevance for young homosexual men?

I consider that by its bias and negativity, the programme was an insult not only to the gay community, but to those outside that community who are heterosexual and married, who see the injustice of the current discrimination, and who wholeheartedly support the campaign for equality. I think the programme was a disgrace to the BBC, and to its reputation for impartiality. I would be pleased to know whether you complied with the relevant Guidelines for Producers.

The Viewer and Listener Correspondence Department replied that the piece had been intended to be supportive and, in fact, 'the programme had complaints that the package was pro-gay propaganda'.

Only by education and proper training will we ensure that journalists understand the issues relevant to gay men and lesbians. But it is also up to the institutions that employ those journalists to create an ethos of fairness and sensitivity, so that such bias does not find its way on to the airwaves – even occasionally. I believe that the BBC is making some headway in that direction, but unless it is repeatedly reminded of its obligations the impetus will be lost.

Liberal fascists and the pink mafia

TV and radio are very much more creative media than newspapers. The gay sensibility has been apparent since the beginning, and the BBC has always attracted a larger than average share of gay people to work within it. Broadcasting, then, is conducive to the particular contribution that gay people can make. Newspapers, on the other hand, particularly the tabloid press, have never been particular magnets for the creative talents of gay people. The working environment, with its rampant machismo and homophobia, has ensured that the gay influence has been small, and those gay people working within it needed to keep their sexuality low-profile. (I once asked a gay man who worked on *The Sun* how he lived with his conscience when he saw what the paper did to his fellow gay men and lesbians. He seemed genuinely bewildered by the question; it had never occurred to him that *The Sun* was particularly anti-gay.) So, while the broadcast media matures in its approach to lesbian and gay issues, the popular press continues in its strident homophobia (the virulence of which is partly restrained by constant threats of statutory regulation if standards are not voluntarily improved). This contradiction has been noticed by Brenda Maddox, who, as media correspondent of *The Daily Telegraph*, speculated in January 1990 about why the press was so unrelentingly nasty towards homosexuals, while television and radio were much less inclined to attack and much more likely to present positive images. Given that, in the main, readers and viewers were the same people, why, asked Maddox, did the papers direct so much hatred at gays, while the broadcast media seemed to be falling over themselves to be kind? She wrote: 'The love that dare not speak its name now proclaims itself in soap operas, chat shows and news programmes. In broadcasting, with certain exceptions, the rage (of the tabloids) seems not to be there.' For some commentators this conundrum has an easy answer. Paul Johnson has said several times in *The Spectator* that there is a conspiracy of what he calls 'liberal fascists' controlling the 'broadcasting duopoly'. All anti-gay voices – such as his own – he claims are excluded from the airwaves. On 21 April 1990 he wrote:

> It is now becoming increasingly difficult, for example, to discuss homosexuality or the related problem of Aids, except in terms approved by the homosexual lobby . . . Although a good deal of pro-homosexual material appears on the

duopoly (of terrestrial television) it is now almost inconceivable that a programme critical of such activities could be broadcast. That is censorship, and all the more objectionable that it is imposed by the controlling elements in the media, rather than the law and Parliament.

The Sun's columnist Garry Bushell also thinks that the terrestrial TV channels are hotbeds of 'political correctness', failing to reflect the thinking of 'ordinary people'. He rages constantly about TV's 'poofter propaganda' and the fact that there is no appetite within the broadcasting establishment for hard right-wing opinions which he claims are widely held by 'the great British public'. Where, he frequently asks, are the voices on telly calling for the recriminalization of homosexuality in order to 'stop the spread of Aids'? Reviewing a public access programme (*Free For All*) about gay law reform in 1991, Bushell wrote: 'You won't find anyone arguing for the return of capital punishment or defending the Isle of Man's stand on perversion here. Everyday views are kept off TV.'[8] Bushell has claimed: 'TV is riddled with a cancerous pink Mafia who are determined to glamorise their own perversion no matter what viewers think.'[9] Richard Ingrams even blamed television's approach to homosexuality for the spread of AIDS:

> It is ironic that the March of Aids has had no perceptible influence on the campaign by the people running TV to make homosexuality respectable . . . One wonders if it has ever crossed the minds of anyone at the BBC or Channel 4 that the spread of AIDS has been greatly assisted by the propaganda campaign. To put it crudely, many are dead and will die thanks to the permissive approach to television that they have helped to promote.[10]

Certainly if opinion polls give an accurate measure of attitudes to homosexuality (and much seems to hinge on what questions are asked and how they are phrased), there remains a substantial well of intolerance. A poll conducted by *The Independent* in December 1993, for instance, showed that 75 per cent of respondents thought that homosexual relationships were, to varying degrees, unacceptable. In the light of this, whenever TV covers homosexuality in popular programming – such as soap operas – the tabloids react with hysterical outrage, claiming that their switchboard – and the switchboards of the TV companies – have been 'jammed' by those 'ordinary people' complaining. (I once checked a tabloid claim that a TV station had been 'inundated with complaints' following an episode of *EastEnders* with a gay story-line. The BBC assured me that they had, on that particular evening, received no more calls than usual.) So are these newspaper 'storms' genuine and spontaneous expressions of outrage or are they provoked and manufactured by the tabloids in order to perpetuate their own agenda?

Storm in a tabloid

We can see an example of this relentless attacking of TV's 'positive images' in coverage of the gay characters who appeared for a time in the BBC's flagship soap opera *EastEnders* (or *EastBenders* as it was branded at the time by *The Sun*). The tabloids had been complaining bitterly for two years that it was insufferable that a gay character should have been introduced into the top-rated TV series at all, it was even more intolerable that he should be a sympathetic and likeable chap who eventually became assimilated into the Albert Square community. Tabloid TV critics argued that the character was unrealistic because he was middle-class (or a 'yuppie') and because he wasn't debauched and promiscuous as homosexuals are generally perceived to be. As Tom Brown wrote in the *Glasgow Daily Record* in November 1987:

> Colin and Barry seem like a couple of nice lads – and I hope they live happily ever after. But I won't have any of their homosexual hanky-panky in my living room. Gay Lib has become Gay Fib – that homosexual behaviour is natural and normal. Well, it's not . . . It is still not a fit subject for a prime-time early-evening TV soap that has become vital viewing for millions of families, young and old.

Forewarned of a scene which was to feature the two gay characters arguing over money, *The Star* could stand it no longer and – following the lead established by *The Daily Express* all those years previously – led its 5 February 1988 issue with a four-and-a-half-inch front-page headline 'Filth'. The sub-heading demanded 'Get this garbage off TV'. After reading an hysterical and completely distorted account of what the scriptwriters had in mind, *Star* readers were invited to ring in to premium-rate phone numbers to vote on whether 'the scene should be shown': 83 per cent said that it should not be shown.

Then came the day when the gay character Colin (played by Michael Cashman) was to kiss his boyfriend Guido on screen. It was 25 January 1989, and the kiss – of the blink-and-you'll-miss-it variety – provoked a classic tabloid controversy. *The Sun* said: 'Furious MPs last night demanded a ban on *EastEnders* as the BBC soap showed two gay men kissing full on the lips. The homosexual love scene between yuppie poofs was screened in the early evening when millions of children were watching.' (And just in case any *Sun*-reading child missed it, a photograph of the shocking peck was reproduced for their edification.) The names of the MPs who were 'outraged' were equally predictable. Right-wingers Terry Dicks and Geoffrey Dickens – already well-known to regular readers of *Gay Times* under the sobriquet 'rentagobs' - could be depended upon to 'thunder' on demand on all kinds of topics, with homosexuality being a favourite. 'It is absolutely disgraceful that this revolting scene went out at 7.30pm', said Mr Dicks, while Mr Dickens opined: 'I think the time has come to reconsider the whole future of *EastEnders*'. *The Sun*, in its usual hyperbolic style, seemed to be suggesting that the whole country had been traumatized by the gay kiss. Was this the truth or was it more likely that the paper had constructed its story long before the scene was ever broadcast? The paper also ran a 'You the Jury' phone-in, in which readers were asked to vote yes or no to the question: 'Do you think TV should show scenes of men kissing each other?' Once more, premium-rate telephone lines were employed to ascertain that 20,223 had voted 'against the scenes' with 6,313 in favour. (The cost of the phone calls was 38p per minute, half of which went to Mr Murdoch. The minimum profit from this piece of gay-bashing would, therefore, have been in the region of £5,000.) Of course the results of these reader votes must be seen in the light of the extremely biased and inflammatory descriptions of the events involved, but even so it does seem to indicate that the majority of *Star* and *Sun* readers would have preferred the scenes not to have been broadcast. But a simple 'yes' or 'no' on a specific question does not tell us what general attitudes are to the coverage of homosexuality on television. After all, a few days after the phone poll, the correspondence column in *The Sun* carried letters from a brace of 'mums-of-two' completely contradicting what the MPs and the paper had said. A Mrs Metcalfe of Cheltenham asked:

> Where has MP Terry Dicks been all his life to call *EastEnders* 'revolting'? When Colin kissed Guido goodnight, my eight-year-old asked why? He accepted my answer that some men prefer the company and love of another man . . . We cannot wrap children in cotton wool. Living with the fact that everyone is different makes for well-balanced human beings.

Part of the explanation for the over-reaction is the strange relationship that tabloid newspapers have with TV. They are fully aware that their readers are avid soap fans and that a front-page lead about one of the prominent actors or a sensational development of the story-line will shift tens of thousands of extra copies. Wendy Henry, who worked on *The Sun* and eventually went on to edit *The News of the World*, was aware of this dependence, and she was quite happy to say that her papers were sometimes little more than '*EastEnders* supplements'.

Proliferating images

The BBC took another drubbing from *The Sun* on 25 March 1988, when it broadcast a play called *The Two of Us* which had been produced for use in schools. The play had already been the subject of a certain amount of controversy after the ending was changed and a scene which showed two teenage boys kissing had been cut from it. The *Sun* editorial said:

At 11.30 tonight the BBC is broadcasting a play about teenage homosexuals. Teachers are invited to record the programme and play it back to classes of 14 to 16 year olds. In notes with the play, psychiatrist Dr. Martin Gay says: 'In many ways, homosexual activity of adolescents is very much part of the continuum of behaviour from puberty through into full adult life.' Our view is that on the basis of the continuum of his own behaviour, Dr Gay should have his head examined. It is wildly irresponsible for the BBC to screen the play. It will be irresponsible for any teacher to show it to his pupils, in direct breach of the new Government rules against making homosexual propaganda in the classroom, and without the consent or even knowledge of the parents. We hope that head teachers will not take their guidance from the BBC or Dr Gay. They should ensure that any videos stay where they belong. Locked away in the closet.

The play itself turned out to be a rather mild affair although well made and thoughtful, with not a hint of prurience or sensationalism. Its point was to illustrate the intolerance that greeted the burgeoning relationship between the two young lads. The play was broadcast to schools in an uncut form and with little controversy in 1991.

When he was about to become the first chairman of the Broadcasting Standards Council, in April 1989, William Rees-Mogg went on a tour of the country to find out for himself what the British public's standards were. He found that 'one hears much more antipathy to homosexuals than might be expected in a tolerant society. Scenes of men kissing do not seem to promote tolerance; they were invariably commented on unfavourably, sometimes with sharp hostility.' In the same month, ITV cut from a recording of a Royal Gala variety show an act by the lesbian entertainer Sandra Bernhardt in which she sang a love song to another woman.

So why is there now such a plethora of gay images on TV? Part of the answer must be the success of the pressure that has been applied over several years by the gay community. There may also be an element of truth in the argument about 'political correctness', and the desire by the broadcasting authorities to take their commitments to equal opportunities seriously. There is also the fact that homosexuality has become an important issue both politically and socially, and one that cannot any more be sidelined. Programme producers are naturally anxious to reflect this shifting focus and so they ensure that the gay issue gets a reasonable hearing. This is not, however, because the majority of viewers want these topics covered. In their book *Power without Responsibility* James Curran and Jean Seaton write: 'It is often argued that the mass media "reflect" society because they are obliged to please their audiences. Yet many researchers have commented on the apparent remoteness of producers from their potential viewers.'[11] They quote from a book about TV production, in which the authors say: 'It is not so much that people don't know what the audience wants, as in the actual process of production people were working more to please themselves.'[12] Some producers strive to achieve the 'Whitehouse effect'. In the 1970s and 1980s producers would pray for Mrs Mary Whitehouse to denounce their programme on the basis that it would increase ratings significantly. This was certainly the case with the Kenny Everett Television Show, which became extremely popular in the wake of a Whitehousian condemnation. Similarly, the inclusion of a gay character in a popular drama would, it was hoped, provoke the tabloid 'outrage mill' into action, so ensuring another ratings winner. In the case of *EastEnders*, though, it should be remembered that one of the original creators, Tony Holland, was an out gay man, and his influence would certainly have had an effect on the introduction of the gay characters. (Coincidentally, Tony Warren, the man who created *Coronation Street*, is also gay, but his influence on the programme ended long before it would have been even possible to contemplate a gay character in Weatherfield. There is no such excuse today, but the producers resist the suggestion vigorously.)

The fact, of course, that there is prejudice against homosexuals should not militate against their voices being heard. There is a large element of racism in our society, too, but few would take seriously the argument that non-white faces should be excluded from broadcasting. (In the days before Channel 4, people from ethnic minorities also had to fight hard for fairer representation of their lives. It would be illegal and unthinkable for the tabloids to mount a campaign to exclude black people from TV – and doubly so if expressed in immoderate language.) And yet still the popular press rails against TV's approach to homosexuality. While TV tries to move attitudes along, the tabloids try desperately to restrain and retard them. 'Radio Five is devoting a weekly programme to homosexuals and lesbians', said an editorial in *The Daily Star* on 15 March 1994. 'Why should this minority get so much special attention? What about programmes for other interest groups such as anglers, pigeon-fanciers, bird watchers, or even ferret-down-the-trouser enthusiasts? But, of course they aren't as vocal and politically fashionable as the gay lobby.' And when, in 1994, *The Sun* discovered that *EastEnders* was to include a lesbian storyline it came up with yet another variation on the theme, branding the programme *BentEnders*. Once more 'the BBC switchboard was jammed' routine greeted the scene of 'French kissing' between the two lesbian characters Della and Binny.[13] The mandatory 'mum' was wheeled out to say: 'My six-year-old daughter saw it, tongues and everything. What was I supposed to say to her?'

The roots of press homophobia

The question then becomes: why are some elements of the press so intransigent in their homophobia? Perhaps the simplest answer is an awareness of the widespread homophobia in Britain, and the wish to appeal to it. Another is that the tabloids like to pander to Britain's rather juvenile and immature sexual attitudes which are composed of part prurience, part prudery, part shock and part titillation. Anything of an 'unusual' sexual nature seems likely to provoke tabloid readers into a mixture of vicarious pleasure and tutting disapproval. As ex-Fleet-Street editor, and now broadcaster, Derek Jameson said in a Radio Four news programme in 1991: 'The essential ingredients of a successful tabloid newspaper are the four S's: sex, sensation, scandal and sport.' The 'tabloidization' of newspapers – reducing them to half the size of broadsheet – has also had an effect on the quality of the journalism within them. Most newspapers started life as full-size broadsheets, but were then reduced in order to attract a popular audience and make them easier to handle. (It is salutary to remember that the archetypal tabloid – *The News of the World* – was, in fact, a broadsheet until 1982.) Naturally, in order to fit the smaller spaces, stories had to be compressed and consequently coverage became shallower. The front-page lead became all-important – the headline had to be bold, arresting and, most of all, it had to out-sensationalize the other papers on the newsagents' counter. The demand for ever more lurid headlines gradually tempted editors to lower their standards and take more risks with the truth. Most of the time they got away with it. The list of untrue front-page stories is almost endless, but the number that have brought adverse consequences to their creators are very few.

Money and influence

To say that the British press is overwhelmingly conservative would be an understatement. The men who control a large proportion of newspapers are tycoons whose success depends on the operation of the freest possible market. At the same time it would be simplistic to assert that the right-wing press always blindly support the Conservative Party. Their only consistency in *any* area is in the protection of their proprietors' self-interests (Tom Baistow described them as 'manipulators of public power for private ends').[14] An example of this ceaseless protection and promotion of their own financial interests can be seen in the treatment of the BBC by all the Murdoch-owned newspapers. *The Sun, News of the World, Times, Sunday Times* and *Today* ceaselessly attack the BBC. Sometimes the criticism is valid, but often it is transparently exaggerated or manufactured. *The Times* has, on many occasions, run editorials about the unfairness of the licensing system, the amount of waste at the BBC and the supposed decline in the quality of its programmes. It seems that *The Sun* is incapable of saying a single civil word about any aspect of the BBC (although it gleans a great deal of easy copy from writing about its programmes). Of course, Murdoch's News Corporation would benefit greatly if the BBC were to be dismantled, and while his papers slate the terrestrial TV stations, Murdoch's satellite TV interests are 'puffed' and promoted. This reached such a pitch that *Private Eye* magazine began a feature inviting readers to send in the most blatant examples of Wapping newspapers' 'free advertising' for Sky Television. In relation to his TV interests, Murdoch's support of the Thatcher government was repaid many times over when he was absolved from the cross-media ownership restrictions by which everyone else was obliged to abide. The fact that Conservative Party policies are most likely to coincide with the self-interest of the press barons means that in most instances the press will support the Tories. As Lord Stevens, chairman of United Newspapers, publishers of *The Daily* and *Sunday Express* and *Daily Star* has said:

> I think it would be very unlikely that I would have a newspaper that would support the socialist party. That isn't what some people call press freedom, but why should I want a product I didn't approve of? I believe it is in the best interests of United Newspapers in terms of profits and shareholders to support the Conservatives.[15]

Mrs Thatcher's free market economic philosophy suited the press tycoons perfectly, and goes much of the way to explaining their almost poodle-like loyalty to her. Thatcher's successor, John Major, had to take the flak for the eventual collapse of the Thatcher dream, and his rough treatment at the hands of the press was an object lesson in not taking Fleet Street for granted. However, despite being the subject of much adverse comment in mid-term, the Tory press invariably return to the fold to give the party undivided support at the time of elections. The shifting political affiliations of those who run the press (these shifts are rarely leftwards, although this is not unknown) was also well illustrated in the 1930s when the ultra-right-wing press baron Lord Rothermere actually used his newspapers for a time to support the British Union of Fascists. 'Give the Blackshirts a Helping Hand' was a headline from *The Daily Mirror* of 22 January 1934. 'Hurrah for the Blackshirts' said the *Daily Mail*.[16] Another of his papers, *The Evening News*, actually ran a competition for the best letter on the theme 'Why I like the Blackshirts'.

There have been attempts to break the strangle-hold of the press barons and to oppose the concentration of the media into so few hands. Unfortunately, the cost of launching and establishing a newspaper is so prohibitively vast that most efforts to balance the press with more left-leaning titles have failed. The left simply cannot access the huge resources that are available to the press barons with their multiplicity of financial interests. It was thought that the advent of the new technology, and the breaking of the print unions, would make the creation of new and different newspapers more feasible, but it proved a false hope. Starting and establishing a national newspaper still remains an impossibility for all but the richest of entrepreneurs – recent estimates put the cost at £10 million, but that is considered a conservative figure. The destruction of the print unions and the use of new technology have simply allowed the existing press establishment to make even larger profits.

In this tradition of relentless right-wing philosophy, the maintenance of the status quo has always been important. The press tycoons know that if a conservative, free market ethos can be maintained, their profits are unlikely to suffer. This extends not only to their political support but also to their approach to social matters. While the liberal end of the press has moved the way of TV, acknowledging the diversity of modern British society and trying to represent it, the popular papers continue to deny the important contribution of minorities. It seems that *The Sun*, *The Star*, *Daily Mirror* and, to an extent, *The Daily Mail* and *Daily Express* are still of the opinion that 'immigrants' are a threat to them, that gay voices must be silenced, that stricter punishment – especially capital punishment – is needed for those who transgress. They promote the opinion that the undeniable changes in society are really signs of its disintegration. The majority of the press still attack any radical reform which might be seen as the beginning of a threat to their own power and privilege. The status quo must be maintained if their power is to be protected.

Prejudice and ignorance

In the light of this, we must also examine personal attitudes which hold sway within the popular press. Much of the anti-gay feeling comes from individual revulsion and dislike. The homophobia of Rupert Murdoch – perhaps the man with most influence on the popular press in Britain – is well documented. In the book *Stick it Up Your Punter* Peter Chippindale and Chris Horrie tell that, while Murdoch acknowledged that sex sells newspapers and that there should be plenty of it, he drew the line at homosexuality. In the early days of *The Sun*, Nick Lloyd wrote a feature about 'what it was like to be homosexual'. The article was made ready for the paper but just before the presses rolled, Murdoch spotted the piece. 'Do you really think our readers are interested in poofters?' he is said to have demanded. ('The question was phrased in standard Murdoch style to inform them that they were not. The feature was spiked.') The book reveals that:

> Murdoch would compare the *Sun* and the *Mirror* page by page every day wherever he was in the world . . . He would lay the papers next to each other and flick through the pages, complaining if he thought the *Mirror* had done better on any particular story. 'Why did you print this dreadful rubbish?' he would ask Lamb [Sir Larry Lamb, the first editor of the Murdoch *Sun*] as he flicked through the pages. 'What's all this crap about poofters?' he would enquire when there was a fleeting reference to homosexuality.[17]

Chippindale and Horrie explain Murdoch's antipathy for all things gay as being partly 'standard Australian macho attitude' and partly a personal conviction that homosexuals represented a dangerous 'mafia' which take over organizations once let in. He had come across what he termed 'the gay network' in Hollywood and New York and 'found that, like the British establishment, it was another club that he was excluded from'. Kelvin MacKenzie, who edited *The Sun* for over ten years, was obviously chosen for the job because he shared – and was prepared to promote – his master's convictions, including the almost pathological homophobia. Indeed, so closely aligned are their opinions that Murdoch was said to refer to MacKenzie affectionately as 'My Little Hitler'. The two men obviously differed in one particular, though – MacKenzie judged that the readers were very interested in 'poofters' and, during his reign, anti-gay abuse and hostility reached a level that caused alarm even in traditionally disinterested circles.

Brian Hitchen, too, has a long history of down-market journalism, and edited *The Daily Star* from 1987 to 1994, before moving on to *The Sunday Express*. Under his editorship, *The Star* carried some of the strongest anti-gay copy ever published in Britain, and much of it has emanated directly from his own pen. (See Chapter 5 for examples.) Derek Jameson has also edited this paper and subsequently *The Daily Express* and *News of the World*. He knows Fleet Street well. He was interviewed for a 1986 BBC *Open Space* programme about gays and the press. He said:

> I'll tell you quite straight. Fleet Street takes the view that homosexuality is abnormal, unnatural, a bit evil because it's wrong and so on. The editors are not going to come out and say 'Be gay, it's wonderful and isn't it great?' They are going to say that gays are not normal, natural people.

Editors of the popular papers do, indeed, encourage aggressive attitudes among their journalists, instances of which appear elsewhere in this book. The rush to outdo each other with ever more trivial 'exclusives' resulted in the standards of journalism in the popular press plummeting to new lows during the 1980s and 1990s. Tabloid newspapers are also supplied with stories and pictures by news agencies, small operations throughout the country seeking material on their local patch. A documentary exploring the operation of one such agency – News Team based in Birmingham – was broadcast by the BBC on 8 June 1994.[18] It gave an insight into the kinds of pressures that journalists find themselves under in order to beat rivals to a story. It also illustrated how grubby and amoral such work can become when common human decency gives way to the quest for an exclusive. Reviewing the programme the following day in *The Daily Telegraph*, Max Davidson wrote:

It was a shocker: shocking because although one knew that this sort of journalism went on, one hadn't really *acknowledged* that it went on; shocking because the people practising it were so indifferent to the unsavouriness of their trade . . . The staff at News Team . . . had been raking muck for so long they had lost their sense of smell. They had fallen into the old journalist's trap of thinking that news is an absolute value and that news-gathering, *ipso-facto*, is a process in which the ends justify the means . . . A murdered white man was marketable, a murdered black wasn't. A black *murderer* on the other hand . . .

Another revealing section of the programme gave an indication of how tabloid news desks construct stories about homosexuality. The news agency was filing a story about a young constable who had been beaten up while on 'cottage patrol' in a city centre lavatory. A woman reporter was ringing the story in to a male colleague:

> *Woman*: '. . . after he was attacked during an undercover investigation into a gay sex circuit . . .'
> *Man*: Into a what? You mean a gay sex ring?
> *Woman*: No, you see homosexuals wear sex rings, don't they? So I thought that sounded a bit odd. A gay sex ring has implications. What about a gay sex circle?
> *Man*: We'll go with sex ring.

The language being employed in this little tale seems to suggest that there was some kind of organized sexual club going on in the lavatory (in tabloid speak homosexual sex is frequently portrayed as occurring in some kind of Masonic or conspiratorial framework) when in fact successful cottaging is almost invariably a matter of luck – individuals turn up when the mood takes them, on the off-chance of an assignation. I have never known of any kind of organized cottaging 'ring', 'circuit' or 'circle'. However, when tabloid newspapers carry stories on the topic the 'shorthand' and ritualized thinking inevitably comes into play. As Nancy Banks-Smith, *The Guardian*'s TV critic, wrote about the same programme: 'When you work with words, you must take good care of them.'

There is evidence that, although some individual journalists thrive in this highly competitive and unscrupulous atmosphere, many are disillusioned and dejected. *Stick it Up Your Punter* is full of tales of traditional journalists who still consider themselves members of an honourable profession, being appalled at what they were called upon to do. One ex-tabloid journalist who was sickened by his work was Terry Lovell, who had been employed by *The People*. He wrote about his feelings in *The Observer*[19] magazine saying that he had become a practising Christian and that he could not reconcile his faith with a career that cast him in the role of Pontius Pilate, crucifying people left, right and centre.

> More and more I read *The People*'s stories with a sense of disgust and anger at its brutal treatment of people's lives, the damage to society of its negative values and attitudes . . . It started with a series of investigations, all successful: the naming of Harvey Proctor for his rent-boy-beating activities, a high-society drugs exposé, and the gay vicars scandal which *The People* tactically broke on the Sunday prior to the commencement of last year's General Synod.

So, while some journalists working on the tabloids may have a conscience about what they are required to do, they will do it anyway. At a conference organized by the National Union of Journalists,[20] Roy Greenslade – once editor of *The Daily Mirror* – explained his decision to run the story of Prince Edward's denial that he was gay. (See Chapter 4 for details.) Greenslade said:

> I knew the story fitted the tabloid agenda . . . It would certainly get the paper talked about. But it was prurient, puerile and implicitly homophobic. I didn't want to do it but as a tabloid editor fighting a war against a paper I knew would have paid thousands for that story, I knew what I had to do. It was a guaranteed seller and I was a prisoner of the job.

At the conference Mr Greenslade insisted that the real ethical problem is embedded in 'the very nature of the private press ownership and the free market'. He accused proprietors of wishing to exert influence or make money or both and cloaking their aims by talking of 'providing a service'. The financial rewards for successful journalists are considerable, but there are also likely to be intense pressures to conform to the political line taken by the paper. In the book *Getting the Message – News, Truth and Power* David Miller and Kevin Williams report how, when one journalist was challenged on a particularly homophobic report he had produced about AIDS, he replied: 'It was that or my mortgage because the editor said, "I am not having any more of your gay loving, junkie loving pieces. We are going to tell it like it is." '[21] Many others, however, do not see that there is any moral dimension to the work they do. Such people are often employed because they will enthusiastically toe the political line required by editors and proprietors. They justify their activities by disingenuously equating the scandal-mongering and muck-raking involved in 'bonk journalism' with serious investigative reporting which serves the public interest. Whenever there are threats to regulate the press by statute, the editors most guilty of low journalistic standards invariably claim that any restrictions on their activities will interfere with the investigation of serious political and financial corruption.

Subs and the backbench

Another important element in the perpetuation of tabloid gay-bashing comprises the sub-editors who re-write, cut and edit the journalists' copy. As well as making the copy fit the space allotted, they ensure that it fits the style and politics of the newspaper. Because space is so tight on tabloid newspapers, their sub-editors are much more likely to intervene in journalists' submitted copy, sometimes changing it drastically. I have challenged many journalists on stories which have been inaccurate, misleading, cruel or unfair. Almost invariably they will claim that their copy was substantially 'changed by the subs'. Often this is just an excuse, but sometimes it isn't. The place of the subs was described by Tom

Baistow in his book *Fourth-Rate Estate*. Baistow says the 'back-bench – a powerful caucus of senior executives headed by the night editor' - directs the subs, who in turn:

> re-write, shape and beef up the copy in a highly-skilled process of synthesis that places great emphasis on bold, exaggerated layout. Straight news has to be a dramatic happening in the 'action' class – terrorist bombings, plane hijackings, hold-ups, train crashes – to oust a good scandal from the splash position. The tabloid editor has graduated from the subs bench, skilled in the mechanics of presentation. In effect, the backbench determines what goes into a popular paper on any given night, subject of course to overall policy.[22]

The subs are also the people responsible for the headlines. Sub-editors will occasionally create a headline which completely misrepresents the story below it. Sometimes this is deliberate, sometimes simple carelessness, often it is the result of stretching too hard for a pun. The sub-editors are answerable to the editor, and frequently it is he or she who demands the changes that result in distortion. In the heated and frenetic atmosphere of a newspaper office, sub-editors might be required to 'massage' facts so that a weak story will stand up. They have been caught out on numerous occasions inventing quotes, changing dates and times, excising important information which then unbalances a story, and generally subverting the journalists' original intention. Anyone who needs samples of the dubious work of tabloid sub-editors should read the books *Lies, Damned Lies and Some Exclusives* by Henry Porter[23] and *Stick it Up Your Punter*.

Often it is imagined by gay activists that 'if only we could educate journalists on the yellow press' we could stem the flow of homophobic reporting. Unfortunately this is not likely. In the case of the reporting of AIDS, much effort was put into 'making journalists better informed', in the hope that they would then produce copy that was more accurate and less sensational. Regrettably, this education process did not extend to the subs' benches or to the editors' offices. While specialist correspondents – particularly in the broadsheets –

dramatically improved their reporting of AIDS, the tabloids continued to use the crisis as a political tool. Only reluctantly, and after much criticism, did they let go of such emotive and inaccurate phrases as 'the gay plague' and 'the homosexual disease'. Andrew Veitch, who was *The Guardian*'s medical correspondent in 1989, won an award from the Terrence Higgins Trust for his reporting of the epidemic. In an acceptance speech he pinpointed the fact that the message he and other responsible journalists were trying to promote had not reached the newsdesks: 'We have failed to get through to the people who really make the papers – the editors, the sub-editors, the guys who decide what goes in the pages, the guys who write the headlines you hate so much.'[24] Similarly, a senior Health Education Authority official was quoted as saying: 'I think we make a mistake in the sense of always talking about journalists because it is the people who actually control what is printed who are crucial and this is an almost shadowy group we don't get to in the normal course of events.' One man who didn't buy this blame-it-on-the-subs argument was Ron Todd, who was General Secretary of the Transport and General Workers Union when, in June 1987, he made a speech at the London School of Economics, criticizing press standards. 'We have to say frankly to journalists that the Nuremberg defence no longer cuts ice; the predictable train of disappearing responsibility which starts with the reporter and goes through the subs will no longer prove absolution.'

Playing on anxieties

Newspaper circulation has been declining steadily for a decade and the competition for readers is fierce. It is in the tabloids' interests to ensure that they give their readers what they want, and what they want seems to be a daily diet of bigotry which reassures their prejudices. David Banks, as editor of *The Daily Mirror*, told *Options* magazine that: 'You basically have to be what your readers are. You have the same aspirations and standards. Deep down, I'm the same person as the men and women who buy *The Daily Mirror*.'[25] Brian Hitchen in the same feature said: 'You need to understand your readers absolutely. You've got to reflect all their hopes, dreams, fears and anxieties.'

It is particularly the *anxieties* which the tabloids target. They have identified groups which their readers are suspicious of and antagonistic towards, and they have ruthlessly encouraged the hounding of these groups. According to Peter Chippindale and Chris Horrie the favourite tabloid hate groups – known in the trade as 'scum' – are:

> Prisoners, criminals, drug-takers, football hooligans, most blacks, homosexuals, militant trade unionists, muggers, students, peace campers, demonstrators, hippies, dossers, tramps, beggars, Social Security scroungers, squatters, terrorists and especially the IRA, vandals, graffiti artists, prostitutes, gypsies, winos, various foreign groups *en masse* and all deviants, especially sex offenders.[26]

To this group we can now add New Age Travellers, militant gay activists, 'the AIDS establishment' and rent-boys.

Contradictions

There are no simple answers to any of the contradictions that arise from the popular press's coverage of homosexuality. Opinion polls repeatedly show that intrusive journalists are held in very low esteem in the public mind, but their work remains in great demand. Most people believe that the private lives of law-abiding citizens should not provide newspaper copy. Yet these same people in their millions day after day buy the very product for which they express such disapproval.

Although the tabloids are, in the main, ultra right-wing in their political opinions, they will occasionally employ a token columnist who puts 'the other point of view'. Ken Livingstone, *The Sun*'s 'red' bogeyman of the 1980s, once wrote a regular column for that paper. And that may also explain why, from time to time, even the most intractably anti-gay newspaper will carry sympathetic stories on a homosexual theme. Even papers with apparently rigid anti-gay editorial stances will sometimes run features that are generally sympathetic and informed on gay topics. These will probably be included in women's supplements or be written as 'specials' by the resident agony aunt. Indeed, these two areas can often provide material that completely contradicts the general editorial approach of the paper on many topics. And so the varied influences at work in a newsroom can, then, result sometimes in coverage that seems inconsistent. The editor cannot be on duty every day, and occasionally must take a holiday. Their deputy will probably share most of their boss's views and be well aware of what is required from them, but there may be subtle differences of emphasis and priorities, and this is why a tabloid newspaper will suddenly seem to have significantly changed tack for a few days.

Convenient and useful though terms such as 'tabloid journalism' and 'the tabloid press' are, they can be misleading. They come loaded with assumptions and prejudices. Not all the tabloids are the same, and they don't take a uniform stance on every issue. Sometimes they take opposing views. One example is the different approach to the AIDS crisis adopted by *The Sun* and *The Daily Mirror*. *The Sun* consistently stated that AIDS is a 'gay disease', whereas the *Mirror* – after a lot of prompting – has been more inclined to follow the government line that 'everyone is potentially at risk'. *The Daily Mail* and *Daily Express* have both followed the line that homosexuals are 'to blame' for the appearance and spread of HIV, while *Today* has been less inclined to apportion blame and more careful in its presentation. *The Sunday Times* has controversially promoted the renegade idea that HIV is not the cause of AIDS. *The Sun* and *Star* have used homosexuality relentlessly as both a political battering ram and a means of titillation. The middle-market tabloids, such as *The Daily Mail* and *Daily Express*, have generally ignored the exposé angle and concentrated much more on what they see as the negative and threatening political ramifications of the gay emergence. Although they have concentrated less on sexual sensationalism, and the private lives of individuals, their intention has been no less sinister and malevolent in intention for that. Some characteristics, though, *are* common to all tabloid newspapers: hyperbole, exaggeration, vulgarity and ruthlessness.

During the 1980s and 1990s, public unease about press intrusion into private lives and personal grief has led to several sharp warnings of Government intervention if the downmarket press failed to mend its ways. There have been several attempts to make self-regulation work (see Chapter 6) but it remains to be seen whether this unwilling restraint will be maintained as the circulation war hots up once again.

Information is presented by tabloid newspapers in a form which the editor and his or her assistants consider is acceptable to the readers. Information about homosexuality, therefore, is generally presented unsympathetically, because it is assumed (not unreasonably) that the majority of the readership is hostile to that minority. We will see, in the rest of this book, how news about gay people is treated; how it is manipulated to reassure readers that their prejudices are reasonable; to score political points and, of course, to feed the insatiable appetite for sexual titillation.

The advent of tabloid broadcasting

Increasingly, though, audiences are turning away from the printed page and towards the screen and the radio for information. The advent of satellite, cable and other means of receiving TV, and the proliferation and success of commercial radio, will soon open up the 'information superhighway' to everyone. In seeing what has gone before in newspapers, it might be possible to prepare for what might lay ahead in TV. The gradual deregulation of TV, and the opening up of other means of communication, mean that it will soon be much more difficult for anyone to control effectively what is broadcast in Britain. In the USA, tabloid TV has already arrived. Half a dozen nightly programmes compete for the downmarket audience – perhaps the most successful being *Hard Copy* and *A Current Affair*, which concentrate on intrusion into private lives, sensational 'human interest stories' and disasters. Ironically, just about all the reporters working on these shows are imported from Britain. The Americans needed the ruthless, amoral skills of Fleet Street's tabloids in order to make these shows work. Wendy Henry, who began her tabloid training on *The Sun* and went on to become the first woman editor of a national paper (*The News of the World*) is prominent in this new arena of trash television. Commenting on this phenomenon Richard Ben Kramer said: 'When news and entertainment is all one business, there is no wall between fiction and fact, as long as it's good commerce.'[27]

Another indication of this trend was the move by consummate *Sun* journalist Richard Littlejohn into radio and then TV. For some time Littlejohn had a morning programme on LBC Radio. Its aim was controversy and within that remit it seemed to succeed. But eventually, in straining for shock value, Littlejohn went too far and was censured by the Radio Authority for comments about the women's movement being 'hijacked by hatchet-faced, shaven-headed dykes in boiler suits, who despise men'. Another complaint concerned comments he made the morning after the age of consent debate (which took place on 21 February 1994). He said on air:

> Curious woman, Edwina Currie. A couple of years ago she wanted to ban all eggs on the grounds that they're a threat to health. Now she demands legalized teenage anal sex – the surest and quickest way of transmitting AIDS . . . I couldn't care less about [the age of consent] but I think the decision to peg it at 18 was about right. However, after seeing the plankton bouncing up and down outside the Commons last night, if I were an MP I'd probably have voted to raise the age to 65 and banned moustaches and earrings as a basis for negotiation. Anything which that lot outside the Commons are in favour of, I'm against on principle. The police should have turned the dogs on 'em – and if that failed, brought out the flame-throwers.[28]

This kind of thing would have passed unremarked in *The Sun*, but the Radio Authority decided that he had incited violence, in contravention of the Broadcasting Act, and that LBC should pay a substantial financial penalty. Unfortunately, LBC being in receivership, no fine was extracted. Similar complaints were made to The Broadcasting Standards Council, which came to a different conclusion about the episodes saying: 'in the Committee's view, the words, distasteful as they would have sounded to many listeners, did not go beyond the limits expected of a programme whose principle stock in trade is offensiveness.'[29]

Littlejohn walked away from the whole episode laughing, and picking up contracts that will bring his filthy and dangerous opinions to a much wider audience. In an article in *The Sun*, Littlejohn moaned that his 'bollockings' from the Radio Authority amounted to censorship. 'There are already adequate laws to prevent incitement to violence,' he said, although it is difficult to think of one that could have been invoked by the homosexuals for whom he was recommending the flame-throwers.[30]

Littlejohn is well aware that his anti-gay ranting can bring in viewers, and when he was given a weekly show on London Weekend Television,[31] the very first subject was, predictably, lesbian mothers. His grossly offensive treatment of the women he had brought in for the discussion caused another guest on the programme to say: 'I'm quite appalled and very nearly walked out. To be on a British TV programme where lesbians are wheeled out for you to make smutty remarks, an absolutely shameless exhibition of vulgarity, where the lesbians have come across with great dignity and you have come across as an arsehole.' This was music to Littlejohn's ears – after all, if you are going to be a 'controversialist' you have to upset people (although not 'real' people), you have to be provocative. He and his producers were pleased with the reaction to the show; from an audience of 658,000, seventy complaints were generated. Littlejohn, like so many before him, sees the defamation of homosexuals as an easy way to success. The only way to stop such abuse is to outlaw the incitement of hatred – whether it be of homosexuals or of anyone else.

As this kind of yobbo programming proliferates, TV regulatory bodies will be helpless to influence it. There are signs that Britain's terrestrial TV stations are also going down the 'tabloid' route, particularly in news values. *The Independent on Sunday* carried out a three-week survey of TV news and found that ITV, in its race for viewers, was 'concentrating on crime and human interest stories and carrying fewer political [and foreign] stories than the BBC'.[32] Jocelyn Haye, chair of the Voice of Listener and Viewer consumer group, commented that ITN's changing priorities were influencing those at the BBC. She said:

> I think both channels are showing a greater tendency to feature the more sensational, emotional, personal stories. There appears to be a bandwagon effect when something really horrific happens. Everyone flogs it to death and issues that have a more profound, long-term effect are given less coverage.

It is difficult to predict what this decline in quality will eventually mean for the representation of lesbian and gay images. In theory, a wider choice of TV means a wider presentation of all shades of opinion. This is the same argument that was put forward when new technology was introduced to produce newspapers. In fact, newspapers remain locked in the grip of the ultra-rich. The extent to which TV remains out of reach of 'alternative' voices has yet to become apparent. Cable TV could, of course, open up possibilities for more gay-produced and controlled programmes, but it seems unlikely that such small-scale operations will ever be able to deliver a service to match that put out by the major operators.

Notes

1. *Broadcasting It* (Cassell, 1993).
2. Prism Press, 1991.
3. HMSO, 1982.
4. 31 January 1991.
5. 15 August 1986.
6. 1991.
7. 14 February 1993, 8–10 p.m.
8. 6 March 1991.
9. 12 February 1992.
10. *The Sunday Telegraph*, 17 August 1986.
11. Routledge, 1993, p. 267.
12. M. Alavarado and E. Buscombe, *Hazell: The Making of a Television Series* (BFI, 1978).
13. 1 July 1994.
14. *Fourth-Rate Estate* (Comedia, 1985).
15. *The Good, The Bad and The Unacceptable* (Faber, 1993), p. 133.
16. 15 January 1934.
17. Peter Chippendale and Chris Horrie, *Stick it Up Your Punter* (Mandarin, 1992), p. 26.
18. Inside Story: *The Tabloid Truth*, BBC1.

19.   13 November 1989.
20.   *The Media We Deserve* – reported in *UK Press Gazette*, 25 April 1994.
21.   Routledge, 1993.
22.   *Fourth-Rate Estate*, p. 46.
23.   Chatto & Windus, 1984.
24.   John Eldrige, *Getting the Message* (Routledge, 1993), p. 137.
25.   May 1994.
26.   *Stick it Up Your Punter*, p. 137.
27.   *The Hunt for Michael Jackson*, BBC2, 25 April 1994.
28.   22 February 1994.
29   Broadcasting Standards Council report, May 1994.
30.   2 May 1994.
31.   *Littlejohn Live and Uncut*, 9 July 1994.
32.   22 May 1994.

Chapter three

Homosexuality as a Political Tool

THE use of homosexuality to make political capital gained momentum in right-wing newspapers in the early 1980s. The creation of moral panics, using one of the last remaining minority groups which it was socially acceptable to abuse, helped the papers to set the political agenda. There is even a suggestion that these inflated 'crises' and 'threats' were hyped up to the extent that they were partly responsible for the ill-considered and badly-judged Section 28. The political exploitation of lesbian and gay lives began in earnest in May 1981, when control of the Greater London Council passed into the hands of a radical group of Labour politicians, headed by Ken Livingstone. Fleet Street's nightmare scenario had come to pass. 'Red Ken' – as Livingstone was dubbed – was promising a completely new direction for the London authority, a direction which was causing alarm in Downing Street and frenzy in Fleet Street. Livingstone had already created something of a furore by visiting the Harrow Gay Unity group in August 1981 and promising that the GLC would work actively to combat all forms of discrimination against lesbians and gay men. And he intended to put money where his mouth was. This was immediately attacked as an espousal of 'buggery on the rates' and caused *The Daily Telegraph* to state in its editorial that 'sexuality should not be a matter for evangelization'.[1] It also reiterated that, unlike Livingstone, it wanted the age of homosexual consent to remain at twenty-one. *The Daily Mail* carried a story about Livingstone headed 'The Commissar of County Hall',[2] while *The Sun* labelled him 'The most odious man in Britain'. The demonizing of Ken Livingstone had begun.

Demons and loonies

Characterizing individuals and groups as sinister and intolerable threats to the established order is a favourite device of propagandists. Nell Myers, once press officer for the National Union of Mineworkers, has seen this technique operating in close up. She wrote:

> Demonology is a device used by those who attempt hegemony; in societies such as ours it is used very effectively through the channels of mass communications. The National Union of Mineworkers and its president (Arthur Scargill) in particular have over the last few years been uniquely subjected to media-nurtured and propagated demonology, deployed in an unremitting attempt to discredit the NUM's fight to save the British coal industry . . . Demonology as a weapon to arouse fear, hostility and forms of hysteria is not of course confined to use against trades unionism nor against groups on the Left . . . look at its deliberate use to create an amorphous panic in attacking heresies such as homosexuality.[3]

The papers certainly pulled out all the stops in order to turn Ken Livingstone into the nation's number one hate figure. No stone was left unturned in efforts to defame him, and when the GLC bravely decided that it would back initiatives to improve the lots of several minority groups in London, it led to the authority being branded 'loony left'. In creating this concept, the tabloids had found the perfect tool for attacking the Labour Party, and others who were perceived to be 'a threat' to the status quo. The GLC's attempts to offer some redress to groups it considered 'disadvantaged' - gays and lesbians, blacks, gypsies, women and the disabled – were presented remorselessly in the press as 'a waste of ratepayers' money'. The purpose of newspaper attacks on left-wing councils which supported gay rights was explained like this in the pamphlet *Out of the Gutter*:

> The primary aim is to discredit the Labour Party, but in doing so, it implies that [lesbian and gay] oppression is normal, 'common-sense'. And it increases pressure in the Labour Party and the Left in general to drop policies aimed at ending our oppression. In no way are lesbian and gay issues seen as relevant to the readership, who it is presumed are heterosexual and prone to be outraged at any expenditure of public money on 'perverts'.[4]

The GLC was as good as its word, and spent £300,000 in grants to various gay groups around the capital, as well as putting up £175,000 to secure the building in Smithfield which was to become the London Lesbian and Gay Centre. Three years after the election, in May 1984, *The Daily Express* was still bashing away at Livingstone. Under the heading 'The great dictator', Peter Grosvenor wrote: 'Would Londoners, now paying rates for daft schemes to support gay movements have voted so convincingly for Labour had they known Red Ken would be running the city?' Opinion polls at the time suggested that yes, they would, and, despite the constant attacks, Livingstone refused to compromise his commitment to equality. He was quoted in *The Evening Standard* in May 1984 as saying: 'Being gay and lesbian is natural for gay men and lesbians. This needs to be understood by the heterosexual majority. The GLC has endeavoured to recognise this in its policy.' (Livingstone even listed the London Lesbian and Gay Centre as his only club in *Who's Who*.) All this was heresy to the Thatcherite philosophy so doggedly supported by most of Fleet Street. It was the antithesis of everything the Prime Minister was promoting. Not that the GLC was the first radical left-wing council in the country. David Blunkett's administration in Sheffield had been promoting unapologetically socialist policies for some time. Manchester and Islington councils had also made small grants to gay organizations in the late 1970s, but these had been low-key and discreet, and had not provoked the hysterical press reactions that were to come later. Journalists saw the GLC differently. Here was 'the enemy' right on the doorstep, only a stone's throw from Westminster, and deeply disturbing to a Government almost obsessively committed to 'self-reliance' and 'individualism'. Livingstone – and his large-scale banner over County Hall announcing the number of unemployed in London – was to become a severe irritation to a Government that was intolerant of any form of opposition.

Homosexuality: the perfect tabloid weapon

The lesbian and gay initiatives were a particular gift to the opponents of the GLC, for here was a minority that ranked high in the tabloid demonology. The queers didn't need help, Fleet Street repeatedly asserted, they needed shoving back in the closet. It wasn't long before the newspapers realized that pre-existing public homophobia could easily be manipulated and encouraged to the detriment of their left-wing foes. The Tory propaganda machine was quick to learn this lesson, too. Local Conservative councillors pored over the minutiae of council business, seeking to uncover anything which they might taint with the 'loony left' label. These titbits would be fed to their press allies who would then inflate and distort them to fit their agenda. So successful was this ruse that eventually the papers succumbed to the temptation not only to exaggerate but actually to invent 'loony left' stories.

Gradually, as more and more London boroughs elected radical Labour councils, a whole mythology was constructed. Anti-racist initiatives were plagued by wild stories about the supposed 'banning' of black dustbin liners and black coffee. Women's committees were – according to the tabloids – 'banning' the use of words like chairman, manhole – even 'girls' in one instance.[5] 'Sexist and racist' books by Enid Blyton were supposedly to be 'banned' from libraries. Gays were prominent subjects of this mythology. A glance at some of the 'loony left' stories would soon leave the casual reader imagining that half the rate precept was being spent on lesbian and gay initiatives. Reports of tiny grants made to lesbian and gay organizations were inflated by huge headlines and accompanied by 'thundering' quotes from local Tory councillors. (In fact, Camden and Haringey, the two most criticized boroughs in London, had total annual budgets in 1987–88 of £138 million and £204 million respectively, of which the lesbian/gay budgets accounted for 0.096 per cent and 0.06 per cent.)

The London *Evening Standard* was, perhaps, one of the most relentless originators of distorted 'loony left' stories. Many of its classic tales were to be subsequently taken up, and further embellished, by the national press. In March 1984 the paper reported the 'outrage' felt by Tory GLC councillors about a grant to gay teenagers. The story, headed 'Rates grant for teenage gays' concentrated almost entirely on the 'disgust' the tiny grant had provoked in the opposition. No information was given as to what the grant was for, or why gay teenagers might need it. The story was given a prominence quite out of proportion to the amounts of money involved, whereas other grants to less contentious organizations were ignored or played down. (For example, a few days before the gay teenagers story, The *Evening Standard* had reduced to three paragraphs the news of a much more substantial grant to a half-way house for the mentally ill. Those three paragraphs were relegated to the last news page). Another frequent trick was to imply that any pro-gay initiative must automatically be detrimental to heterosexuals. The message was clear: if they're giving something to gays, they must be taking it away from straights. An instance of this was when, in 1985, the Birmingham Gay Community Centre applied to the local council for rates relief. Both *The Birmingham Post* and *The Birmingham Evening Mail*[6] chose to link this application with the fact that the council was likely to refuse a similar application from a 'hard-pressed' scout group. The gays would receive their grant at the expense of the scouts. What the papers failed to say was that over three thousand other groups had also made applications for financial support from the Council.

Many right-wing commentators were totally thrown by this sudden emphasis on groups whose needs had been traditionally regarded as 'irrelevant'. The kind of socialism being promoted by left-wing London authorities was anathema to many journalists, who struggled to make sense of it. Peter Simple in *The Daily*

Telegraph even propounded the theory that gay people had been coralled and identified as 'a group' (in the same way as 'the Irish, women, blacks and the handicapped') so that their vote could be 'manipulated by the Left'.[7] Simple's theory totally ignored the previous fifteen years of non-party political self-organization in which the gay community had been engaged. He also ignored the fact that the Labour councils he referred to were losing more votes than they were gaining as a result of their pro-gay policies. The tabloids, though, were much less confused. When Hackney council proposed to include gays in its equal opportunities policy in December 1984, *The Daily Express* fumed: 'This is appalling foolishness. Despite the propaganda of militant homosexuals and trendy theorists, most of us still recognise the truth: homosexuality is deviant.' *The Sun* said: 'If it weren't such a dangerous idea it would be laughable. Impressionable youngsters have enough difficulty coping with adolescence as it is. We can only assume that in Hackney, the loonies have taken over the asylum.' In both these editorials, classic propaganda techniques are discernible. Both proceed from the apparently incontrovertible assumption that homosexuality is utterly undesirable and to be discouraged at all costs. Anyone who argues with this logic is automatically mad (or, more accurately, 'loony'). The reason they are mad is because they not only encourage children to be aware of homosexuality, they actually encourage homosexuals to come into contact with children. And as every good tabloid reader knows, homosexuals cannot be trusted with children (and if they don't know it, it will be repeated until they *do* know it).

'Positive images' were, indeed, to be opposed at all costs. Haringey Council in North London had formed a Lesbian and Gay Unit with the intention of not only providing support to the local lesbian and gay population but advising all council departments on the needs of homosexual ratepayers. The Tories on the council played the 'gays-are-evil-and-they're-stealing-your-rates' ticket for all it was worth. One local paper, *The Hornsey Journal*, even brought its publication date forward a day during the 1986 local council elections in an attempt to influence the result. The paper carried a huge headline 'HARRINGAY' and emphasised the council's commitment to 'positive images'. The ploy failed in that instance, and Labour was returned with an increased majority. But opposition continued to mount and the pressure from Fleet Street was unabated. Sometimes it seemed that local authorities were doing nothing but discussing gay issues, and giving 'special rights and privileges' to lesbians and gay men. Every proposal, every idea – wherever it came from and however unlikely – was presented in the papers as settled council policy. John Smith, the *The Sunday People*'s so-called 'Man of the People', commented:

> What a gay day it is among the left-wing lunacy of Hackney Council. The benevolent London borough is putting together a £1,000,000 package to safeguard the rights of homosexuals. They want to set aside parks for them with wardens making sure the poor darlings are not harassed by the 'straight' population. They also plan 'gay only' days at the baths and sports centres, and special library facilities for homosexuals. It's a pity they couldn't show similar concern for the Post Office worker who has taken them to court after waiting four years for them to repair his council house. Presumably the postman wasn't a poof. Not being homosexual can be a hell of a handicap in Hackney.[8]

None of the reported 'package' was ever seriously considered, but *Sunday People* readers might well have been left with the impression that it would all be in place by the following week. We also see in this another example of the gays-are-stealing-from-straights argument.

The distortion, disinformation and lying reached such a pitch that eventually the Association of London Authorities felt obliged to put out a leaflet entitled *It's the Way They Tell 'em* trying to counter some of the stories that the press had invented. The leaflet revealed that Bernie Grant, who at the time was leader of Haringey Council, had been reported in *The Mail on Sunday* as having banned 'black bin liners' because they were 'racially offensive'. It was sheer invention. So also was the report in *The Daily Express* that Ealing's Labour council had 'banned' the use of the term 'Wendy house' because it was sexist; *The Daily Mail* reported that the 'loony left' had re-written 'Baa Baa Black Sheep' because it was 'racist':

'Playgroup leaders have been told that in future children should sing "green" sheep instead' the paper lied. *The Daily Mirror* even reported that one council had: 'banned references to family life during sex lessons in its schools. Teachers have been told to drop the word "family" because it discriminates against homosexuals.' Funny as these stories might have appeared to some people, there was something sinister about the tabloids' blatant fabrications, and the fact that they made no attempt to defend themselves against charges of lying. Democracy was not being served by these deceptions, and the disadvantaged groups that the councils had set out to help were actually receiving even *more* discrimination because of the policies.

The inclusion of 'sexual orientation' in equal opportunities policies was often presented by Fleet Street propagandists as the giving of 'special rights' to homosexuals. This was particularly true in the areas of housing and jobs where 'equal ops' were portrayed as the granting of 'priority' treatment. *The Daily Telegraph* reported that Islington Council was giving gay couples 'preferential treatment' in housing. This was not true – the council was simply saying that gay couples would be considered in the same way as everyone else for council housing. John Junor in *The Sunday Express* wrote: 'Once again the London Borough of Ealing is advertising for a child care officer . . . saying Ealing's new council will welcome applications from "lesbians and gay men" . . . Isn't that akin to setting alcoholics free in a liquor shop?[9] *The Sun* followed this up with 'Lefties seek gay for boys home job'. In fact, Ealing Council's Equal Opportunities statement is carried in all recruitment advertising. This ad was no exception. Far from 'seeking a gay' for the job in question, the ad simply said gay people would not be barred from applying. The 'protection of children' slur is, of course, one of the most insidious and frequently recurring subtexts of those blustering about the 'loony left'. The late Jean Rook, who was a columnist on *The Daily Express*, was commenting in 1985 on a decision by Greenwich Council to promote 'a better understanding' of homosexuality in schools. She wrote:

As a 1985 mother, I'd sooner burn that classroom speech [in defence of Oscar Wilde] than deliver it to an increasingly warped and bent section of society which ill-names itself gay. Gay? They are a miserable bunch of fanatics who spend their lives dismally pretending to revel in what they are. And outrageously trying to recruit others . . . Now my backlash is complete . . . to red Hell with Oscar Wilde.

Jenny and other children

Then, to coincide with the local Government elections and those for the Labour-controlled Inner London Education Authority in 1986, *The Sun* devoted its front page on 6 May to the headline 'Vile book in schools'. It concerned a small book, originating in Scandinavia and published in Britain by the Gay Men's Press, called *Jenny Lives with Eric and Martin*. The book told the story of Jenny, who is living with her father and his male lover. It advocated tolerance. 'Pupils see pictures of gay lovers,' was *The Sun*'s sub-heading over a breathtaking piece of distortion. According to *The Sun*, *Jenny* was 'a shocking schoolbook showing a little girl in bed with her homosexual father and his naked lover' and, worse still, it was available to children in ILEA schools. *The Sun* also labelled its election eve story 'exclusive' even though its sister paper *The News of the World* had 'done' *Jenny Lives with Eric and Martin* a full three years before, and *The Islington Gazette* had used it the preceding week as a means of attacking the local council. Not to be deprived of such a juicy weapon, *Today* headed its coverage with 'Scandal of gay porn books read in schools'. The commentators were quick to follow up this concerted attack. John Junor in *The Sunday Express* wanted to know: 'Which porn shop is peddling this filth? No porn shop . . . the Inner London Education Authority.'

Complaints to the Press Council about *The Sun*'s coverage of the *Jenny Lives with Eric and Martin* saga resulted in the paper receiving a severely slapped wrist. The Council described the paper's coverage as 'exaggerated and misleading' saying:

> According to the evidence before the Press Council the book was held by ILEA at a teachers centre, not in schools and was

not available to pupils. The authority had said it should only be used with older pupils in particular and exceptional circumstances after their parents had been consulted. Under the main headline 'Vile book in schools' *The Sun* said it was being made available to junior schools by education officials and in another headline reported 'Pupils see pictures of gay lovers'. The paper itself chose to reproduce across four columns a picture captioned 'Perverted . . . a page from the book showing Jenny in bed with her gay dad and his naked lover' thereby giving the picture and its caption far wider dissemination than otherwise it might have had. Although the story did not say so, there is no doubt that the book was available to London children either through other channels than schools and the ILEA. However, the misleading but clear implications of the headlines was that the book was then in schools and had been seen by children there. The complaint against *The Sun* is upheld.

Then came *The Daily Mail*'s claim that there was a 'Row over call for gay education in schools'. The 'row' was, in fact, constructed by *The Daily Mail* when members of the Campaign for Homosexual Equality distributed a leaflet to all candidates in the ILEA election asking them to remember that not everyone is heterosexual and those who aren't might need some information and support relevant to their needs. In the hands of *The Daily Mail* that simple plea became: 'children should be taught that relationships between men and women aren't necessarily normal'. Meanwhile, a feminist group in Haringey was campaigning against racism, sexism and heterosexism. *Today* turned this around to become: 'A feminist group in a left-wing borough has been attacked for trying to turn people into homosexuals.' This deliberate confusing of the words 'heterosexism' and 'heterosexual' lead to the claim that the group was 'pushing their ideas in schools' with the clear intimation that they were trying to turn children into homosexuals. *The Daily Mail* took this story up, too, elaborating it to claim that the group was: 'urging Harringey council to publicise lesbians as loving, caring, perfectly normal women with special teaching on the subject in the borough's schools plus the promotion of books like The Joy of Lesbian Sex in local libraries'.

It seemed the papers would stop at nothing to punch this message home. No one was safe from having their words twisted to suit the tabloid agenda. Dr John Habgood, the Archbishop of York, for instance, appeared on the front page of *The Daily Mail* under the heading 'Primate: Ban These Gay Lessons'.[10] The sub-heading said that the Archbishop had made 'an outspoken attack on the teaching of positive attitudes to homosexuality'. But when Ian Wardle of the Leicester Branch of the National Union of Teachers wrote to Dr Habgood about his supposed comments, the prelate replied:

> My main purpose in giving an interview to *The Daily Mail* reporter was to say something about AIDS and in particular to stress the importance of a compassionate understanding of homosexual victims of the disease. Questions about education were entirely secondary to this main purpose, though in the event they received the greatest prominence. As is usual with the tabloid press the headline bore no relation to anything I actually said or believe, and I have been careful throughout all my interviews on the subject to make the point that I am not in any way opposed to young people at an appropriate age learning about homosexuality and having their questions answered in a straightforward manner.[11]

When challenged on this brazen distortion, *The Daily Mail* refused to comment, and letters remained unanswered. *The Daily Express* also joined in the growing hysteria with an editorial which read:

> The line between teaching children not to be hostile to homosexuals and leaving them with the impression that homosexuality is acceptable or even normal is an extremely fine one . . . too fine. That is why those left-wing councils who seek to promote 'positive images of homosexuality' to children as young as three are behaving with scandalous irresponsibility.

Despite this deluge of 'children have to be protected from gays' propaganda, Labour's majority was increased in all the boroughs regarded as 'loony left' and the Inner London Education Authority. But others in powerful positions had obviously begun to believe the unfair – but continuing – propaganda. At the time, Kenneth Baker was Education Secretary and was playing the 'protect our children' card with great vigour. Writing in *The Sunday Telegraph* he said: 'When it comes to aggresive promoting of homosexuality, it is wrong. There is a difference between encouraging and accepting homosexuality.'[12] To help out with this campaign, The London *Evening Standard* ran a front-page frightener under the heading 'Beware this dirty dozen'.[13] It referred to twelve books which the ridiculous back-bencher Peter Bruinvels wanted 'banned' from schools. Among the titles were several with gay themes. It was an extraordinary piece of propaganda with little purpose than to turn up the heat on the sex education debate that was raging at the time.

Tabloid homophobia had reached such an hysterical pitch that even the broadsheets were beginning to get worried about the way things were developing. Generally reluctant to criticize their fellow journalists, commentators on the more liberal wing of the press began to question what was happening. Ian Aitken in *The Guardian* wrote:

> One can shake one's head sadly over this sort of thing and turn gratefully to one's more tasteful choice in newspapers. But the fact is, things are getting worse rather than better; a substantial section of the press is plumbing depths never before experienced in this country . . . yet I confess I have no idea what can be done about it. Perhaps Rupert Murdoch is the price we have to pay for liberty. If so it is a shamefully heavy one.[14]

Some Tories were disturbed by the rampant hatred that elements within their own party were promoting. One was Brian Meek, leader of the Tory group on Lothian Council. Writing in *The Glasgow Herald* in November 1987 about the rise of the 'rabid right', his thoughts had been prompted by the rantings of Paul Johnson, who had written approvingly in *The Daily Mail* about 'a hardening of attitudes to abortion, capital punishment, the rights of homosexuals to be treated in a liberal fashion and the suppression of violence on television.' Brian Meek concluded that Johnson wouldn't be happy until 'you were forced to have a baby, but hang it if it were gay'. After demolishing Johnson's facile arguments about abortion and hanging, Meek wrote:

> Then there are the homosexuals, the supposed destroyers of everything that is decent in our society. By allowing them, in the privacy of their own homes, to conduct their sleazy affairs we are corrupting the nation. How? I know homosexuals. I suspect you do too. They have never posed any threat to me or any of my heterosexual friends. Many are talented, gifted men who have made great contributions to music, to theatre, to the very culture of which we are supposed to be proud. Yes, there are dirty old men who prey on young boys and they should be locked up. There are thousands more who prey on young girls.

Such criticisms had no effect upon the tabloids and the abuse continued unabated: Commenting on Camden Council's Lesbian and Gay Unit, *The Daily Star*'s 'Angry Voice' columnist Ray Mills wrote: 'They employ four full-time woofter apologists . . . Mills has a positive view to offer: These filthy degenerates should be kicked up their much-abused backsides and locked up in their closets.'

Eventually, at the Tory party conference of October 1987, Mrs Thatcher signalled her exasperation with 'loony left' education policy, and said in her closing speech: 'Children who need to be taught respect for traditional values are being taught that they have an inalienable right to be gay'. This was the signal needed by the gang of puritanical MPs who had made several attempts already in the House of Commons to curb what they saw as 'the promotion of homosexuality' and the 'indoctrination' of children. They insisted that a full-scale campaign to 'normalize' homosexuality was under way, and few tabloid readers would have argued with them after enduring four years of their papers' insistence that the Labour Party had conspired with the 'homosexual lobby' to infiltrate every school in the land and brainwash children with perverted ideas. Indeed, Paul Johnson was even trying to use AIDS for party-political advantage. He wrote in *The Daily Mail,* under the heading 'AIDS: the danger that Labour ignores at Britain's peril':

> During the past five years, as evidence of the AIDS peril has grown, the Labour Party has step-by-step committed itself to policies which place homosexuality on a moral par with normal sex and encourage its expression . . . On the issue of AIDS and the homosexual connection, Labour is playing politics with human lives. As the public grasps this fact there could be awesome political retribution.[15]

Woodrow Wyatt echoed these sentiments in *The News of the World*:

> Some Labour councils encourage AIDS with grants to homosexual centres. So do Labour education authorities telling children that homosexuals living together are as stable as married couples. They also encourage children to experiment with sex. This is murder.[16]

Such was the level of abuse and distortion, that Bernard Levin was moved to write in *The Times:*

> Homosexuals are being portrayed – portrayed literally as well as metaphorically – as creatures scarcely human; they are being abused in not just the old mocking way but in the foulest terms, meant with deadly seriousness; they are experiencing an increasing discrimination over a wide range of situations; already voices have been raised demanding the 'cleansing' of schools as they have been for purging the church.[17]

The end product

The climate was ripe for Tory back-bencher David Wilshire to introduce an amendment to the Local Government Bill (on the final day of the committee stage), stating that a local authority should not 'promote homosexuality or publish material for the promotion of homosexuality . . . promote the teaching in any maintained school of the acceptability of homosexuality as a pretended family relationship by the publication of such material or otherwise'. Initially the Labour Party accepted the amendment – only Bernie Grant, who had once been leader of the dreaded Haringey Council, spoke out with any force against it. To its credit, *The Guardian* was quick to pick up the dangers of this amendment, and the morning after its acceptance the paper's editorial stated that there was 'no more unpopular group of people in this country today than homosexuals' and accused the Conservatives of using this fact to become the 'anti-gay party'. It said that Labour should oppose the motion, claiming the party had the choice of being 'popular or principled'. Clause 28 – as the amendment was termed – led to an enormous protest and to an unprecedented politicization of the gay community in Britain. In that sense it had proved counterproductive for some of its most enthusiastic supporters.

A bludgeoning for Kinnock

Of course, once the effectiveness of the anti-gay 'smear' technique had been proved and perfected, it was liberally applied in other areas of life disapproved of by the Tory press. Not only could local authorities be blackguarded for supporting gay rights; the unions and the national Labour Party could be similarly attacked, using the same blunt instrument. In 1986 the Labour Party was being pushed, sometimes reluctantly, into supporting gay issues. Despite desperate efforts to distance itself from the taint of the 'loony left', Labour found itself stuck with pro-gay policies which its national conferences continued to pass with gratifying regularity. *The Daily Express* was pleased to inform its readers a few days before that year's Labour Party Conference that 'Gay Lib poses a new threat to Labour hopes'. The paper considered that, because a couple of gay rights motions had been proposed for that year's agenda, it would cause 'an embarrassing new storm'. The storm, of course, was a familiar one – a similar tempest had blown up at the previous conference, whipped up entirely by the Fleet Street wind machine. Meanwhile, the TUC conference had overwhelmingly passed a couple of supportive motions at its conference. The motions had been opposed by only one speaker, Frank Sweeney, but he was the only person quoted in *The Sun*'s report of the event. ('Gay people are absolutely vile. They corrupt anything and everything they touch' Mr Sweeney had said.) Not a single word of the many speakers in support was reported.

As the 1987 General Election approached, Fleet Street went into overdrive. Despite the fact that Neil Kinnock was trying to moderate perceptions of the party, the 'extremist' imagery was still being propounded in the papers. Charles Moore wrote in *The Daily Express*: 'Labour is the pro-homosexual party. Until recently its preoccupation with "gay rights" was considered a bit of a joke. Now it's beginning to stir up real rage.'[18] Indeed it was, but the rage had been created, and was being further inflamed, by the right-wing press. As the day of the election approached, the heat was turned up further. Ken Livingstone, who was then standing as a parliamentary candidate in Brent East, spoke, in his usual supportive way, at a gay rights conference in Camden. This was manna for the tabloids: 'Red Ken to defy Neil and speak out for gays' blared *The Sun*.[19] In fact, Livingstone had simply expressed support for some ideas for law reform that had been floated at the conference and he promised that Labour would give them full consideration if it gained power. This was then distorted to appear as official Labour Party policy. *The Sun* mendaciously claimed: 'Labour leftie Ken Livingstone has smashed the party's new moderate image by promising to introduce special laws for gays and lesbians. And he claimed later that Neil Kinnock was backing his move.' In an editorial, *The Sun* said:

> Labour is now publicly pledged to introduce legislation to protect homosexuals against 'discrimination'. The pledge was given at a meeting . . . by one Kenneth Livingstone . . . He has in mind a law similar to the Race Relations Act. On that basis it would enable any homosexual or lesbian to blackmail any employer who denied him or her promotion. It would protect any propagandist who sought to persuade schoolchildren that homosexuality was not merely normal but superior to heterosexual activity.

On 6 June that year, *The Daily Mail* pulled the same trick. It featured on its front page the headline 'The Left's plan for a gay charter' reporting that 'Labour bosses are being urged to support a gay rights bill'. What in actual fact had happened was that *The Daily Mail* had obtained a copy of proposals from a gay pressure group, the Labour Campaign for Lesbian and Gay Rights, calling for changes in the law which discriminate against homosexuals. This was pretty standard fare; all political parties were being pressurized by gay groups to include promises of reform in their manifestos. However, these reasonable demands were utterly twisted by *The Daily Mail* which listed them as:

- Male prostitutes to be allowed to *solicit for prostitution* without fear of arrest.
- All homosexual offences, *including gross indecency* in public places, to be abolished.
- Age of consent for *sex between people of the same sex* to be lowered to 16.
- Law of blasphemy to be removed.
- Members of the armed forces to be allowed to *indulge* in homosexual relations *without being disciplined*.

My italics emphasize the paper's use of emotive words and phraseology which did not appear in the original report. In fact, the LCLGR report consisted of a draft proposal for a Lesbian and Gay Rights Bill to be introduced into Parliament by some future Labour government. It was wide-ranging, covering partnership and adoption matters as well as suggesting the abolition of discriminatory legislation. *The Daily Mail*'s report selected only those sections dealing with sexual offences, putting a completely different emphasis on what was actually in the report.

Throughout the weeks leading up to the General Election (held on 21 June 1987), the press repeatedly used the 'Labour-is-the-gay-party' ploy. *The News of the World* ran 'My love for gay Labour boss' over two pages,[20] while *The Sun* gave the whole of one front page to the headline 'Labour picks rent boy as school boss'. Another *Sun* classic read: 'Lesbian plots to pervert nursery tots'. And so determined were the tabloids that Mrs Thatcher should return that the 'gay smear' technique was also used against the Liberals. When David Steel mentioned his party's commitment to reforming the law relating to homosexuality on a radio programme, *The Sun* headlined: 'Lower gays' age of consent, says Steel – Liberal leader's gaffe is set to split the Alliance'. Of course, it was all hyperbole and there was no such 'split' over this issue.

Immediately before the 1991 local council elections, the 'loony left' was dusted off once more. *The Daily Star* revealed that 'loony' Newham Council in East London was considering naming some streets after 'gay heroes' as nominated by the council's Lesbian and Gay Advisory Group. 'Vidyapati Drive, Tseko Simon Nkoli Road and Audre Lord Avenue could soon be appearing on the local map,' the paper told its incredulous readers.[21] A week earlier, *The Newham Reporter* had told its readers quite straightforwardly that these possible street names 'were suggested in order to provide positive images of black people, women, the disabled and homosexuals'. Not to be left out of the propaganda jamboree, *The Daily Mail* told how 'hard up' Hackney Council was 'offering special courses for black lesbians who have lost their lovers'. The Tory leader on the council, Joe Lobenstein, said that he had 'no objections to doing something for black people in need. I am against giving privileges to lesbians who lead an unnatural life.' *The Sun* came up with the headline 'Doh, a deer, a female queer' and told of 'The lesbian version of The Sound of Music' which was to be staged with the 'support of two loony left councils, Lewisham and Greenwich'. And, in line with the well-established formula for these kinds of stories, the Tory leader of the council was quoted as 'exploding': 'What a load of utter rubbish. Using community charge payers' money for this kind of thing is totally wrong'. Having carried the story, *The Sun* could not resist embellishing it with its own style of mockery, 'gaying' familiar songs and titles in an unfunny and embarrassingly juvenile way: 'ideas for song titles and other gay musicals, including Idle Vice; Climb Every Mountain, forge every dyke; Sex-queen, going on seventeen; My Favourite Shirtlifters; Oklahomo; My Queer Lady . . . etc.' Birmingham Council, too, was one that the Tories had lost to Labour and which they were desperate to regain. In the approach to the election, Birmingham Labour group were constantly portrayed as extremists and 'loonies'. *The Birmingham*

Evening Mail said on its front page: 'Labour to woo teachers in gay mag'.[22] If we look carefully at this headline we will see that it had been constructed to induce maximum fear among parents. The story itself had been created from almost nothing. The council had an equal opportunities policy, which included sexual orientation. By 1991 that was not in the least bit unusual. As part of its commitment to making sure everyone had a fair chance of getting jobs, Birmingham had stated that it would 'advertise such posts in the relevant minority press'. On came Tory group leader Reg Hales to say: 'This is the trendy Lefty road, followed by Liverpool and the London boroughs, and it is sad to see Birmingham going the same way'. This story, as presented by *The Birmingham Mail*, did not just 'happen' – it is not, in fact, an event at all. It had to be carefully created, angled and headlined in such as way as to make it seem like a serious issue. It takes a special skill, perfected over many years, to conjure up scare stories from such flimsy material.

But perhaps the most blatant and unpleasant use of the gay cudgel to bash Labour was provided by *The Sun* when, on 3 October 1991, it headlined 'Labour will allow gay sex at 18 – Kinnock sparks AIDS fury'. This exaggerated story was accompanied by an almost unbelievably crude editorial headed 'Save our teenagers from AIDS'. It read:

> Nearly 2,500 Britons have died from the disease Aids. The vast majority were homosexuals who caught it through unnatural sex. Teenagers need to be protected from them on moral grounds and for health reasons. Few people would argue with that. But along comes the Labour Party with plans to lower the age of consent. Gay sex would be legal at 18, not 21. Eventually under Labour it could be as low as 16. If that's the kind of Britain you want, you know who to vote for.

(Only three years after this editorial was written, it was, paradoxically, the Conservatives who made parliamentary time available for a debate which led to the age of consent being reduced to eighteen.) But the use of racism and homophobia as a means of selling newspapers and influencing the outcome of elections was now well established. It seemed that the blitz on the lives of homosexuals was never-ending, that the denigration of the needs of gay people would never cease. Even after the so-called 'loony left' had been disowned by the national Labour Party and largely hounded from power, the tactic of portraying Labour as the 'gay-lovers' party would emerge over and over again. But then came the sea change.

A new regime

Mrs Thatcher was suddenly ousted from power to be replaced as Tory leader by John Major, who had been her Chancellor. He appeared a much more moderate and affable personality, a blessed relief after eleven years of unfettered bigotry. Major did not hold the iron-cast views of his predecessor and his social conscience was not grounded in the 1950s as hers had been. When, in 1992, he had to face the electorate on his own terms, he appeared to be sending out signals to the gay community that he was prepared to look sympathetically at their cause. Gay rights activist Sir Ian McKellen was invited to Downing Street for a chat with the PM, and, in February of that year, *The Sunday Telegraph* was telling us: 'The Prime Minister has signalled his support for equal opportunities for homosexuals, fuelling expectations of a free vote by MPs on reducing the age of consent for male homosexuals if he is returned to power.' The 'signal' came in the form of a supportive letter to the chairman of the Tory Campaign for Homosexual Equality (TORCHE). In just five lines, Major managed to avoid any mention of the words lesbian or gay or even homosexual. Major wished the group well and hoped it would become 'a valuable forum for discussion of these issues'. *The Sunday Telegraph* said that 'Ministers are still nervous about alienating supporters by moving too fast on the reform of homosexual laws'. The 'signal' however was sufficient to provoke another backlash in the tabloids, with *The Daily Star* asking backbench Tory MP (and long-time opponent of gay rights) Geoffrey Dickens what he thought of the prospect. Mr Dickens, in his usual overblown style, said that he would fight the proposal to change the law 'tooth and nail'. He said: 'They don't have a snowball's hope in hell of getting this through . . . There is a small minority of paedophile homosexuals who want to corrupt and ensnare youngsters. They must be stopped at all costs.' At the same election, a Tory MP, Alan Amos, who was fighting to retain his seat for Hexham, was arrested on Hampstead Heath after being discovered in a car with another man. The police alleged that there had been more than conversation in progress when the the two had been disturbed. No criminal proceedings were instituted, but the news of the arrest was leaked to *The Sun* (presumably by someone in the police force) and resulted in Mr Amos resigning his candidature. He said at the time that what had happened had been 'childish and stupid' and that he did not deserve the 'squalid reporting' he got from the press. That gave the very papers he was criticizing the green light to go to town on him. *The Sun* said: 'He should not put the blame on the press. So far as we know no newspaper lured him into a public haunt of homosexuals. The blame is entirely his own. And the shame.' *The Star* said that it was his own choice to: 'wander at dusk at a place which has been turned into a no-go area for decent families by perverts practising what many people . . . would call another dirty, dangerous and anti-social habit. His downfall must be sad for him. But he shouldn't try to tar us with his own muck.' *The Daily Telegraph* had the same opinion: 'Even in a relatively liberal and enlightened age, conduct that may be acceptable as long as it remains wholly private becomes intolerable when it is exposed to the public gaze. Mr Amos cannot blame his tragedy on the messengers.' But it was to pre-empt a Sunday newspaper exposé that Hexham's Liberal Democrat candidate, Jonathan Wallace, decided to come out voluntarily. 'I'm gay and proud of it,' he said, but that did not spare him having to endure *The Star*'s 'hilarious' front page 'Hold on to your seat!'

All this prompted Elizabeth Grice to ask in *The Daily Telegraph*: 'is the single man an electoral liability?' She checked out several Conservative Associations and found that all male candidates were being 'carefully screened' before nomination, so as to avoid potential 'scandal'. The last thing they wanted was for their MP to find his way on to the front page of *The News of the World* or *The Sun* – exposed as homosexual. So, it seemed that the dead hand of Rupert Murdoch and his editors were now dictating who was to be selected for Parliament (or, at least, who was not). The selection procedure, however, seemed as fallible as ever it had been, and the 'outing' of gay MPs by tabloid newspapers has continued. However, the 1992 General Election saw one more outing for the 'loony left' and on the eve of the election[23] (when opinion polls were indicating that Labour had a serious chance of taking office) *The Sun* ran a classic summary of all the lies they themselves had created over the years under the heading 'Nightmare on Kinnock Street':

> Planning applications – including loft conversions, home extensions and garages – will have to be approved by gay and lesbian groups if Labour are elected. Housing spokesman Clive Soley has decreed that the scheme will be operated by every council in Britain. Town chiefs will be forced by law to consult homosexuals over planning decisions – as well as ethnic groups, the elderly and disabled.

This was distortion *par excellence* and prompted Clive Soley to complain to the Press Complaints Commission, which ruled:

> The newspaper told The Commission that their story was based on a cutting from a seemingly accurate story which had appeared several months earlier in another newspaper and to which Mr Soley had apparently not objected. The Sun accepts that perhaps they should have made clear that the reported arrangements were only proposals but argue that the proposals were undoubtedly serious and they had no reason to believe that a Labour Government would not have enacted such legislation. The drafting of the consultation document did not permit the distorted interpretation published by The Sun and clearly referred to consultation with the local community on relevant planning policies and procedures and not to individual applications. The complaint is upheld.[24]

This adjudication came five months after the election, which the Tories had won seemingly against the odds. Whether this piece of 'horror journalism' had caused the vital C2 voters to switch intentions at the last moment we will never know, but that did not

stop Kelvin MacKenzie boasting that it was *The Sun* 'wot won it for
the Tories'.

The Major factor

By the time of the 1994 local council elections, a different
political climate was apparent. John Major's 'decency' was being
seen as weakness and he was proving to be the most unpopular
Prime Minister since opinion polls began. Fleet Street's traditional
loyalty was being sorely tested. Its adulation of Mrs Thatcher had
been complete, but Major commanded no such unquestioning devo-
tion. Suddenly papers like *The Sun* and *The Daily Mail* were found
to be criticizing the Tories in a way that would have been unthinkable only two years before. But it was a Conservative Government
that had allowed the age of consent to be lowered, and had made a
number of other legal reforms in the arena of gay rights. Then another
Tory (Michael Brown, MP for Brigg and Cleethorpes) was outed by
The News of the World,[25] after it revealed he had had an affair with
a twenty-year-old man. The information was obtained by deception.
A *News of the World* reporter, Mazher Mahmood, was tipped off by
a member of the Conservative Party (who was paid £10,000 for his
trouble). The reporter then posed as a diplomat and inveigled
himself into the confidences of one of Brown's friends. Using hidden
tape recorders, he provoked the men into indiscreet conversations.
The justification for this intrusion into private lives was that Brown
had broken the law. At the time, although Parliament had voted for
the age of consent to be lowered to eighteen, the change had not been
enacted and the legal age was still twenty-one. Even so, although
Brown was forced to resign his Government position there was no
question of his resigning his seat. Significantly, he received a great
deal of support from his parliamentary colleagues, indicating how
profoundly attitudes had changed. Rather than being condemned
for being gay – which would have been inevitable only a few years
before – Brown was being sympathized with as yet another victim of
press brutality. *The Sun* even reported that 'John Major has ruled
that it is OK for his ministers to be gay. The premier says they will

not be sacked unless they behave irresponsibly – such as cheating on wives or having affairs with under-age boys.'[26]

The paper quoted an unnamed 'Government source' as saying: 'The days when a minister could lose his job simply for being gay are gone. There is no more reason why a single male MP should not have boyfriends than girlfriends.' *The Independent*, however, was confused by this, and in an editorial commenting on *The Sun*'s story said:

> Mr Brown's problem lies not in his sexuality but in having notionally broken the law . . . Unfortunately for MPs, the public expects those who act as legislators not to break the laws that Parliament passes, however obsolete and unfair they may appear. That applies equally to heterosexual MPs. If one of them were found to be having a relationship with a girl of 15, he would probably be in more serious trouble than Mr Brown, who is receiving strong support from his constituency association . . . What matters, as the only MP to have 'come out', Labour's widely admired Chris Smith, has commented, is not whether someone is straight or gay, bachelor or married, but how good they are as an MP or minister.[27]

The Daily Mirror, anxious to score some anti-Tory points and yet not be seen as gay-bashing, tried to play both ends against the middle – and failed. It said in an editorial:

> Among the ailments of which this Government is dying is terminal sleaze. An MP's sexuality or private life must never in itself be a bar to holding office . . . Voters have formed an indelible impression that Mr Major presides over a party which behaves as though it is living through the last days of the Roman Empire.[28]

Further advice was proferred to Michael Brown in *The Guardian* by Francis Wheen, who brought out another dilemma faced by the MP:

The Brown affair is the least scandalous [of a series of sexual exposés] yet. If the MP in the case were some pious zealot like John Selwyn Gummer – or better still Ian Paisley – one could enjoy watching him wallow in his hypocrisy. But Michael Brown is no hypocrite. Rather courageously for a right-winger, he has consistently supported gay rights. He was one of only three Tories who opposed the wretched Clause 28, and a few weeks ago he voted to lower the male homosexual age of consent to 16. So why shouldn't he have a boyfriend? Would the Mirror think it sleazy if a young, unmarried MP took up with a 20-year old woman? . . . I can understand his desire to sue the News of the World, but I hope he'll reconsider. A libel suit would rest on the assumption that it is 'defamatory' to suggest he is gay – which in turn would imply that homosexuality is shameful. Such defensiveness gets you nowhere . . . I prefer the line taken by another MP friend of mine, the Labour front-bencher Chris Smith. He 'came out' a decade ago, and since then has been left happily unmolested by the tabloids. To stick with the hunting metaphor: where's the fun in chasing a fox that won't run?[29]

The rise of political correctness

Although these events were indicative of a change in thinking in the sensible press, the right-wing division was being as socially conservative as ever. It had now discovered an alternative means of opposing reforms that it perceived as a threat to its vested interests. That new weapon was 'political correctness'. The concept of political correctness had originated on the university campuses of America. There, the idea of 'disadvantaged groups' had, apparently, been taken to ridiculous lengths. It was described by Alexander Chancellor in *The Daily Telegraph* as:

a phrase invented in America to combat through mockery a new Orwellian world of Newspeak, and it has been used to good effect. It has done a lot to stop the disease taking root in

Britain, where people now seem to me to be more in fear of being labelled 'politically correct' than of expressing 'incorrect' attitudes.[30]

According to right-wing observers of the phenomenon, the English language was being mangled in an attempt not to offend groups like 'Red Indians' who were now to be referred to as Native Americans, and people from ethnic minorities who would henceforth be referred to as People of Colour. The philosophers of the right maintained that plain speaking had become impossible and anyone refusing to use this new and 'ridiculous' terminology was to be persecuted from their job by the new 'fascist armies of the politically correct'. *The Daily Mail* even reported, with some contempt, that the makers of the board game Scrabble: 'are to remove racial epithets and other terms offensive to minorities from The Official Scrabble Players Dictionary. Included on the list of newly-banned words are "nigger", "spic", "dago" and "jew" used as a verb for bargaining.'[31] In March 1993, *The Sun* told us that: 'The White House is grinding to a halt – because of the Clintons' obsession with giving enough jobs to blacks, gays and women. President Bill Clinton, driven by his wife Hillary, is determined to be seen to be politically correct.' *The Sunday Times* reported:

> When the head of one of the transitional teams that shaped policy for Bill Clinton asked the White House recently why it had not offered him a job in the new administration, the reply was baffling. 'Your transition team had no OGs and this is considered unacceptable,' he was told. Translated, the message was clear: because his team included no openly gay men, he was considered unwilling to encourage diversity in government.

In the London *Evening Standard*, Alexander Cockburn suggested that political correctness has led to a 'lesbian take-over of the White House'. He wrote:

> The highest-level gay or lesbian government officer now graces the Department of Housing and Urban Development.

Roberta Achtenburg, formerly a lesbian city council person in San Francisco is Deputy Assistant Secretary for Community Development. She is also Clinton's liaison to the politically potent gay and lesbian movements. The sense that somehow the dykes have taken over is swiftly susbstituting itself as demon fear among bible-thumpers who previously reckoned that [gay men] were pulling the strings.

The idea that the employment of one open lesbian in the whole of the Clinton administration constituted a 'take-over' is an indication of how defensive attitudes to homosexuality still are. And the opinion was rapidly forming that any homosexual in any job was not there on his or her merits but only because of political correctness. No humane and compassionate person would really oppose the replacing of words like 'nigger' and 'poofter' and 'mongol' with less violent and insulting terms like 'African American', 'gay' or 'a person with a learning disability' – unless those people were trying to make political capital from it.

British journalists grabbed the concept with both hands and began using it for their own purposes. Richard Ingrams in *The Observer* wrote:

The schedules of Channel 4 are usually a good guide to what is politically correct. So I was interested if somewhat alarmed to see a whole hour being devoted to promoting Ludovic Kennedy's campaign for the legalisation of euthanasia. If I am right, it looks horribly as if euthanasia has now joined abortion, gay rights, doing away with nuclear energy and saving whales as something we all have to be in favour of.

Notice how Ingrams has craftily made it seem that all the above listed issues are the province of 'the politically correct' (aka 'loonies') and can therefore be disregarded by all sensible people. And then we have Garry Bushell writing in *The Sun* about the gay character in *Casualty* (BBC1): 'Inevitably Ken is painted as a sympathetic character rather than a sleazy kharzi cruiser. This is because TV drama is life as Big Brother Beeb would like it to be, rather than how it is, and "positive images" are a must for all minorities.'[32] Bushell makes out that any attempt to portray gay people as whole human beings with a full range of emotions is nothing but 'political correctness' and in Bushell's book, PC is just one more left-wing conspiracy aimed at undermining the lives of 'real folk'. Astute readers will know, of course, that Mr Bushell is peddling a political agenda of his own which is as dogmatic as that of any 'loony lefty'.

The right-wing press has been full of stories about the 'legions of the politically correct' who, they maintain, are stifling free speech. To hear them tell it, you'd think it was almost impossible to criticize anyone with a black skin, a gay orientation or a disability. The only problem with their argument is that their pages are full of abuse for these groups. So we should be careful about those who oppose political correctness – and remember that attempts to make it sound like a sinister undermining of 'traditional values' are generally creating a stick with which to beat reformers and progressives.

Such had become the obsession with political correctness in the straight press that I was forced to return to the subject in March 1994, after Jane Brown, a school headmistress in Hackney, East London, was splashed over the papers when she refused tickets for a performance of the ballet *Romeo and Juliet* on the basis that it was 'too heterosexual'.

> Here was a heady brew to sustain the fantasy world that [the right wing press] has created: political correctness gone mad; a loony left-wing council and – the icing on the cake – a lesbian in charge of 'our' children.
>
> The political correctness ticket was played for all it was worth. 'Romeo, Romeo, where art thou homo?' was *The Sun*'s front page announcement of the story.
>
> 'Don't laugh at political correctness. It could seriously damage your freedom,' wrote Brian Hitchen, pig-like editor of *The Daily Star*. 'There is always somebody eager to explain to [our kids] why the act of buggery is romantic and acceptable in a society gone mad. Cherished books of childhood are scorned as racist or sexist. Black dolls are outlawed by muddle heads who see nothing wrong in

smoking dope but go batcrap over golliwogs. Potty politically correct teachers have even changed the words of the nursery rhyme to Baa, baa, white sheep.' (Notice how Hitchen recycles the loony left mythology in this new context.)

Richard Littlejohn, *The Sun*'s self-proclaimed 'irritant of the year' (wouldn't His Master's Voice be more appropriate?) was quick to take up the cudgels. 'She is almost certainly anti-American, considers African wood-carving a higher art form than anything Michelangelo ever turned out and believes disabled lesbian mud-wrestling more 'relevant' than Beethoven. Otherwise she would never have been appointed. Jane Brown is what you get from job adverts in *The Guardian* – where strict adherence to the doctrines of political correctness is more important than an ability to actually do the job.'

Mr Littlejohn is unimpressed by Ms Brown's record of improvements at the school in the face of overwhelming disadvantage, and seems unaware of the esteem in which she is held by the people who really know whether she is doing a good job or not – the parents. For it was they who threw this poisonous slander back in the face of the press. Instead of forming a lynch mob, as the sick tabloids were encouraging them to do, they stood shoulder to shoulder with the embattled headmistress and told the Fleet Street muck merchants to eff off. 'She must be sacked immediately,' said Littlejohn. 'She should be kicked out of her present job on her non-heterosexual ear and never allowed to teach again,' said John Junor in *The Mail on Sunday*.

'Get lost', said the parents and school governors by way of response.

Just as it had broken the original story, the London *Evening Standard*[33] was the first paper to confirm that Jane Brown was, indeed, a lesbian ('a hatchet-faced dyke' as Littlejohn put it in *The Sun*) and then the hunt was on for the dirt about her private life.

Jane Brown was besieged. The street where she lives was so cluttered with reporters and photographers that no traffic could move on it. Her neighbours were harassed and abused when they refused to supply the titillating details. The children at Kingsmead School where Jane Brown works were 'wound up' by all the attention. Years of valuable work on tolerance and understanding were blown out of the window.

Then the hate mail began. From all over the country – indeed, from all over the world, for this had become an international controversy – the anonymous green-ink brigade began bombarding Jane with threats to her life. It became so bad that at one point she needed police protection.

Meantime, the then Education Secretary, John Patten, was in something of a cleft stick. A rumour was circulating that the story had been planted in the London *Evening Standard* in order to distract attention from the fact that, in the same week, he had had to 'stand down on just about every recommendation he has made'. Government embarrassment over the failure of Patten's half-baked schools policies needed to be minimised. The story's 'political plant' theory was given further credence when it was revealed that the original remarks had been made in the previous September. Where had the story been in the intervening six months?

Patten's much vaunted legislation to put power into the hands of parent-governors had also back-fired on him, because the very people he has empowered are refusing to suspend a woman whose 'politically correct' philosophy he detests. ('We should be in no doubt about either the scale or danger of the PC advance. It is dangerous and if allowed to spread without challenge it could alter the nature of British life,' Patten wrote in *The Daily Mail*.)[34]

The Times Educational Supplement took a calmer look at the issue and said: 'The affair has highlighted the dilemma common for any teacher working in a multicultural, cosmopolitan borough, over where to draw the line between sound equal opportunities policies and political correctness.'[35]

Ah yes, political correctness. Suzanne Moore in *The Guardian* was calling the bluff of the rampaging right-wingers: 'Change is what it is all about. And that's why I ask what the opposite of political correctness is . . . it is not tolerance. Instead, PC is being used to lunge at the heart of anyone who suggests that there is something wrong with the status quo. There are may things wrong with the notion of political correctness, chief of which is that it mirrors so precisely the faults of its opposition. Both understand that language is a vehicle for ideology. Both camps seem to think that language, literature, indeed culture is a fixed rather than a fluid entity, that the substitution of one word, one text, one sentiment for another somehow changes everything. Both are appallingly literal, concentrating on text at the expense of context. Why else, for instance, have we had to endure another spirited defence of Shakespeare, one of the "dead white males" least in need of resuscitation? It appears that those so vehemently opposed to the concept of PC are doing very nicely thank you; the world may be full of kykes and dykes, whingers of all descriptions who want a piece of the action, but that's tough. The fact, though, that some of them may even be getting it means something has to be done.'

That 'something' often leaves a trail of broken lives: Jane Brown being just one.

In the May 1994 issue of *Gay Times* I was pleased to be able to record:

> At the same time Jane Brown received some support from a surprising source when *The Sunday Express*[37] sent an undercover reporter to the Kingsmead Estate, where her school is situated, to find out why parents are supporting her so determinedly. They discovered that Kingsmead School is 'a beacon of hope for the rest of the estate'. Ms Brown is making a difference to the lives of the children who live in circumstances that would have shocked Charles Dickens.
>
> *The Sunday Express* was big enough to admit that Jane Brown's decision about the ballet was 'far from being about petty political correctness' and much more concerned with the play's portrayal of violence and gang warfare, which is rife in the Kingsmead.

Of course, this admission that the newspapers' portrayal of Jane Brown as a left-wing lesbian extremist was unfair and distorted came too late. The damage to her reputation had been done and references to her in future will always be coloured by the initial branding of her as a dangerous, politically motivated, threat to the development of children.

In the same issue of *Gay Times*, I reflected once more on the abuse of homosexuals using 'political correctness' as an excuse for piling on the obliquy. This example was centred on that year's Oscar ceremony:

> Tom Hanks had just won best actor Oscar for his perform- ance in *Philadelphia*, which was hyped as the first main- stream Hollywood film to deal with AIDS. In his tearful, but unconvincing, acceptance speech he had said that gay men who had died of the disease – and many of them had been his friends – were 'angels walking in the streets of heaven'. The speech might well have been embarrassingly overblown and over-rehearsed, but I suppose it was made with the best of intentions. I don't suppose he can have known that any mention of homosexuality on television brings a compensat- ing torrent of hate from the British press.
>
> Leading the charge of the Right brigade was John Junor of *The Mail on Sunday*[38] who said: 'Should Hanks be congratulated for his acceptance speech in which he sought to glorify men who died from AIDS? I know many actors don't have much behind their ears and that Mr Hanks was in a state of euphoria. Even so, I could hardly believe my ears when he described them as "Angels walking in the streets of heaven" . . . Isn't that a bit hot? I would agree if Mr Hanks were talking of innocent victims, haemophiliacs who had died because of being transfused with blood, but homosex- uals who contract the disease through their own promiscu- ity? If they're in heaven just who the hell is in the other place?'

The more liberal papers eventually caught on to the use to which political correctness was being put. Mike Hornby, writing in *The Independent on Sunday* said he had seen through the manipulative harping on political correctness by bigots who wanted an excuse for their bigotry. He wrote:

I don't want to be accused of political correctness myself, but
. . . No, sod it. Actually I don't give two hoots. We have
reached the stage where one only has to say, politely, that one
disapproves of, for example, the charming contemporary
custom of pushing excreta through the letter boxes of Asian
families, and otherwise humane people start to sneer about
social workers and *Guardian* readers.[39]

He recalled his childhood in the late 1960s and early 1970s when
Asians were 'pakis'; Afro-Caribbeans 'coons'; girls 'scrubbers' and
everyone told 'Irish jokes and Biafran jokes and queer jokes'. He
thinks things have improved since then:

> *Love Thy Neighbour* and *The Black and White Minstrel
> Show* are hardly likely to be revived, and Bernard Manning is
> now confined to the Northern club circuit; but I cannot . . .
> find it in my heart to grieve for their absence, and if that
> makes me sound like a bleeding heart, drippy, pinko pansy,
> well, I'm sorry . . . Elsewhere it looks like business as usual.
> Local councillors with Nazi sympathies, drunken Tory MPs
> interrupting important debates with moronic homophobic
> abuse, terrifying assaults on Asians in the East End of
> London.

The use of homosexuality as a political tool is likely to continue so
long as it proves effective. But it can prove effective only while
homophobia remains so deeply entrenched, and can be so easily
manipulated by those with a political axe to grind.

Notes

1. 20 August 1991.
2. 30 May 1981.
3. *Bending Reality* (Pluto Press, 1986).
4. Andy Armitage, Julienne Dickey and Sue Sharples (Campaign for
    Press & Broadcasting Freedom, 1987).
5. *The Sun*, 8 April 1992.
6. 14 November 1985.
7. December 1984.
8. 18 November 1984.

9.   24 July 1988.
10. 21 November 1986.
11. *Outlaws in the Classroom* (City of Leicester Teachers' Association (NUT)), 1987.
12. 14 September 1986.
13. 22 October 1986.
14. 8 May 1987.
15. 4 November 1986.
16. 9 November 1986.
17. 28 December 1987.
18. 6 March 1987.
19. 19 May 1987.
20. 17 May 1987.
21. 8 May 1991.
22. 22 April 1991.
23. 8 April 1992.
24. Reference 92–397, 7 September 1992.
25. 'Tory whip in gay sex triangle', 8 May 1994.
26. 10 May 1994.
27. 11 May 1994.
28. 9 May 1994.
29. 11 May 1994.
30. 10 May 1994.
31. 11 May 1994.
32. 29 September 1993.
33. 27 January 1993.
34. 11 February 1994.
35. 8 January 1994.
36. 28 January 1994.
37. 3 April 1994.
38. 27 March 1994.
39. 13 March 1994.

Chapter four

You 'Out' but
we 'Expose'

REPORTING from New York on 2 October 1989, the
London *Evening Standard*'s correspondent, Clive Barnes, said that a
US gay magazine called *Outweek* had:

> initiated a policy of trying to drag reluctant gays out of the
> closet, even if they are kicking and screaming . . . by
> publishing a list of about 50 people in a box marked 'Peek-a-
> Boo'. There is no explanation of the list, but if a name is
> included beside that of such uncloseted gays as Barney Frank,
> people can draw their own conclusions.

And so the phenomenon of outing was introduced to an apparently
fascinated British public. (The term 'outing', though, wasn't actually
coined until March 1990, when *Time* magazine reported that gay
activist and writer Michelangelo Signorile had revealed that a
recently deceased high society millionaire, Malcolm Forbes, had
been gay.) Writing in *The Sunday Correspondent* about this new
phenomenon, Christopher Hitchens said:

> The American language is usually more than ready for a new
> word, but the verb 'to out' is having some difficulty gaining
> acceptance. To be 'out' is to be an admitted homosexual, and
> to 'come out' is to declare the fact. To be 'outed', however, is
> to be exposed as a homosexual against one's will. In the old
> days this was known as fag-baiting or queer-bashing, and

was done by 'crusading' moralists. To be subjected to outing today, however, is to be outed by homosexuals intent on making a point.[1]

After years of tolerating abuse and betrayal from influential closet cases, someone – probably Signorile – thought up this new strategy for hitting back. In the USA, radical gays had become determined that the rich, famous homosexuals who remained in the closet would no longer enjoy their straight privileges at the expense of the rest of the gay population ('You slimy, hypocritical bastards' as one of Signorile's columns was headed). Any closeted politician who supported anti-gay initiatives could no longer feel that he was invulnerable in his treachery. No well-loved entertainer who was hiding his or her sexuality could be sure that passing for straight was the safe option it had previously been. Interviewed in *Gay Times*, Michelangelo Signorile said that he had posthumously 'outed' Malcolm Forbes so that:

> history wouldn't be distorted, so that it's clear that gays are everywhere, not just the bottom of the pile, and because a powerful man like Forbes felt unable to speak out over the AIDS crisis because he wanted to remain in the closet. There is an element of revenge in it, but it's also about claiming figures in the political establishment. I don't want to help gay people remain emblems of heterosexuality.[2]

Writing in *Rouge*[3] magazine about his book *Queer in America: Sex, the Media and the Closets of Power*,[4] Signorile says that his main aim in promoting outing as a political act was to 'equalise discussion of homosexuality and heterosexuality in the media':

> Every day the media discusses aspects of public figures' heterosexuality when these facts are relevant to the news story whether or not these subjects want these facts reported and no matter how private they may be. But most of the 'responsible' media refuses to reveal public figures' homosexuality, even when relevant – except of course when such

revelations play into their homophobic agenda. The heterosexual media thereby becomes the enforcers of the closet,
opening it only when it is to their advantage and not ours. I
therefore advocate open discussion in the media of the
homosexuality of *all* public figures – and *only* public figures –
when relevant to news stories – and only when relevant to
news stories – regardless of the subjects' deeds or misdeeds.

Clive Barnes was horrified by this kind of thinking and he articulated in his article what was to become a Fleet Street litany: 'Surely
people should be allowed to come out of their appropriate closet in
their own time. No-one needs this kind of smear coercion.' *The
Daily Mail*'s US correspondent, George Gordon, said of the outers:
'This fascist army is doomed to failure' and rapidly made outing a
platform for a generalized attack on homosexuals, using AIDS as a
familiar vehicle.

The whole outing exercise was, in fact, the last desperate
throw of angry gay activists who had failed to convince the
world that Aids was as much a threat to the community at
large as it was to homosexuals . . . It is as vicious and nasty as
anything dreamed up by the Nazis in denouncing Jews . . . a
tool of psychological terrorism. It was redefining the concept
of suggesting that a gay community is a genuine, inescapable
minority into which one is born, from which one derives
advantages and to which one owes inherent allegiance. It
brands as immoral the attempt by prominent gays to escape
the social penalties of homosexuality and advance the claims
of moral kinship.

Outing comes to Britain

It would be another two years before outing really became a
major issue in Britain. The direct action group OutRage! had caused
a minor stir when, in March 1991, it had 'besieged' Cliff Richard at
a film studio where some of its members were acting as extras on

Derek Jarman's film *Edward II*.[5] The gay activists had demanded that the veteran pop star should 'come out of the closet'. In its usual overstated and melodramatic way, *The Sun* reported 'the gays . . . tried to break down the rehearsal room door' and it claimed that they chanted: 'Come out of the closet Cliff and declare yourself a full-blown homosexual.' This seems rather a clumsy chant, and not one that any self-respecting gay demonstrator would lumber himself or herself with. The people who had actually taken part in the spontaneous episode say that there was no attempt to break down doors and, in fact, the whole thing was rather good-humoured. Commenting on this incident, however, John Smith, a columnist on *The People*, wrote:

> Who the hell do these gays think they are, acting like some liberation lynch mob? I don't know if Cliff Richard is homosexual and frankly I couldn't care less if he is in the closet, out of the closet or on top of the wardrobe. That's his business. It certainly isn't the business of a bunch of braying bully boys carrying the banner for gay rights. What about Cliff's right to privacy?[6]

Leaving aside the almost laughable hypocrisy of anyone at *The People* having the temerity to talk about respect for privacy, Mr Smith's comments came after many years of media attempts to get Cliff Richard to admit that he was homosexual. I would imagine that every newspaper and magazine in the land has, at some stage, asked Cliff 'Are you gay?'[7]

But outing obviously intrigued Fleet Street. On 2 July 1991, *The News of the World* carried an article about the appearance of a few outing posters around the West End of London. These followed the same format as the American ones – a large photograph of a celebrity, with the legend 'Absolutely queer' underneath it. 'MPs face "you are gay" smears in poster war' the paper announced. However, the most famous of the posters was the one naming Jason Donovan, which was later to bring the outing saga to an unpleasant head.

On 16 July 1991, *The Independent* carried an interesting, well-informed feature on the American outing campaign which had concentrated on film stars and other popular entertainers. *The Independent*'s piece was subsequently lifted by *The Sun*, which headed its version 'Branded queer by evil gays'. The article was suffused with moral indignation at what the paper called 'these sinister sex slurs'. It did not, of course, restrain itself from reproducing the offending posters in their entirety.

Outing had all the elements of a successful tabloid story. It would enable the public's apparently endless appetite for information about the sex lives of celebrities to be fed while, at the same time, allowing the papers to adopt a ludicrous tone of righteousness. Because the story broke during what is traditionally the 'silly season' (high summer when Parliament is in recess, the courts are not sitting and there's not much real news around) the papers had the space and resources to do the topic proud. *The Sunday Times* decided on 28 July to feature an outing story on its front page. The paper claimed that there was now a threat to bring the outing campaign to Britain in a big way – naming MPs, actors and even a member of the Royal Family. The threat was emanating from a mysterious, previously unknown group called FROCS (Faggots Rooting Out Closet Sexuality) which, according to the paper, would also name judges, policemen and other prominent closet cases. This was a gift to the editors strapped for genuine news, and during the following week the whole British press went into outing overdrive. Journalists tried desperately to track down this unknown 'terrorist' organization that, for a few glorious days, seemed to be threatening the whole fabric of society. Peter Tatchell – seemingly the only known spokesperson for the 'militant' end of the gay movement – featured large and, once again, became the focus of Fleet Street's hate. *The Sun* said:

> Peter Tatchell squealed like a stuck pig because newspapers revealed his homosexuality when he stood as a Labour parliamentary candidate. Invasion of privacy, he protested. Now hypocrite Tatchell is backing a spiteful campaign by gays to reveal the sexuality of public figures.

Every other national paper commented in a similarly hysterical fashion. The supposed campaign was a 'cruel and squalid . . . witch hunt' according to *The Daily Star*;[8] 'spiteful and vicious' (*The Sun*); 'bitchy and scabrous' (*The Daily Mirror*); 'downright nasty' (*The Independent*); 'McCarthyism' (*The Daily Telegraph*); 'despicable and vicious' (*The Daily Mail*); 'cruel' (*The Daily Express*); 'an unacceptable infringement of privacy' (*Today*). Such excitement – but where was this campaign? How was it to be successful without the help and co-operation of the very newspapers that condemned it? A few posters, seen by a tiny minority of the population, hardly warranted distress on this scale, but the papers were on a roll – even though very little was actually happening. Hundreds of column inches were devoted to outing during the week. Even the broadsheets joined in the chorus, taking the opportunity to reproduce the American posters which had named Jodie Foster, Tom Selleck and Whitney Huston.

Some people in the gay community were heartened by the press reaction, feeling that at last we were being regarded as a real force to be reckoned with. But others felt it threatened the small degree of respect that conventional campaigners, working within the system, had established over the years; the use of such terms as 'terrorists' and 'bullies', and the sheer hysteria of the coverage, was making them nervous. After the controversy died down, A. E. Cairns put into words (in *Rouge* magazine) what many who opposed Michelangelo Signorile were thinking:

> What right does this self-appointed vanguard of the gay community have to blackmail gays and lesbians to come out of the closet? Everyone, gay or straight, surely has the right to choose the lifestyle which suits them. Why do they have to be the subject of pressure, however subtle, to conform and identify themselves publicly with the gay community? The philosophy of who is not for me is against me is the genuine voice of fanaticism which has no place in the liberalism of the gay and lesbian community. There is no place in such community for the thought police of groups who wish to expose gays and lesbians against their will.[9]

The newspaper commentators saw in outing another opportunity to heap abuse on to gay people. They took pot shots not only at outing but at gay life in general. Outing was to unleash a positive torrent of vituperative homophobia in the press. Lynette Burrows, in *The Sunday Telegraph*, wrote:

> The aim of outing is to improve the civil liberties and general acceptability of homosexuality by demonstrating how many covert homosexuals there are doing a useful job in public life . . . It is as if a group who wanted hard drugs legalised were to publish a list of those pop stars who sniff cocaine, in the hope that their fame would commend their vice.[10]

She said that the 'common man' does not glean his concept of right and wrong from observing the activities of those who consider themselves to be 'the best people':

> So are there any factors which might make the common man change his opinion that the Bible had it roughly right when it described homosexuality as wrong and dangerous, or is there even anything in 'outing' which might cause the common man to think he had misjudged the homosexual lobby? . . . The instinctive repugnance which ordinary people feel for the practice of homosexuality has little to do with religion, as can be seen from the rabidly anti-homosexual regimes like the Nazis, which punished it with death, and from our own society which has become more openly and crudely anti-homosexual as our religious tolerance wanes.

From outing, Burrows ranged over the whole gamut of anti-gay thought, venting a depth of hatred that was awesome to behold. After several thousand words of muddled reasoning, religious self-delusion and sheer irrational prejudice, she eventually reached the conclusion that young men are:

> persuaded out of their role as husbands and fathers of the next generation by the practice which is the literal death of all that most parents have lived for and all the treasures of the temperament, intellect and talent that they have nurtured. This is not an idle fear to be dismissed as mere prejudice; it is

the healthy response of families and of a society which knows themselves to be threatened.

Much similar comment followed from other sources, but still there was no evidence of the start of any widespread outing campaign. The tabloids had, as usual, cooked up another 'major gay scandal' out of next to nothing. In the end, FROCS, too, turned out to be a hoax. An *ad hoc* group of young men had got together to play the papers at their own game, and they had succeeded beyond their wildest dreams. As the intrepid press pack eventually tracked them down, Lofty Loughery and Shane Broomhall – the men at the root of it all – realized they had better come clean. The British libel laws are punitive, and are not tempered by a constitution guaranteeing free speech, as in the USA. At a hastily convened press conference at the London Lesbian and Gay Centre, they said they had never had any intention of launching a massive poster campaign. Reporters who had flocked to the Centre in the hope that the story was about to take on a new impetus were bemused to find that the laugh was on them. 'Nice to know that the gays have a sense of humour, even though it is a queer one,' said the London *Evening Standard*, through pursed lips. *Today* newspaper, however, did not see the joke and was claiming that it was not they who had been duped, but Peter Tatchell, who had been forced to become the spokesperson for the secretive (and, as it turned out, putative) outers.

Jason and The Face

The outing controversy seemed to be over until the style magazine *The Face* covered it again, this time reproducing the Jason Donovan outing poster which, foolishly, it had doctored. Over the front of the T-shirt that Donovan was wearing had been printed the words 'Absolutely Queer'. He decided to sue *The Face*, and the journalist who had written the feature, Ben Summerskill (then editor of *The Pink Paper*). The case reached court in April 1992. The jury decided that Donovan should be awarded £200,000 damages for the 'smear' on his reputation.

Donovan emerged from court to read a statement claiming that the trial had not been about homosexuality, but about the doubts cast upon his honesty. Gay protesters were on hand with posters reading 'Gay is not libel' and 'Being gay is no shame'. The newspapers were cock-a-hoop at the result and once more went into a frenzy of anti-gay headlines. '£200,000 glad not to be gay' said *The Daily Star*;[11] 'Too hunky to be gay' said *The Sun*; while *The Sunday Telegraph* was pleased to announce: 'Jason win gives gays a straight answer.'[12] This kind of response cut deeply into the sensitivities of gay people all over the country. Just who had been insulted by what? After all those years of campaigning and coming out, it was still considered £200,000-worth of a 'slur' even to suggest that someone might be gay, even though the judge had said during the trial that it was 'very debatable' whether it was any longer defamatory to call someone a 'queer'.

The Parliamentary closets

The Jason Donovan debacle was not the end of the outing saga: it was to re-emerge during the campaign to lower the age of consent. Opening the batting was Stephen Fry, who, in a *Spectator* article in November 1993, repeated an assertion he had made previously in *The Sun* that 'the present Cabinet contains six adulterers and at least two homosexuals' and that, because of this, they should not be pontificating at the rest of us about 'morality'. This outraged John Junor who wrote in his column in *The Mail on Sunday*:

> Is he just making a wild, unfounded allegation? I very much hope so. But if it is otherwise, and Mr Fry does have information denied to rest of us, then why having gratui-tously raised the matter, doesn't he have the guts to name the two ministers? There are 20 men in Mr Major's Cabinet. Each of them is married. Which two of them, according to Mr Fry, are leading double lives? Isn't it damnable that, thanks to Mr Fry, even the 18 innocent ones are from now on going to be under suspicion?[13]

It was at this stage that the all-purpose 'militant gay lobby' was resurrected in *The People*, which ran a front-page headline claiming 'Sixty gay MPs face being "outed" by militant homosexuals'.[14] An unnamed, but allegedly 'furious', back-bencher was quoted in the article as saying: 'Various gay groups are threatening MPs who they know are gay'. However, no specific groups or individuals who proposed to carry out this campaign were identified. It was all extremely vague – in fact one could go so far as to say entirely fabricated – but the issue of outing was back on the agenda. *The Independent*, taken in by the fantasizing of the tabloids, said in a leading article: 'Outing is wrong . . . It would be a bad day for democracy if MPs' voting decisions were affected by unwarranted intrusion into their private lives.'[15]

But the rumours would not go away. As the age of consent debate approached in early 1994, the Government was embroiled in a humiliating farrago caused by a speech Prime Minister John Major had made at the Conservative Party conference the previous year. In it he had called for a return to 'traditional values' under the slogan Back to Basics. Major's ministers had, one after the other, tried to blame the nation's ills upon one-parent families and non-traditional ways of living. The Back to Basics phrase returned to haunt the Tories when several Ministers were subsequently exposed by newspapers as adulterers. Two other prominent Tories were shown to have fathered illegitimate children and *The Sunday Times* found out that one back-bencher (a millionaire called David Ashby) had gone on holiday with a male friend and shared a bed with him – 'in order to save money'. (Incidentally, Ashby was outed not by a 'militant gay lobby' but by his wife and sister who had, in a fit of pique, given the stories to the paper.)

It seemed almost certain that the tabloids would top their revelations with the outing everyone was anticipating – that of a cabinet minister. Tension was heightened when, on 6 February, gay footballer Justin Fashanu tried to sell to *The People* stories of 'three in a bed sex romps' he purportedly had with high-ranking Tories. He had demanded £300,000 in exchange for the evidence. (By that time, anyone who wanted to know the names could have read them in the satirical magazine *Scallywag* which had published a list of sixteen Tory MPs it alleged were gay. Unfortunately it provided no supporting evidence and so was disregarded by the rest of the papers. *Scallywag* is produced by a group of militant heterosexuals.)

The People did not take Fashanu's bait, having come to the conclusion that the footballer couldn't deliver.

In the midst of all this came news of the 'scandalous' death of Tory MP Stephen Milligan, caused by self-strangulation during a masturbation session at his home. He had been wearing items of women's clothes when his body was discovered. Although there was not a shred of evidence that Milligan was gay (but plenty to show that he wasn't), the tabloids seemed incapable of grasping that many transvestites are heterosexual. *The Sun* made an immediate connection: 'Kinky MP: cops quiz gay Fashanu'. Fashanu had claimed to *The Sun* reporters that he had known the dead man and described him mysteriously as 'the weak link'. In *The Daily Express* he was quoted as saying: 'I knew him and I knew he was homosexual'. However, the following day, after a visit from the police, Fashanu was backtracking, saying that he *hadn't* known Milligan and that his tales of sex with Tory MPs were a total fabrication. He also denied that he had tried to sell the story to *The People*, but the reporters involved had taped their conversations with him, and these were broadcast on the television show *The Big Story*. Fashanu left the country a few days later, leaving John Junor wondering whether what he had said had been true and, if so, maybe he had been paid off by someone other than *The People*.

The Daily Mirror was wise after the event and condemned Fashanu under the headline 'Fash the trash'. It said:

> For years he touted to the highest bidder the tale of his claimed affair with a Government minister. He demanded money – usually £5,000 – to name the senior Tory who gave him a tour of the Commons, during which he jumped on the Speaker's Chair. He also said he shared a bed with a married Minister.[16]

None of the papers made any mention of their own eagerness to believe anything anybody tells them about homosexuality, however outlandish. Their desire to make a connection between Stephen Milligan and an alleged 'gay circle' within the Government was so desperate, there seemed to be an element of wishful thinking in taking Justin Fashanu and his agent at their word. Whether

Fashanu's claims of affairs with ministers were true or not, the papers had fallen victim once more to their own prurient need for sensation.

On 21 February 1994, the House of Commons voted to lower the age of consent for gay men to eighteen – and not sixteen, which would have made it equal with heterosexuals. Two days later *The Daily Star* was still playing the outing threat for all it was worth: 'A top politician is to be publicly named as a homosexual by gay activists,' the paper announced on its front page. 'They will "out" him because he voted against lowering the age of consent to 16 . . . Last night opponents of the gay movement said they were appalled because there is no evidence against the MP.' Once again, there was no indication about who the sinister gay activists might be. This lack of detail did not stop *The Daily Star* venting its rage against gay people generally in an editorial in the same issue:

> Famous gays try to sound ever so responsible when they plead their case on TV. But the vicious militants behind them (no pun intended) reveal the truth of their nasty campaign. Piqued over the Commons vote which fell short of their demands, they now threaten to 'out' a prominent politician. This is nothing less than a callous blackmail attempt. No responsible newspaper, magazine, TV or radio station would fall for it.

The editorial ended with a plea to the police to prosecute the perpetrators of this outing 'blackmail'; but for all *The Daily Star*'s raving, at the time of writing the supposed gay Cabinet minister remains safe and secure in his closet.

Of course, without the co-operation of the straight media, gay attempts at outing can only be very small-scale and localized. As far as I know, no British gay magazine has used the outing weapon. Even if it did, with its limited circulation, it is unlikely to have much impact. An Australian gay magazine, *OutRage*, tried, in May 1994, to out a priest who had written a virulently anti-gay article in the daily paper, *The Australian*. The priest had launched a ferocious attack on the annual Sydney Mardi Gras, perhaps the largest gay event in the world, writing that it was 'an affront to every family in

Australia'. He also complained that its screening on TV was 'an attempt to establish the homosexual lifestyle as an alternative.' A columnist on *OutRage*, Peter Blazey, revealed in its May edition that the priest, then a teacher, seduced him when he was a fifteen-year-old schoolboy and also seduced a number of other boys at that time. Reporting the outing, *Capital Gay* said:

> There has been no media response to the *OutRage* article, which is Australia's first outing in print. 'I suppose there is a bit of journalists' solidarity going on,' Adam Carr, the acting editor of *OutRage* said. 'Not that [the priest] is a real journalist, but there are nervous closets all through the media and so I suppose they feel obliged to cover up for each other'.[17]

This was not the case with Phil Webb, who in 1991 was elected on to the local council in the quaint little English village of Wimbourne in Dorset. Webb was a well-known local figure, a determined 'alternative lifestyle practitioner' – he had 'spiky dyed hair', is unemployed and bisexual. This latter point was not something he wished to be known publicly, but when someone suggested he should stand for mayor, the more traditional elements on the council thought it was too much. Two unnamed councillors rang the local paper and told the journalist about Webb's sexuality. This resulted in the headline 'Yes, I am a bisexual says would-be mayor' and a great deal of furore in this small town. A leader in *The Bournemouth Evening Echo* said: 'Two Wimbourne town councillors called the *Echo* to tell us that one of their colleagues, Philip Webb, who had been nominated as mayor, was bisexual. They did not like it. They planned to put a stop to it but they did not want to be quoted.'[18]

Of course, without the paper's help, Webb's sexuality would have remained private, as he desired. (He has been quoted as saying 'I didn't want to stand on a soapbox for gay rights. That choice has been taken away from me'.)[19] As it turned out, the story was picked up by *The News of the World*, which informed the nation that 'Mr Mayor wants it both ways'. At that point, Webb was forced to come out to his family, which he says was 'painful'. Everyone involved in Phil Webb's outing was heterosexual.

However, in October 1994, a gay-instigated outing did succeed in a small way. It started when *The News of the World* discovered that a newly-appointed Bishop of Durham, The Right Rev. Michael Turnbull, had been convicted of gross indecency twenty-six years before. The paper carried lurid details of the 'cottaging' arrest[20] and then revealed that Bishop Turnbull had made a statement supporting the Church of England's line that homosexuality was incompatible with the priesthood. This they used as justification for their outing – they weren't being anti-gay, they asserted, but anti-hypocrite. However, the revelation did revive the debate on gay priests and much comment followed – some of it highly critical of the church's muddled and unjust stance on homosexuality. The new Bishop, however, refused to resign, announcing that he was not a homosexual and never had been. Outrage! mounted a protest at his enthronement and the University of Durham Union Society held a debate on the motion 'This House supports its new Bishop'. During the debate, a former Franciscan friar, Sebastian Sandys, made a speech of opposition in which he outed three other senior Church of England figures. Those names were reproduced in *The Guardian*[21] and then in *The News of the World*[22] – albeit tacked inconspicuously on to the end of news reports. Despite the low-key nature of the outing it was, in fact, the very first successful one perpetrated by the gay community rather than the press, although of course the collusion of the press was needed in order to make it effective. Given the cries of horror that had preceded the event, when it actually happened it passed without comment from the other papers.

Press outings

One of the points Michelangelo Signorile makes repeatedly is that the press are interested in outing only when it is on their own terms and suits their own purposes. Despite the modest gay-generated outing mentioned above, the practice is overwhelmingly a tabloid speciality.

The self-righteous tabloid cant about the 'spite', 'cruelty' and 'McCarthyism' of outing rings hollow when we examine the evidence concerning their own activities on this front. Indeed, the level of malice employed by the press in outing of gay individuals has been quite remarkable. One of the first victims was Labour MP Maureen Colquhoun, who had been hounded by the press to reveal her sexuality and eventually, in 1977, did so. She was promptly de-selected by her constituency party in Northampton North – which said that it had done so because of her 'unsatisfactory record'. Only *The Daily Mirror* backed Ms Colquhoun's right to stay, saying that the constituency's attempt to blame her record amounted to 'hypocrisy'.[23]

Peter Tatchell and Bermondsey

Perhaps the most famous case was that of Peter Tatchell, who stood as a Labour candidate in Bermondsey in the by-election of February 1983. The press suspected that Tatchell – who had, in *Sun*-speak, become 'Red Pete' - was gay, and intended to use this to destroy his chances of winning the seat. There followed what *Gay News* described as 'the most homophobic by-election of our time' and 'the most long, drawn-out pillorying of a homosexual since the 1950s'.

The problem for the papers was that at the time they had no hard evidence of Tatchell's homosexuality. *The Sun* and *The Daily Mail* set themselves the task of uncovering this proof, and Tatchell became the subject of intense journalistic attention. The reporters began to 'monster' Tatchell – phoning him up at all times of night and day, sifting through his rubbish, pestering his neighbours and family. Some journalists even toured gay clubs offering money to anyone who could produce one of Tatchell's lovers. None of this proved fruitful. But then came a tip to *The Sun* that Tatchell had attended the Gay Olympics in San Francisco. *The Sun* editor Kelvin MacKenzie expended huge resources to try and confirm this, but without success. However, true or not, MacKenzie was determined to run the story. Tatchell describes how he was doorstepped by *Sun* reporters.

> At one point, three of them waited outside my workplace for five hours in unseasonal cold and pouring rain to question me about an alleged visit to the Gay Olympics . . . I told them I had known nothing about the event before I went on holiday and did not attend it. Despite my denials, they kept up non-stop pressure on me for the next three days and three nights to force me to 'confess'. In the end I am sure they knew the story was a fiction . . . in reply to my denial and warning of possible legal action, one of the *Sun* reporters actually said to me: 'Sue us. So what? What's a few thousand pounds to us? This is a good story and we're going to use it.'[24]

After much lying, deceit and betrayal, *The Sun* got what it needed to justify the front page headline 'Red Pete "Went to Gay Olympics"'. The story was a smear job of epic proportions and was described in *Stick it Up Your Punter* as 'containing no evidence to prove the truth of the allegation, yet leaving all but the most careful readers with the impression that it was fact'. The editor of *The Sun* knew that the Gay Olympics story was not true, but he had constructed it in such a way that no one could be under any illusion but that 'Red Pete' was, indeed, a poofter.

This was, of course, only a small part of the virulent press campaign which led to Tatchell's defeat by 9,300 votes. Tatchell complained about *The Sun*'s and *The Daily Mail*'s lies and distortions, but all to no avail. The day after the by-election, *The Sun* ran a full-page editorial replying to the complaints under the heading 'The truth hurts – lies, smears and Peter Tatchell': 'Like the famous horizontal heavyweight, Peter Tatchell casts around for excuses and villains to explain away the disaster of Bermondsey. He whines that he was victim of a campaign of smears and lies . . . Peter Tatchell was a victim all right. A victim of the truth.' *The Sun* had, once again, exercised its enormous power to mislead. It made loud noises about the press serving democracy but, in this instance, *The Sun* served its own political allies. Peter Tatchell was outed, his political career was severely damaged.

Bill Buckley

The appetite for outing among tabloid newspapers reached its zenith, however, during the 1980s when it seemed that no gay person – public or private – was safe from the threat of appearing in a scandal-sheet. The list of victims seemed endless. The first one to be reported in *Mediawatch* was in July 1984 when Bill Buckley, who was at the time a presenter on the TV programme *That's Life*, appeared on the front page of *The Sun* under the headline 'That's Life star stole my guy'. The story was told from the point of view of 'pretty Marcia Newby'. She claimed to be the girlfriend of a man called James, who was then, according to *The Sun*, sleeping with Bill.

Bill Buckley wrote in *Capital Gay* about his experience of being outed by the press. He said that he had emerged from the experience relatively unscathed.

> When the reporter knocked on the door without warning, I flipped. I heard myself, to my eternal shame and discredit, denying our relationship and going into the 'just good friends' routine. I had also assumed that my embryonic career was over. And what happened? Not much. The tabloids hounded me for a couple of days and then transferred their interest to Martina Navratilova's sexual preferences . . . My mistake was to have hidden my sexual preferences in the first place. Everyone at work knew about me, but not the viewers.[25]

He went on to advise any famous gay person thinking of coming out to go ahead and do it. 'I'm still earning a living, and the guy I allegedly stole from his girlfriend and I are still together and very happy.'

Russell Harty

The case of Russell Harty, a broadcaster and journalist who was very popular as a TV personality during the 1980s, was very different. On 1 March 1987, *The News of the World* headline blared: 'TV Harty in Sex Scandal' over a story which rested on the evidence of Dean Cradock, a twenty-year-old rent boy, described in the paper as 'a handsome six-footer'. The story told how Harty had engaged the services of Cradock through the medium of the Ecstasy escort agency. The rent boy visited him at his flat in Earls Court to give the star a 'massage' and allowed his bottom to be smacked. For this, Cradock received £60. It hasn't been revealed how much *The News of the World* paid him to dish the dirt on Harty.

Harty was seriously distressed by *The News of the World*'s outing. Although he was not a self-denying homosexual, Harty had not allowed his sexuality to become public knowledge. The revelation of it in such a way, however, unleashed a long and relentless period of pursuit by the press pack. What was described as a 'siege' began at his other home, in the village of Giggleswick, Yorkshire. According to an account of what followed: 'Reporters sat on his doorstep, searched through his dustbins, harassed neighbours, chased his car and forced their way into the public school in the village, where he had once been a master.'[26]

Reporters kept up these visits to Giggleswick for almost a year, attempting to bribe children and even the local vicar for information about Harty's life. At least a few Fleet Street hacks were feeling uncomfortable at what they saw as Harty's persecution. They were disturbed by the viciousness and gratuitous cruelty that was being inflicted on an otherwise popular man. Alix Palmer, a columnist in *The Star*, wrote: 'Even if some of the stories are true, why should they alter our judgement of someone who, from time to time, occupies our television screen? Either he entertains us or he doesn't.'[27] But the chase was on, and it was a depressingly familiar scenario. The tabloids needed to outdo each other and each was determined to be first to have the story on its front page.

The intrusions continued for a year and, according to playwright Alan Bennett who was a good friend of Harty's, the revelations and the almost obsessive speculation about his private life caused Harty to overwork to the point of collapse. He was, said Bennett, so convinced that the undignified nature of his outing would mean the end of his career that he found it difficult to turn down any offer of work. 'One longed for him to say "so what?" ' says

Bennett, 'But not surprisingly with his livelihood at stake, his cheek failed him.'

On 4 May 1988, Harty was admitted to St James's Hospital, Leeds, with acute liver failure brought on by Hepatitis B. On the same day *The Sun* had run yet another feature about him: 'Over the past eighteen months,' the paper claimed, 'Russell has been linked with teenage rentboys and was reported to have been sharing his home with a teenage boy.' Reporters flocked to St James's, trying to find out more, presumably with the intention of escalating the 'scandal' further. It had not escaped their notice that he was suffering from a disease which is often sexually transmitted. Indeed, even while Harty lay in the intensive care department, battling to survive, *The News of the World* ran a particularly ugly story saying that: 'A desperate manhunt was under way last night for handsome Jamie Wilson – TV star Russell Harty's live-in toyboy lover. Doctors fear dark-haired Wilson, 23, could be under sentence of death because of their gay affair.'[28] The wording of the last sentence seems to suggest to readers that Wilson's life was threatened not by Hepatitis B but by homosexuality – a 'disease' much more to be feared in the minds of tabloid editors.

Russell Harty died on 8 June 1988. At a memorial service, Alan Bennett's appreciation of his old friend rapidly turned into a no-holds-barred attack on the Fleet Street press pack which, in his opinion, had harried Harty into his grave. He told of the scenes at the hospital as Harty fought for life.

> One newspaper took a flat opposite, and a camera with a long lens was trained on the window of his ward. The nurses would point it out when you visited. A reporter posing as a junior doctor smuggled himself on to the ward, and demanded to see his notes. Every lunch time, journalists took the hospital porters across the road to the pub, to bribe them into taking photographs of him.

In an article in *The Sunday Times* in December 1989, Michael Neve wrote rather wearily of the injustice that had been done to Russell Harty by the tabloid press.

Russell the wit, Russell the tease was suddenly on the front page for quite different reasons. What was camp had now become real. He was now Harty the promiscuous homosexual. Harty, the user of young, male rent-boys. Harty, the gay who broke the law. Slowly, the life of Russell Harty began to turn into his death. The death first of all of his public persona, then of Harty himself. Harty did not have Aids. Nor has there been any proof that he died of Hepatitis B through any kind of sexual contact. The craving for Harty to be dying for these reasons replaced the idea of death itself. Harty's death was not his own: it was what people wanted. It wasn't enough that he died; a moral had to be drawn, and the News of the World was there to draw it: 'Harty caught the killer virus because he was gay'.

Alan Bennett's scathing condemnation of the press's ruthlessness was supported in many quarters, but *The Sun*, which had begun the persecution, of Harty, did not take kindly to the drubbing it had received. It said in an editorial:

> It is absurd for . . . Alan Bennett to criticise the 'gutter press' for hounding Harty to an early grave. And it is nauseating for showbiz stars at Harty's memorial service to cheer Bennett's claims. Stress did not kill Russell Harty. The truth is he died from a sexually transmitted disease. The Press didn't give it to him. He caught it through his own choice. By paying young rent-boys to satisfy him, he broke the law. Some, like ageing bachelor, Mr Bennett can see no harm in that. He has no family. But what if it was YOUR son Harty bedded?

Rent boy mania

By this time 'rent boy' stories were becoming increasingly popular. On 25 October 1987, *The Sunday Mirror* thought it was on to a good thing when it led its front page with 'Shame of MPs' nights in gay bar'. This time a rent boy by the name of McCallion told the paper how he had provided 'sex services for £30' to a 'bachelor MP' – who was named in the article. The MP in question denied the story completely, but his protestations were met with contempt by the paper. However, the following day *The Guardian* revealed that the rent boy in question was now backtracking over the allegations. He told the Press Association that he was a heroin addict and that: 'the words implicating the MP had been put into his mouth by a journalist when they met in The Golden Lion Pub in Soho. "'I'm a junkie and I needed some stuff, so I took his money," he said.' McCallion insisted that he had 'never even talked' to the MP. Despite this, no further action was taken against *The Sunday Mirror*.

In November 1987 *The People* also outed several gay vicars in a famous story on the Sunday before the Church of England's General Synod were to debate a motion on homosexuality. The lurid article was personally cruel, but politically effective. This was followed by a further spate of outings provided by rent boys. Harvey Proctor, then a Conservative MP, found his career crashing around his ears as *The Sun* outed him with the headline 'Naked Arab boy and Tory MP'. The actor Gorden Kaye – at the time starring as René in the top-rated TV comedy *'Allo 'Allo* – discovered in January 1989 that *The News of the World* was about to out him after it had been approached by a rent boy whom Kaye had befriended. He was given this news by a journalist from *The People*, who suggested that he should tell them everything in order that they could do a 'spoiler' article on the same day.

Having seen the routine many times before, Kaye realized what he was in for, and consulted his lawyer, Oscar Beuselink. Beuselink contacted Ernie Burrington, deputy chairman of Mirror Group newspapers on the morning of Friday 20 January 1989. The ploy was simple. If they gave the story voluntarily to *The Daily Mirror*, it was possible that they might get more sympathetic coverage, and, in the process, snatch the shock-horror-scandal weapon out of the hands of *The News of the World*. The manoeuvre worked perfectly. The story was handed over to journalist Hilary Bonner, who obviously liked Kaye immensely and had no desire to rip him apart. She wrote in the following day's *Daily Mirror*:

Gorden Kaye is a gentle, kindly man who happens to be a homosexual. And yesterday he believed his world lay in ruins. It was bleakly obvious that he had spent a long and sleepless night. The eyes were tired and sad. The hands shook a little as he fidgeted nervously with his packet of cigarettes. Only the day before we talked, he learned that lurid details of his secret gay sex life were about to be exposed.

She allowed Kaye to explain that he did not consider himself very attractive, and that in his loneliness he had turned to rent boys he picked up in Soho for company. The feature was completely sympathetic and robbed *The News of the World* of yet another victim in its long list of cruel exposés. Instead of being presented as a monster of corruption – as would have been likely if the *News of the World* journalists and sub-editors had dealt with the him – Gorden Kaye was shown to be rather cuddly and unthreatening. 'Gorden Kaye is a homely type, fond of comfortable sweaters and slippers,' Bonner wrote, as if to reassure her readers that even homosexuals are human beings. In his autobiography *René and Me*, Gorden Kaye recounts what happened after that:

> My ordeal was not over. Representatives of several news-papers pursued me over that weekend, including *The News of the World* reporter who told me in writing that her newspaper had never intended to write an exposé of my sex life, that they did not have the relevant information, that it was in fact another newspaper that had been following me for months and that, in their words 'You have been stitched up.' I suggested to *The News of the World* that that should then be their story, but they instead chose to print an article that was not based on a proper interview with me. Among other things it contained the comment by Mr Geoffrey Dickens MP that, because of revelations about my private life, I should immediately resign from playing René in *'Allo 'Allo*, 'since this is good family entertainment, and people are never going to watch the show in the same light again.'[29]

Kaye notes that *The News of the World* then launched a readers' phone-in asking whether he should resign or not. He called it their

'Nuremberg phone-in'. (The result showed that readers wanted Kaye to stay by a ratio of ten to one.) In the end, the BBC refused to give in to the moral outrage some papers were trying to whip up, and Kaye remained with the series for several more years.

Perhaps the most notorious use of rent boys was in the Elton John case – a detailed account of which can be found in the book *Stick it Up Your Punter*. When *The Sun* invented lie after lie about his private life, John was in the unusual position of being able to issue a serious legal challenge. In a spectacular misjudgement, Kelvin MacKenzie tried to call John's bluff and continued to print fabricated stories about him hoping that he would back down. Instead, John won a record libel settlement of £1 million from *The Sun*, and taught the paper a salutary lesson.

One can only speculate on the long-term effects these gratuitous outings had on their other victims. In 1988 *The People* and *The News of the World* used rent boys to expose two more gay men. One was a partner in a famous drag act, the other a minor TV celebrity. *The News of the World* then outed Pam St Clements by reporting on its front page under the heading 'EastEnder Pat's gay secret'. The 'secret' was that she was living with 'a big, butch-looking lesbian.'

Martin Bowley

Martin Bowley QC had been chairman of the Bar Committee in 1986 and a Crown Court judge on the South-East circuit. Letters that he had written to his lover, Philip Lafferty, had been stolen by a man in Loughborough, Leicestershire. The man told Lafferty that he would return one letter for each time that the young man slept with him. If he refused, the blackmailer said, he would send the letters to the press. Lafferty did not give in to the blackmail, and the man carried out his threats and sent the letters to *The Sun*. On a BBC *Open Space* programme, broadcast in 1988, Lafferty explained what happened next.

> The newspapermen came round to my house. They wouldn't go away until I let them in, and they started to ask questions

about Martin. I said they had no right to any of the things they had and showed them out. I rang Martin up the following day and told him what had happened.

Bowley immediately took legal advice and tried to have an injunction issued to stop publication of the letters. Despite promises to the judge in chambers that they would not publish either the letters or the photographs, *The Sun* published both. Bowley contends that they were in breach of copyright. Lafferty was so shocked when he saw what *The Sun* had done to Bowley and himself that he took an overdose. 'My sister took me to hospital,' he said, 'and the journalists followed us there, taking photographs and asking my sister if she was my girlfriend because she was pregnant at the time.' Martin Bowley resigned his judicial position, and *The Sun* – despite aiding and abetting a blackmailer – walked away from the whole affair laughing.

The list grew longer and longer. A Sea Lord Admiral featured in an outing story in *The People* when a young man, whom he had treated with great kindness, went to the paper to reveal every detail of their brief affair.[30] *The News of the World* then outed a famous hat-maker after a hotel porter with whom he'd had sex told the paper about the event in great detail.[31] Not to be outdone, *The People* found out that a 'rugged yacht tycoon', with some distant connection with the Royal Family, was gay. 'He and his gay lover, 18 years his junior, have set up home at a luxury London Docklands flat. Their saucy goings-on will rock the Palace' the paper said, more in hope than certainty. Over the page, the 'amazing double life' formula, which was becoming so familiar in these exposés, was trotted out yet again. Even though both men were quite open about the affair, *The People* seemed incapable of imagining that it wasn't a matter for amazement and faint disgust (even though a neighbour was quoted as saying 'Everyone here knows about Nick and David. We just treat them as a normal couple.'). *The People* then outed a gay man employed as a butler in Downing Street.[32] The paper splashed the story on the front page and several pages inside. All it amounted to was a statement that the man was gay and that, after loyally serving Mrs Thatcher, he was continuing his duties for Mr Major. The inference was clear, though: a gay man should not have a job in Downing Street – even as a butler. This piece illustrates the depths to which tabloid newspapers will stoop when victimizing gay people, totally disregarding their personal feelings and threats to their livelihoods.

Another 'amazing' exposé concerned a first division soccer player who, according to *The People*, had 'run away with his gay young lover' to San Francisco, 'AIDS capital of the world'. The story was provided by the man's disaffected wife and was headed: 'Sordid truth . . . he now dresses up in frocks'. There was a photograph of the man dressed in Widow-Twankey-style drag, obviously at a fancy-dress party, but no other evidence of a serious interest in transvestism, which the headline had suggested. Another TV star, Matthew Kelly, was outed by *The News of the World*.[33]

Dirty tricks

Of all the underhand methods that newspapers have used to unearth gay celebrities (and increasingly non-celebrities, such as teachers, policemen, vicars and judges – together with their partners), perhaps the *agent provocateur* method is the most disgusting. This was the technique *The News of the World* used to set-up an ageing gay clergyman in June 1989. The paper ran a headline: 'Evil fantasies of kinky canon', and described how the canon had told its reporter about his sexual fantasies, including 'ogling youngsters on the beach' and 'gay orgies'.[34] What came over most strongly in the two-page feature was the uninhibited terms in which the 'confession' was couched. It wasn't clear why the canon had chosen to talk in this unguarded fashion to a reporter from such a notorious rag. Nor was it clear from the article how or where the alleged interview had been obtained. I was suspicious that the clergyman had been tricked into speaking in the way he did, and that his ramblings had been secretly tape-recorded. *The News of the World* was not anxious to reveal its methods to me and, in an exchange of correspondence, refused to discuss them. I made a complaint to the Press Council, hoping that it would be able to persuade the paper to admit that it had used subterfuge to incriminate its victim.

Despite repeated attempts to get it to own up, *The News of the World* side-stepped the issue and refused to reveal how the story had been obtained. But then the canon was forced to resign from his post as business manager of the Church of England Synod and the full truth came tumbling out. *The News of the World* reporter had insinuated himself into his victim's confidence by posing as a 'friend and admirer'. Over dinner – at which wine had flowed abundantly – he had encouraged the clergyman to speak of his sex fantasies and had clandestinely taped the musings.

Accepting the canon's resignation, the Archbishop of Canterbury, Robert Runcie, said: 'I believe the manner in which the journalist obtained and used the material from the Canon . . . was deplorable.' Meanwhile, the canon's bishop said: 'That a journalist should go into the Canon's home with a concealed tape recorder, cajoling him into fantasising about his private life is deplorable. More deplorable is the fact that a national newspaper should print a story based on material obtained in such a deceitful manner.'

On 9 July 1989, *The News of the World* admitted that it had used a hidden tape recorder and duped the canon. But instead of apologizing, the paper repeated, with lurid embellishments, all the original allegations. The victim was cruelly humiliated all over again, being referred to as 'vile' and 'the camp canon' and 'the kinky clergyman'. This detestable bullying was accompanied by a sanctimonious editorial threatening to sort out 'the powerful gay Mafia within the church' and trying to justify its lying and cheating: 'From time to time newspapers feel justified in using clandestine methods in reporting matters which are in the public interest. We believe the conduct of the Canon . . . was such a case.' The paper said that the Press Council had 'as a broad rule' frowned on subterfuge and deceit but had 'many times recognised the legitimacy of such techniques'. In fact, the Press Council sanctioned the use of such methods only when the public interest was being served. In this instance, the clergyman involved had done nothing illegal or antisocial, beyond articulating – in the privacy of his own home – some rather juvenile sex fantasies. He was punished many times over for that. At his request, I withdrew my complaint from the Press Council. I understood that to pursue it risked bringing even greater sorrow to him. *The News of the World* had already demonstrated its wrath on those who dared to challenge its dubious methods. In *The Independent* Bishop Patrick Roger wrote: 'That [the Canon] should have been driven to this [resignation] is a poor reward for his years of faithful ministry both to his parish and to the General Synod. Many members of the Synod were distressed . . . by the behaviour of *The News of the World*.'[35]

A catalogue of persecution

The vicious circulation war in which the Sunday tabloids were engaged was driving journalistic standards lower and lower. There seemed, at that time, to be at least one outing every week. On 29 July 1989 *The People* outed the vicar of Dulwich who, they claimed, held 'gay orgies' at his vicarage. On 20 August *The People* told of 'Queen Mum's priest in gay sex scandal' which, within the first three paragraphs, contained the words 'perverted', 'vile', 'seedy', 'kinky', filthy' and 'corrupt'. On 2 August, the same paper led with 'Top lawyer exposed in rent boy scandal', which described the latest victim as 'sordid', 'kinky', 'bizarre' and 'squalid'. In the wake of these spiteful cases came the outings of Kenny Everett and Michael Cashman. *The News of the World* even revealed Michael Cashman's address and the name of his local pub.

Perhaps the most ludicrous example was that of Roy Barraclough, an actor who was, at the time, playing a part in *Coronation Street*. The 2 April 1989 edition of *The People* announced on its front page 'Bet Lynch's hubby is gay'. This front page was, in effect, an outing poster that reached the eyes of ten million people all over the country. There was nothing to the story except the revelation of Barraclough's homosexuality. No rent boys, no vengeful lovers, no law-breaking. Barraclough was cornered by *People* reporters while on holiday in Greece. 'I am gay and proud of it,' said the actor. 'I am discreet and what I do behind my own front door is up to me. Still, I am honest and as you've asked me, I can't deny it.' The fact that there was nothing further to report did not prevent the sub-heading 'Roy's amazing double life'. But there was nothing 'amazing' nor duplicitous about Barraclough's personal life. It was all up front, which rather took the wind out of the story.

(Coincidentally, Julie Goodyear, the actress who played Barra-clough's screen wife, had already been outed, this time by *The Daily Star*, under the headline 'Julie lesbian shock . . . Bet Lynch's gay life'.)[36] The harping on the perceived 'double life' aspect – which is what most of these outing stories did – served to reinforce in the minds of readers that gay people were, by their very nature, secretive, deceitful and that their lives were hidden from the view of 'ordinary' folk. Whenever the story was based on the testimony of prostitutes or spurned lovers it was inevitably angled to be 'sleazy' and to make the individual involved seem distant and divorced from everyday life. Gay people who considered themselves to be decent individuals found they were being portrayed in newspapers as monsters of corruption. It also strengthened the perception of homosexuals generally as exotic, antisocial and sex-mad. There were very few balancing stories of the gay people who were making a creative contribution to life in Britain; that would not have fitted the picture. Even those pop stars and actors who had come out voluntarily were frequently mocked or belittled. Jimmy Somerville, one of the first popular singers to stand up unapologetically for gay rights, is often derided in the tabloid press for his sexuality ('He's ugly, he's bad-tempered and he's gay' – *The Sun*.)[37]

A royal outing

One of the most frightening threats to the Establishment during the anticipated 'gay outing campaign' was that a member of the royal family would be named, but FROCS, if it had carried out its campaign, would have been too late. *The Daily Mirror* had beaten them to it on 19 April 1990, when it ran a huge spread about Prince Edward. The Queen's youngest son had been cornered at a party by a journalist who asked him directly: 'Are you gay?' The Prince responded by saying: 'It's outrageous to suggest this sort of thing. It's so unfair to me and my family . . . The scurrilous rumours are preposterous. They cause hurt not only to me but to my mother, father, brothers and sister. How would you feel if someone said you were gay?'

From this somewhat over-the-top denial, The *Daily Mirror* constructed a huge splash covering three pages. The story was spun out with an enormous amount of quite gratuitous gay-bashing revolving around an unedifying potted biography of the Prince. He had been, the paper said, plagued by rumours about his sexuality from his early teenage years when he was known as a 'mummy's boy'. Later, in Buckingham Palace ('where homosexuality is a way of life among many royal servants') it was suggested he was a 'closet queen'. His closest friends apparently knew him as 'AC/DC – a ditherer unable to make up his mind one way or the other'. At Cambridge he was known as 'a wimp'. At a charity show a journalist is supposed to have said 'He behaved liked a ballerina with a ladder in her tights'. Moving on to the Royal Marines (from which he made an ignominious exit) he was 'dubbed the Apple Juice Kid' because he wasn't a great drinker like the other rookies. He made an even 'worse gaffe' by joining 'the darlings and dear boys of theatreland'. He rapidly became known – according to the *Daily Mirror* – as 'Mavis'.

This little trip through royal life demonstrates very clearly how gay men are thought of by tabloid journalists. It is unclear whether they really imagine that all gay men fit the age-old stereotype of the effeminate 'luvvy', or whether they are just too lazy to think beyond it. Another explanation is that they have a vested interest in keeping such imagery current. It makes their job easier if they can use such shorthand when writing stories aimed at belittling gay individuals or intended to defame the whole gay community.

Gill Anderton: an ironic outing

One of the more welcome outings of the 1980s was provided by *The News of the World*, when it revealed that Manchester Chief Constable James Anderton's daughter, Gill, was a lesbian.[38] Many gay people felt it was poetic justice that the man who had initiated one of the most virulent anti-gay backlashes of the decade (see Chapter 7) should be shown to have fathered one of the 'monsters' he so abhorred. Reporting the incident, *The Pink Paper* said the story had been 'remarkably positive', allowing Gill Anderton to tell in her own words how she knew she was a lesbian at the age of thirteen, how she came out to her family and of her current life with ambulance driver Carole Newton in South London. However, *The News of the World* couldn't help decorating the story with a few favourite stereotypes: that they drank 'a pint of lager each', that they behaved 'just like a boy and his girlfriend'.

Wendy and Patsy

Much of the frenzy for outing in the 1980s must be laid at the door of the editors of *The News of the World* and *The People* – at that time, Wendy Henry and Patsy Chapman. Both had long apprenticeships in the ways of tabloid muck-raking. Ms Henry got her break on *The Sun*, under the tutelage of Kelvin MacKenzie. She shared his penchant for foul-mouthed vulgarity and tasteless journalism and so seemed a natural choice for editor of *The News of the World*. However, she went too far, even for the blunted sensibilities of her employer, Rupert Murdoch and, on 18 December 1989, Ms Henry edited her final edition of *The News of the World*. It contained two double-page spreads on gay themes. One concerned 'rampant homosexual' Cary Grant and the other the outing of the soccer player already referred to. Speculating on the fall from grace of Britain's first female national newspaper editor, James Dalrymple wrote in *The Independent* that it might well have been her obsession with homosexuality which put the final nail in her News International coffin. 'She seemed keen on stories of gay relationships, the more bizarre the better . . . It is well known that Mr Murdoch does not like homosexual stories.'[39] As has already been noted Ms Henry has subsequently exported her 'skills' to America where, for a while, she edited the notorious 'supermarket tabloid' *The Globe*, and then moved into the lucrative and expanding tabloid TV market.

Ms Henry's frequent use of rent boys as informants did not go without criticism from other quarters in Fleet Street, however. Peter McKay, in the London *Evening Standard*, said:

> The rotten little creeps who have been parading through newspaper offices are unfit for any kind of work that does not involve the self-absorbed acting out of tedious fantasies

about themselves. An appallingly hypocritical theme has been developed which is designed to cast sympathy upon the rent boy and greater odium on his alleged client. This is the old 'fallen woman' gambit. Having spouted the details, (no doubt for gain) the rent boy suggests that male prostitution was his only way of making ends meet (so to speak) in the cruel Thatcher economic climate. The News of the World said of their latest squealing, pig-tailed rent-boy: 'Dean is now unemployed and has given up his life of vice'.[40]

The Star offered a different explanation:

> If you have been wondering why these verminous rent boys have been emerging from their lairs to tell their stories, it is because business is at a standstill. AIDS has deprived them of a living, so they have been making a buck by selling their sordid kiss-and-tell memoirs – or should that read spank-and-tell?[41]

In his column in *Today*, ex-Fleet-Street editor Derek Jameson placed the blame squarely where it belonged: 'The shame falls not on the head of those betrayed, but rather on those who open their purses to these scavengers. I feel more guilty than most. I once edited *The News of the World*.'[42]

Your life in your hands

Of course, the best way to defeat the newspaper outers is to open the closet door voluntarily. Sir Ian McKellen has certainly been spared the shock-horror headlines by pre-empting tabloid innuendoes about his private life. Labour MP Chris Smith also decided that being honest was safer than trying to hide. He came out at a protest rally in Rugby in 1984, announcing to a crowd of a thousand: 'My name's Chris Smith. I'm the Labour MP for Islington South and Finsbury and I'm gay'. He wrote an article in *New Socialist* in January 1985 about the value of coming out, in which he said:

> The form of oppression from which most gay and lesbian people suffer is one that forces them to hide their true

sexuality and affections . . . I felt strongly in standing up in public and saying I was gay, that honesty and openness are the major weapons that people can use against that form of oppression. The more people who do that, the better. But it's very hard to do, and I still feel constrained in many other ways.

Smith's simple act of courage had deprived the tabloids of the weapon they would – in the right circumstances – have used against him. Instead of a sensational exposé, Chris Smith received congratulations from *The Observer* and was given the front page of the *Islington Gazette* to explain his decision to his constituents. He has written:

I had thought the tabloid press would go to town over what I had said, but they uttered not a word. It took *The Sun* about four months to get round to carrying an article about it . . . What I think had been achieved was the removal of any titillating, salacious innuendo-value in the whole exercise. I am led to the overwhelming conclusion that you counter prejudice and sniping criticism best by being open, clear and confident about who and what you are.[43]

AIDS outings

As HIV and AIDS began to claim the lives of prominent people, it was no longer enough to drag people out of the closet; the papers now seemed anxious also to inform the world who was HIV-positive or had AIDS. Stephen Barry, former valet of the Prince of Wales, was described by journalists as 'trembling with distress' when they called on him to check whether rumours about his HIV status were true. Barry tried to claim that he simply had a persistent throat infection, but the newspapers were zealous in telling the truth about him. He died a few months later in 1986 from an AIDS-related condition. On 2 July 1988, the front-page lead of *The People* was about a porter at a children's hospital who was HIV-positive. The man was described as 'a menace' – but the body of the story showed such a description to be totally unfair and unjustifiable. The man was simply doing his job and was behaving very responsibly. It was not clear how *The People* had obtained the confidential information about this man's health status, or why they had decided to use it when it came into their possession. At the time, the paper was owned by Robert Maxwell, who was gaining great personal publicity for his supposed support for various AIDS and HIV charities.

In March 1988, *The Sun* discovered that Henry Tennant, a gay member of 'an aristocratic family' was HIV-positive. This was duly revealed on the front page.[44] *Sun* journalists then started a pursuit of Tennant around the world, determined to make more of their story because they considered it had some tenuous 'royal' connection. This remorseless hounding caused Tennant's father, Lord Glenconner, to complain about the press's behaviour towards his son, saying that he would not have to endure it if he were suffering from cancer. This prompted *The Sun* to issue one of its sickeningly pious editorials: 'First it is not "hounding" to report the news. Secondly, people contract cancer totally by chance. AIDS usually occurs through a sexual choice.' I wrote in *Mediawatch* at the time:

> To say such thinking is wicked seems insufficient. To justify the intolerable harassment of a man who is already under such enormous strain is almost unbelievable. And to say that dragging the details of his medical condition on to the front page is 'news' is contemptible.

One Sunday paper paid a bribe of £100 for the confidential medical records of two doctors. Despite a court order banning them from publishing the information, the paper went ahead and was subsequently fined £10,000 for contempt of court for the headline 'Scandal of the docs with AIDS'. 'Ice Star Curry's AIDS Agony' was another giant front-page lead of *The News of the World* on 2 August 1992.

In May 1993, the tabloids were conjecturing about the health of comedian Kenny Everett, who had never really recovered from his initial press outing. He decided that he would put paid to that speculation and revealed that, yes, he was HIV-positive and had known about it for four years. In the same week, Holly Johnson, a singer who had attained fame in the 1980s with the group Frankie Goes to Hollywood was revealed to have AIDS by *The Sun*. Johnson was furious about this outing by a paper he despised. He had, in fact, made the decision to go public with the news of his condition and had chosen to make the revelation in *The Times*, reasoning that in doing so there would be at least a chance of avoiding tabloid-style sensationalism. In an interview with *Gay Times*, Johnson said:

> Seeing pictures of Freddie Mercury on the cover of the papers looking emaciated, that was really vile. Just knowing that the tabloid journalists were going to wait until they got a really bad picture of me and print the story anyway. And I didn't want it to come out in a negative way like that. Because there has been enough of that kind of badgering, let's face it. But I was also scared. I'd read stories where gay men's flats had been burnt to the ground. Horror stories. I didn't know how people were going to react.[45]

He gave *The Times* a long interview, but, before it could be published, its sister paper, *The Sun*, curiously managed to hijack it and robbed Johnson of the dignity he was hoping for. 'For the man who told the world to "Relax – make love not war" – and boasted of the joys of promiscuous gay sex, it was the ultimate punishment,' said *The Sun*'s screeching, moralizing and judgmental story. The paper's columnist, Richard Littlejohn, seemed almost pleased and, all too predictably, gloated: 'It's not the best of weeks for the "we're all at risk" brigade. Kenny Everett and Holly Johnson, the latest celebs to declare they have the AIDS virus, are both notorious homosexuals.' The miles of comment and, in the main, heartless criticism that emanates from the press when someone is discovered to have died from AIDS also has nasty repercussions. Many have been portrayed as monsters of promiscuity and depravity after they died: Freddie Mercury, Rock Hudson, Liberace, Denholm Elliott, Rudolph Nureyev to name but a few. As Oscar

Moore, a man living with AIDS, once said: 'The whole thing is a double-edged sword. When people get outed by their deaths, it is a bitter blow to the gay rights movement, for it perpetuates the myth that there is no homosexuality without AIDS.' The fascination with celebrity 'AIDS victims' continues, and, although the tabloids continue to lecture about morality, they show no sings of restraint when it comes to making money from other people's misery.

Notes

1. 22 April 1990.
2. June 1990.
3. Issue 17, 1994.
4. Abacus/Random House, 1994.
5. 13 March 1991.
6. 17 March 1991.
7. Cliff told *The Independent* in April 1994: 'Teasing is fine, I can take that. It's when they speculate, it's really upsetting. Imagine how my mother feels when people write that I must be gay. How dare they? It's all so vulgar and unnecessary.'.
8. 29 July 1991.
9. Issue 17, 1994.
10. 4 August 1991.
11. 4 April 1992.
12. 6 April 1992.
13. 21 November 1993.
14. 2 January 1994.
15. 15 January 1994.
16. 10 February 1994.
17. 29 April 1994.
18. 20 April 1994.
19. *Independent*, 9 May 1994.
20. 26 September 1994.
21. 22 October 1994.
22. 23 October 1994.
23. 28 September 1979.
24. *Battle for Bermondsey* (Heretic Books, 1983).
25. 18 April 1986.
26. *Stick it Up Your Punter*, p. 298.
27. 4 March 1987.
28. 8 May 1988.
29. Sidgwick & Jackson, 1990, pp. 154–5.
30. 4 December 1988.
31. 11 December 1988.

32. 9 December 1991.
33. 14 October 1990.
34. 4 June 1989.
35. 12 August 1989.
36. 29 September 1986. An interesting analysis of that story can be found in the booklet *Out of the Gutter* published by The Campaign for Press and Broadcasting Freedom.
37. 22 December 1987.
38. 20 March 1988.
39. 19 December 1989.
40. 2 March 1987.
41. 5 March 1987.
42. 7 March 1987.
43. R. Healey and A. Mason (eds), *Stonewall 25* (Virago Books, 1994).
44. 29 March 1988.
45. April 1994.

Chapter five

Facts and Opinion: Bias and the truth

THE expression of opinion – sometimes strong and controversial opinion – has always been an essential element of a newspaper's make-up, but opinion and news are supposed to be separate and distinct in newspapers. The Press Complaints Commission's code of practice, to which each national newspaper editor is a signatory, states: 'Newspapers, whilst free to be partisan, should distinguish clearly between comment, conjecture and fact.' This clause, however – like so many others in the code – is routinely disregarded. Emotive and inflammatory headlines make frequent appearances on tabloid news pages and the reports beneath them are often written from a strongly moralistic or disapproving point of view. The line between partisanship and deliberate distortion is often so thin as to be invisible; frequently the facts contained in partisan news stories are so selective or strongly slanted that they become misleading. The manipulation or omission of balancing information can make stories fit the newspaper's political agenda more easily. This is particularly true of gay-related stories in the popular press, which are almost always written from a strongly condemnatory standpoint.

Even if the body of a news report, as written by a journalist, is relatively neutral, it can be made to appear negative by the inclusion of quotes from sources that oppose gay rights, such as authoritarian back-bench MPs or conservative religionists. Frequently, no balancing quote from the other point of view will be included. An example comes from *The Daily Express* about the Civil Service equal opportunities policy, which extends to lesbian and gay employees:

> A top-level Whitehall inquiry was launched last night into the gay civil servants' cash scandal. The Daily Express yesterday exclusively revealed how homosexual staff get extra relocation expenses for their lovers. Thousands of pounds of taxpayers' money is helping gay couples from the Home Office set up home in different parts of the country . . . Ann Winterton, Conservative MP for Congleton said 'This is a disgraceful waste of public funds and it needs to be looked into as a matter of the utmost urgency. One hopes it will be stopped immediately.' Her husband Nicholas, Tory member for Macclesfield said: 'One should go to the very top, to Mr Major, to stop this. There is supposed to be a shortage of money, yet we are paying it out to people who have an unnatural lifestyle. It is a disgrace.'[1]

This was definitely 'partisan', but did that permissible bias allow readers of *The Daily Express* to make a considered judgement about the issue under discussion? Or did the newspaper create the reader's opinion by giving a one-sided version of events which totally left out the views of the gay protagonists? Also, the claim that 'homosexual staff get extra relocation expenses' would suggest that gay couples are being given special or priority treatment. This is not true. They receive exactly the same allowance as would a heterosexual couple in a stable relationship. The story also suggests that it is wrong that homosexuals should get *any* money from the taxpayer, whether they are entitled to it or not. The claim that: 'Thousands of pounds of taxpayers' money is helping gay couples from the Home Office set up home in different parts of the country' does not make clear that they are moving house and incurring expenses at the behest of their employer. (Nor – if it comes to that – that homosexual people pay taxes too.)

Another example of extreme bias and condemnation is a front-page report in *The Daily Star* relating to the same story.[2] The page was headed 'Sod off!' in large, reversed-out print. Yet another example of this from *The Star* was published in their issue of 22

January 1994 under the heading 'Storm over cash for gay jail visits'. It concerned what the paper described as 'a shock Government plan' to allow homosexuals to visit their jailed lovers with taxpayers footing the bill for travelling expenses.

> Last night furious MPs hit out at the 'scandalous' Home Office move. Tory MP Geoffrey Dickens raged: 'I am amazed. A lot of people will be infuriated by this ridiculous plan. Homosexuality is already a curse in prison. That the Government is thinking of adding to the problem at our expense is absurd.'

The article then went on to quote Dr Adrian Rogers of the Conservative Family Institute as saying: 'Homosexuality is a disease-ridden activity widely condemned by most societies. It should not be encouraged, condoned or supported.' After that came Stephen Green of the Conservative Family Campaign, who said: 'This is completely outrageous. It is part of the drive by the homosexual lobby for equality between homosexuality and hetero-sexual love and marriage. Such equality does not exist in God's law, natural law or British law and the public will not tolerate it.' No attempt was made to put the other side of the argument and no balancing quotes were included. A few days later, the Home Office announced that the plan had been scrapped.

Fair comment?

If the news pages of a newspaper are at least supposed to *aim* at factual accuracy, no such pretence of balance is needed in the comment and feature sections. No newspaper would be complete without a 'leader' column in which its opinions are trumpeted and its politics stated. Columnists, polemicists, pundits and commen-tators are also an essential part of newspapers, reinforcing their character and opinions. Columnists can garner a large following, and sometimes their writings will provoke a wider discussion of issues in the news. Editors recognise the value of having identifiable 'star' columnists with whom readers can become familiar and whose columns they can look forward to reading. An ideal columnist will be in possession of strongly held opinions which he or she will be able to express with eloquence, authority and wit. Many have gained considerable reputations, and their carefully considered views have become respected by ordinary readers and policy-makers alike. Indeed, columnists can have an important role in interpreting the events of the day, presenting them from a different angle and making them easier for the casual observer to understand. In these days of carefully constructed public relations exercises and news management, it could be argued that commentators are more important than ever. It should be their job to cut through the often misleading 'information' which is pumped out by sophisticated PR firms and press offices. A good commentator will be aware of the tricks of the trade and will be able to see through the weasel words and meaningless façades which are constructed to conceal mistakes or misdemeanours by governments or corporate bodies. A skilful columnist can give insights into the motives of those in the public eye, and background information and opinion that would be inappropriate in the news pages. The best commentators can inform, provoke and infuriate with equal ease. However, in the rush to become a 'name' columnist, some journalists have sacrificed reasonable debate in favour of gratuitous controversy. They confuse offensiveness and reasoned criticism. The art of insult and abuse has been refined to such an extent by some journalists that even TV and radio producers seek them out to spice up dull programmes. As one columnist has admitted, journalism is becoming a 'performance art' which requires the columnist to be entertaining and provocative as well as informed and informative. This is fine, so long as provocation does not become an excuse to slander and malign innocent people.

Far from recognizing and challenging the 'factoids' which are created by vested interests trying to gain publicity for commercial products and by pressure groups, columnists are often guilty of taking such dubious information at face value. For instance, a religious pressure group called the Washington Family Institute issued a report claiming that 'a homosexual lifestyle reduces life expectancy from 75 to 42'. This ludicrous and unprovable 'statistic' was widely quoted in the British media during the run-up to the age of consent debate in 1994. Lynette Burrows in *The Sunday Telegraph* quoted it uncritically, giving no indication about what the figures were based on.[3] It also turned up in a House of Lords debate on the age of consent.

In the propaganda war gay groups, too, have also occasionally overstated their case. For many years there was a common assumption that the Kinsey Report of 1948 had concluded that one person in ten was 'a homosexual'. Even a cursory reading of Kinsey (see Chapter 1), however, will reveal that he never made such a claim. Gay campaigners did little to contradict this statistic – and many actively promoted it, conscious that 10 per cent was politically hard to ignore. Columnists and commentators began to question the statistic only when they felt under threat from the progress of gay rights. Then, in the early 1990s, several studies conducted throughout the Western world seemed to conclude that the proportion of people who were, at any given moment, leading a homosexual lifestyle was more likely to be nearer 1 per cent – or even less. 'Confirmation' came in a large-scale study of Britons' sexual habits which was exploited by *The Daily Mail*.[4] 'The Gay Myth and the Truth' was its enormous front-page headline announcing that: 'The most exhaustive survey ever conducted into British sexual habits has buried the claim that one man in ten is gay . . . the key finding is only 1.1 per cent of men had a homosexual partner in the year prior to the interview.'[5] *The Sun* said:

> We've been conned by the gay lobby. For years they've told us that one man in ten is homosexual. Governments pump millions into AIDS propaganda as gay actors mince into Number Ten. Teachers tell children that homosexuality is normal. A campaign grows to make gay sex legal at 16. But now the truth is out: A survey shows that barely one man in 90 is gay. The loud-mouthed luvvies should belt up.[6]

The Star was pleased to tell its readers that the survey was 'Glum for Gays' because 'there aren't many of them'.[7] Commentators ignored the fact that even if the 1.1 per cent statistic were correct, it matched the proportion of the population that is Jewish almost exactly. No one would dare suggest that because of the small size of the Jewish minority their human rights should be disregarded. Gay people know from their own experience that although 10 per cent is undoubtedly an over-estimate, 1 per cent is equally wide of the mark. Indeed, the survey's authors had said in the book: 'the prevalence estimates of homosexual behaviour based on these data must be regarded as minima'. The refusal rate for the survey was *forty per cent*. As Peter Kellner wrote in *The Sunday Times*: 'Imagine you are a gay teacher, army officer, Tory MP or a married man with a gay lover. Would you be part of the 60 per cent or the other 40 per cent? And if you joined the sixty per cent would you tell the truth. All of it?'[8] None of these caveats were of interest to the tabloids who presented the 1.1 per cent estimate as settled fact. Here was a new 'reason' to dismiss the gay community and its demands for justice.

Vigorous debate is, of course, an essential element in a democracy and sometimes strongly held opinions must be forcefully expressed in order to challenge injustice. But, too often, commentators and opinionated columnists in the tabloid press aim their attacks at people who are relatively defenceless and have little power to answer back. This is a one-way debate, and any retort or correction is usually relegated to the correspondence column – at the editor's discretion – several days after the event.

In this chapter, and throughout the book, we will see many examples of the abuse and insult aimed at homosexuals – as individuals and as a community – by opinion-formers in the press. Many of these attacks are motivated by pure homophobia: there is no pretence of rational criticism or reasoned objection, just raw detestation. Such irrationality would not be permitted in relation to any other serious subject. Raw and unbridled racism, for instance, would not be tolerated in a newspaper column; vicious homophobia, however, seems perfectly acceptable. The same applies to the letters columns. No newspaper would publish a blatantly racist letter in its readers correspondence column, but they think nothing of including violently hateful anti-gay diatribes. (For instance, 'Lesbians and gay men are under divine wrath and curse . . . a gay has no right even to give an offering to the House of God . . . No wonder the noose of nuclear disaster is tightening round the neck of this generation' a clergyman was allowed to rant in *The Observer*.)[9]

Because it suits their case, pundits on the popular press refuse to acknowledge that 'gay' means anything other than 'having anal sex'. The idea of 'gay' being a political construct or a word to describe a whole style of life seems beyond their comprehension. At the same time, acknowledging that human sexuality might even be more complicated than the simple gay/straight split is something journalists only occasionally attempt. Life in the tabloids has to be simple: you are either black or white, gay or straight, good or bad – and no space for Mr In-between. Perhaps that is one of the greatest disservices that newspapers do to society at large.

Some journalists hide their homo-hatred behind spurious 'rationales' which are easily deconstructed by people who have thought more carefully about the issues. These artfully created justifications for gay-bashing are dangerous in that they reassure a public that is already deeply homophobic that its prejudice is rational, reasonable and acceptable. Homophobic individuals who might be restrained from acting on their violent impulses might find it easier to disregard such restraint when their morning newspaper reinforces their prejudice and appears to be almost condoning violence.

Columnists on the broadsheets have more space to develop their arguments and to look more closely at their subjects, and are generally better informed. This does not mean that they are always fair in their conclusions. Many commentators will give precedence to their paper's dogmatic political or religious viewpoint rather than their own convictions. Ambition overcomes conviction in many instances, and fair-minded men can become nasty propagandists in order to climb Fleet Street's slippery pole. Deductive reasoning gives way to self-delusion. A signed column is obviously an expression of a personal opinion – but that opinion is given authority by the fact that a national newspaper feels it is reasonable enough to be disseminated to a large audience. Crude hate-mongering should have no place in newspapers. The prominence given to 'opinion pieces' also means that far more people read what the columnist has to say than will read any contrary point of view or correction in the letters column. The behaviour of some columnists and commentators in the British press makes a convincing case for some kind of legislation to protect *all* minorities from incitement to hatred.

Right of reply denied

If an expression of opinion is particularly extreme, news-papers will occasionally grant a 'right of reply' to the opposite point of view. This was evident during the campaigns which were organized at the time of 'Clause 28' and during the age of consent debate. Regular commentators in right-wing papers such as *The Sunday Telegraph* developed arguments justifying the implementation of Clause 28; they also argued for the age of consent to be left unchanged. Occasionally their arguments were so patently unfair that they had to be challenged. Very occasionally, people prominent in the campaigns – such as Sir Ian McKellen, Michael Cashman and Peter Tatchell – were given space to put the alternative point of view. More often, though, the abuse and misrepresentation of gay people passes without any contradiction. Although the Press Complaints Commission says in its code of practice that 'A fair opportunity for reply to inaccuracies should be given to individuals or organisations when reasonably called for', there is no compulsion upon editors to grant a right of reply, and quite often – even in extreme cases – they do not. The Press Complaints Commission and its predecessor, The Press Council, has frequently castigated newspapers for denying groups and individuals the right of reply to serious misrepresentation, but the papers concerned have been unrepentant. In 1978, *The Leicester Mercury* wrote a vicious editorial – headed 'Not in our columns' – attacking a local gay phone service, Gayline. The editorial made reference to paedophilia and concluded that the activities of the group ('a parading of perversion') were not a fit subject for a family newspaper and therefore there would be no further mention in *The Leicester Mercury* of the 'sexual extremists' that ran Gayline. The group was horrified to be presented in this way and asked for a letter to be published distancing themselves from paedophilia and other untrue accusations made in the article. The editor refused. This caused such anger within the gay community that a demonstration was organized to march through Leicester, passing the offices of the newspaper.

Gayline complained to the Press Council. In the ensuing correspondence the editor of *The Leicester Mercury* told the council that he did not think that homosexuals were a 'responsible group' and that 'homosexualism was an unnatural practice abhorrent to most people' associated with 'perverted interest in children'. He said that he would not accept homosexuals at their own valuation. The Council's report says: 'He would not afford militant homosexuals the remotest chance to recruit through his columns young people at a time of decision in their lives'. The Press Council's subsequent adjudication supported the editor, saying:

> Leading articles are intended to convey the opinion of the newspaper concerned which may of course be controversial and is very often partisan. There is no absolute right of reply to it and the editor of a newspaper is entitled to exercise his discretion as to this on the facts of each particular case provided he does so responsibly and in good faith. The leading article in question did not identify particular individuals or organisations as being the special object of its attack. It dealt with a subject on which the Editor was entitled to express the strong view he held. It was a matter of discretion for him to decide whether, having regard to what he considered the moral issues involved, he should provide a platform for those taking a different view. The Press Council does not consider that in the circumstances of this case his discretion was exercised in a way that was open to legitimate attack. The complaint against the *Leicester Mercury* is rejected.[10]

Given that the chairman of the Press Council had written in the same annual report that year that 'any organisation identifiably attacked . . . is morally entitled to, and should be given the opportunity to, make a reasonable reply' this seems an extraordinary outcome. In his book *People Against the Press*[11] Geoffrey Robertson draws attention to the 'intellectual poverty' of this adjudication when it is set against a ruling made by the Australian Press Council on an almost identical case in the northern Queensland city of Townsville. There the local paper, *The Townsville Daily Bulletin*, had launched an attack on a gay group which had recently been established to change the law. The paper said the group was 'dedicated to the propagation of practices which are reprehensible, against the order of nature and morally degenerative'. The paper said that it would not give any further publicity to the group and denied it a right of reply. The Australian press watchdog said:

> The Australian Press Council, while reaffirming that a newspaper which purports to serve the general public has the right to advocate any point of view it thinks proper on a question of public controversy, emphasises the duty of such a paper, when it has published arguments favouring one point of view on such a question, to give reasonable publicity to countervailing arguments . . .
>
> *The Townsville Daily Bulletin* is a paper of general news coverage. The Council is clearly of the opinion that such a paper, while within its rights in condemning in the terms of the editorial the proponents of reform of the law on the relevant topic, is under a strong obligation as a matter of ordinary fairness to hold its columns open to a reasonable reply.
>
> The *Bulletin*'s refusal to do this was not only an act of suppression and intolerance, it was a rejection of the duty, which must be accepted if freedom of the press is to retain the support of the public, to respect the right of the general reader to be informed of the arguments on each side of a public debate upon which a paper has expressed its own views in favour of one point of view.

There is still no clear policy regarding rights of reply and automatic corrections in British newspapers. The editor's discretion – and his or her prejudices – will dictate whether homosexual groups and individuals are allowed to put a different point of view when they have been traduced.

Friendly voices

However, as gay rights has risen on the political agenda, some journalists have become better informed about the issues and this has resulted in improved analysis and comment. It is much more likely in the 1990s than at any other time that editors will seek out and commission gay people to write about their own experiences and to comment directly on the events affecting their lives. We have commentators in the liberal press who know, like and sometimes admire gay people, and who have shaken off the annoying stereotyped images that infest the tabloids, and have come to understand what we are aiming for. The late Jill Tweedie was an early example of the more thoughtful columnist who treated gay rights with some seriousness and honesty. As long ago as 1971 she was writing in *The Guardian*:

> these young homosexuals, by their very acceptance of the normality of homosexuality, challenge the status quo . . . And they are beautiful to see. It is lovely to be with men and women who are not ashamed to express their affections openly, in the normal heterosexual ways, the hand in hand, the arm in arm, the occasional cuddle, the quick kiss. Suddenly, watching them, the whole evil, squalid image of homosexuality crumbles – are these bright young faces corrupters of children, lavatory solicitors, the something nasty in our woodsheds?[12]

Nowadays such stuff might seem patronizing, but at the time it was a welcome relief from the grinding negativity. It also indicates how radically things have changed and how much more we expect from serious journalists now. Bernard Levin, too, was an early champion of the rights of gay people to live their lives unmolested. In his *Times* column on 24 April 1980 he was defending John Saunders, a caretaker at a residential camp for schoolchildren in Perthshire who had been fired after it was discovered he was gay. An Employment Appeal Tribunal had refused to rule that Saunders had been unfairly dismissed on the grounds that:

> there are people who believe that homosexuals are a greater risk to the sexual integrity of children than heterosexuals, and in deference to that prejudice they would refuse Mr Saunders a declaration that his dismissal was unfair . . .
> There is no evidence, *as was agreed by the employment tribunal which ruled against Mr Saunders*, that homosexuals

are any more likely than heterosexuals to seduce children in their care (and it is worth stressing that the children at Aberfoyle camp were *not* in Mr Saunders's care anyway – he was a handyman, not a teacher, supervisor or group leader). That being so, those who ran the camp had no business dismissing him because of the prejudice of others, the tribunal had no business ruling that the existence of that prejudice rendered this dismissal fair, and the Scottish courts have no business upholding that ruling. I hope they will not.

In fact the Scottish courts also refused to uphold Mr Saunders's appeal. Levin has written about gay issues several times since, and always from the liberal, supportive point of view. But voices such as his and Tweedie's were rare, and when one found them they were grabbed like nuggets in a gold rush. The homosexual who was searching in his or her newspaper for some kind of validation of his personal life and feelings was much more likely to discover a torrent of abuse, vilification and unmitigated hatred.

Since those early days, when sympathetic or informed opinion about homosexuality was hard to find, the situation has changed considerably. More recently, people like Suzanne Moore, Matthew Parris, Nicholas de Jongh and John Lyttle have been bringing regular and serious discussion of gay cultural and political issues to the broadsheet reader.

Commenting on a tabloid 'storm' which had resulted in the cancellation of a BBC 'perk' (which involved giving a £75 'wedding gift' and some time off for a 'honeymoon' to both straight and gay couples under the terms of their equal opportunities policy), Francis Wheen wrote angrily in *The Guardian* that: 'a perfectly decent and unexceptionable policy should be ditched overnight merely because a couple of oafish back-benchers and homophobic leader-writers make a fuss . . . The cancellation of the wedding-presents . . . represents gutlessness of a rare order.'[13] Claudia Fitzherbert in *The Daily Telegraph*, commenting on the same issue, wrote: 'Is it not curious that it is the very same people who revile homosexuals on the grounds that they are degenerate, promiscuous and out of sync with the monogamous mores which make for a stable society who are most vociferous in their indignation when these same monsters of depravity make a show of their long-term monogamous commitment?'[14] Occasionally 'an alternative voice' is permitted into the pages of newspapers so as to demonstrate 'fair play'. Consequently, union leader Frank Chapple has been a columnist on *The Daily Express* and 'Red' Ken Livingstone on *The Sun*. Richard Ingrams has written a column for *The Observer* – not his natural milieu.

Unfriendly voices

It is inevitable that anti-gay hostility will find its way into the opinion pages of the right-wing papers. Some of the bogeymen and women of the press that have been active during the years I have been writing *Mediawatch* have become familiar names to my readers. George Gale and Jean Rook were particularly annoying homo-haters during the early and mid-1980s. Paul Johnson is another virulently homophobic polemicist.[15] Garry Bushell, Brian Hitchen, Richard Littlejohn, Lynda Lee-Potter, Richard Ingrams, Julie Burchill, John Smith, Peregrine Worsthorne, Geoffrey Wheatcroft, Mary Kenny, Lynette Burrows, John Junor, Chaim Bermant, Colin Welch and a host of others have produced thousands of column-inches of spiteful, hateful invective about events in the history of the gay struggle. All have tried to retard our progress in some way – and for motives that were not always immediately apparent to their readers (such as a strong attachment to authoritarian religious dogmas).

One of the most important duties of the political and social commentator on the right-wing papers (as opposed to the gossip columnist or purveyor of showbiz trivia) is to construct apparently rational arguments in support of the paper's political line. An editorial in the *New Statesman and Society* described this cabal of newspaper 'opinion formers' in this way:

> There are, at most, a hundred or so journalists who fix the prevailing 'consensus' - who determine what views get expressed in print . . . Editors, columnists, political editors, a handful of respected lobby correspondents, the occasional old-hand independent operator – they were all selected in the

first place to be in sympathy with their proprietors' political ethos, and they will not have departed far from it since. They speak with one voice because, by and large, they are *of* one voice.

Almost entirely London and lobby-based, limited in their social and professional circles to an extent that often exceeds even the parochial small-town MP, their opinions are those of a self-reinforcing oligarchy. They test those opinions against the opinions of their peers – other journalists who have the same restricted world view as themselves – seeking confirmation and approval within those same narrow circles. They run – and hunt – with the pack.[16]

Examples of this 'great minds think alike' syndrome are not difficult to find. On 20 May 1991, William Rees-Mogg was writing in *The Independent* about AIDS:

> The 'unzip a condom' approach to the HIV epidemic reminds one of the filter tip response to the issue of cigarette smoking and cancer. It is not wrong, but it is a distraction from the real issue. The Judeo-Christian sexual code has a function to provide for the care of children, and also like Jewish dietary laws, to prevent the spread of disease . . . That is, in some ways, a similar approach to that of Alcoholics Anonymous, which is also prepared to accept the logic of abstinence and the need for community support . . . In Christian terms, sexual morality is determined by spiritual needs, but in Darwinist terms, Christian morality is a strategy for survival.

Three days later, Mary Kenny wrote in *The Daily Mail*:

> Condoms, in short . . . are just not enough to combat AIDS . . . Parallels can be drawn with organisations like Alcoholics Anonymous. AA does not say: 'Practise safer drinking' to those in the grip of alcoholism. It teaches people to build up a taboo against drinking, and then shows them the joys of sober living through community and, indeed, spiritual support . . . If something is killing us, we develop an instinct to

stop doing it. Morality has acted as a strategy for survival. We had believed that modern medicine had rendered such strategies obsolete. But, once more, history teaches the old lessons that if we don't have certain moral standards, we perish.

Less subtle, but also uncannily similar, were two other columnists, Bernard Dineen in *The Yorkshire Post*[17] and Cliff Graham in *The Newcastle Evening Chronicle*. A quick comparison shows that not only are they of the same mind on the topic of AIDS, but that those opinions are expressed in terms so similar as almost to pass into the realms of the psychic:

> *Dineen* (*Yorkshire Post*): Anyone who doubts the extent of homosexual promiscuity should examine gay periodicals such as The Pink Paper . . . Its advertisements make it clear that caution is not in fashion. Yet any attempt to reveal the facts about gay promiscuity provokes an outcry from activists.
>
> *Graham* (*Evening Chronicle*): You should examine some of the gay magazines. The advertisements make it clear that caution is not in vogue. Yet if anyone dare to write about gay promiscuity he or she is shouted down by the activists and branded a 'homophobe'.
>
> *Dineen*: These shrill activists do a disservice to their fellow homosexuals by their pretence that they represent 'the gay community' when in fact there is no such entity.
>
> *Graham*: The activists pretend to speak for the 'community' when there is in reality no such thing.
>
> *Dineen*: Their pretence that AIDS is some kind of badge of honour – recklessly living for today without thinking of tomorrow – is sinister and perverse.
>
> *Graham*: By pretending that AIDS is some sort of badge of honour . . . these people anger ordinary people.

Another favourite why-oh-why style of opinion piece which crops up at regular intervals is the all-out attack on gay lifestyles. The first is from *The Daily Telegraph* and written by Chaim

Bermant, who is also a columnist in *The Jewish Chronicle* where he peddles a similar line. It illustrates the dogmatic thinking of a rigid religionist, riddled with predictable stereotypes and offering up horrifying authoritarian solutions to the perceived 'problem' of homosexuality:

> Gays are reverting to queers but given their disposition should they not be calling themselves kamikazes? I ask the question in all seriousness, for they not only seem to have a death wish for themselves, but an apparent readiness to inflict death upon others . . . The 1967 Act was intended to remove the stigma of illegality from homosexual practices and end the pariah of the homosexual. But, if politicians could have foreseen what was to follow, the Act would never have been passed . . . Where they had been retiring and discreet they became strident, assertive, even aggressive . . . They tried to push their teachings in schools . . . the homosexual way of life is a desperately sad one. Their gaiety, where it exists, is extremely ephemeral. There is little love in their lives and their promiscuity is an attempt to snatch a moment of bliss in physical gratification . . . inherently sterile . . . Their relationships are generally brief . . . efforts at proselytisation . . . gays are pushing their luck and seem to think they can win over public sympathy by alienating it . . . [18]

And here's one by *The Glasgow Herald*'s columnist John Macleod:

> There is a myth of homosexuality, a crafted image of gentleness and civility. The reality is a culture of perversion, obsession and hatred. It is murder, like that of Joe Orton, battered to death by his gay lover. It is homosexual rape, today such a hazard in Kelvingrove Park that Glasgow University Union now buses students home. It is paedophilia . . . it is serial killing like Dennis Nilsen . . . It is simple yobbery like the lesbians who abseiled from the gallery of the House of Lords . . . Streets at night swarm with homosexual prostitutes . . . Homosexuality is unnatural, antisocial and

wrong. And if it is madness to say, then . . . I delight in madness.[19]

Stereotyping is, of course, an essential tool for any propagandist. For columnists, the pre-existing images of homosexuals make it easy to maintain the negative mythology, a mythology which stubbornly clings on, despite efforts to dislodge it. The effeminate, handbag-waving pansy makes frequent appearances in the tabloid press, as does the leather-jacketed clone and the rapacious child-corrupting sexual athlete. The pipe-smoking, man-eating, butch lesbian is also a favourite. These crude images are still peddled – in words and pictures – even though just about everyone in the country now knows a lesbian or gay man who doesn't fit them.

One man who obviously does believe these stereotypes is Roy Kerridge, who wrote an article in *The Spectator* entitled 'Predatory homosexuals':

> Strange are the rules of homosexual 'love and marriage'. An older man, having persuaded a younger man to live with him, humiliates the boy by bringing ever younger teenage boys back to his flat for tea and sympathy. Often the older man and his younger partner indulge voracious and voyeuristic sensations by going out *together* in pursuit of young boys . . . 'Gay clubs' often have rooms attached to the dance floor where group sodomy can take place, sometimes with whips, chains and handcuffs as handy props. In a sense, many popular 'gay clubs' are brothels . . .[20]

So wildly bigoted was this piece that in the following issue equal space was given to Adam Mars-Jones to rebut it:

> Homosexuals are the softest of soft targets. They – I suspect I have left it too late to modulate gracefully into the first person plural – are poorly placed to rebut even the most preposterous description of homosexuality. *This isn't true of me*, many gay people may think, *but perhaps it is true of the majority of my minority. How can I know?*

The gay conspiracy theory

A more insidious example of how this construction of a mythology works is in the case of the 'powerful homosexual lobby'. It is not clear where this lobby is supposed to be situated, who is supposed to run it or how it is funded. It has been 'known about' (at least by newspaper columnists) long before the Stonewall lobbying group was ever thought of. In fact, the first reference I can find to it was in a 1982 issue of *The Daily Express*, when columnist John Akass wrote of the 'powerful homosexual lobby' and the 'gay publicity machine'. At the time, the Campaign for Homosexual Equality, with its couple of thousand members, was the most prominent gay organization in the country. But the idea that there was some kind of hidden fifth column of influential homosexuals, pulling strings in high places, doing favours for each other to the detriment of 'ordinary people', a kind of sinister Masonic conspiracy, was one that had powerful resonance. People can't see this malevolent 'influence' being wielded because the 'secret army' hides in a 'twilight world'. All the same, many are prepared to believe that such a conspiracy exists.

George Gale had been slating gays for years in *The Daily Express*. In 1986 he moved over to Mirror Group newspapers where the diatribes continued unabated (until, that is, he was summarily fired after a torrent of protest from *Mirror* readers who were appalled by the reactionary views being peddled by Gale). In *The Sunday Mirror* he wrote: 'I don't mind what homosexuals get up to so long as they don't frighten the horses or spread AIDS. But like the great majority who lead normal and natural sex lives rather than abnormal and unnatural ones, I get fed up with the gay lobby.'

Garry Bushell, perhaps the most persistent hate figure in the gay community, was speaking in 1990 against a motion at the Oxford Union calling for more gay rights. His performance came during the week that the Press Council upheld a complaint against his use of the words 'poof' and 'poofter'. Following that adjudication, *The Sun* decided to reproduce the text of Bushell's speech under the headline 'We must defeat this militant gay cult'.[21] Once more the 'militant gay lobby' was invoked, as well as all the other familiar bogeymen beloved of anti-gay propagandists. Bushell began with the familiar assertion that homosexuals 'stoke up public intolerance towards themselves' by 'their own attitudes behaviour and demands':

> Now they want homosexuality to be thought of as just the same as heterosexuality. They want our children to be taught that their perversion is normal. Militant homosexuals have become a powerful anti-democratic lobby attempting to silence their critics ... Another major factor in changing public attitudes is AIDS which for all the propaganda of gays is plainly spread in the vast majority of cases either by the use of shared needles by drug addicts or by sodomy ... they are a militant cult seeking to pervert and convert others. The Times cuttings library is full of court cases of homosexual seduction, of the corruption of innocence ... The mass of people have no great sympathy or understanding for homosexuals ... most of all they want the homosexuals to leave them alone. Especially their children.

The speech failed to stir participants in the Oxford Union debate and Bushell's proposition that gay rights should be curtailed was overwhelmingly rejected – a fact which *The Sun* signally failed to mention. However, this idea of the 'powerful gay lobby' or 'gay rights cabal' or 'gay Mafia' or, later, 'the AIDS brigade' or 'powerful AIDS establishment' was eventually brought to a head by *The Sunday Telegraph* when it carried a piece of polemic entitled 'Is there a homosexual conspiracy?' by Graham Turner.[22] On the front page of that day's edition of the paper had been an opinion poll which apparently indicated that 'two-thirds of the British population' was anti-gay. (It was a telephone poll conducted among 460 people.) This seemed to justify, as far as the paper was concerned, Turner's paranoia about the infiltration of the 'gay lobby' into every aspect of British life. The article, which depended for its effect on an inordinate number of unattributed quotes, suggested that the major British institutions – TV, the Church, medicine, the Government, the civil service – were all in the pocket of 'the gay lobby'. According to Turner, only positive images of gays ever appear on TV because the BBC and ITV are 'liberal' and crawling with homosexuals; and the Church is reluctant to condemn homosexuals outright because there are so many in high places. According to critics quoted in the article, the medical establishment is all part of the collusion, too, because it takes too much notice of the lay members of its advisory bodies and won't allow anti-homosexual comment in the *British Medical Journal*. The Terrence Higgins Trust – an AIDS education and support organization – came in for particular suspicion and was presented in the article as little more than a conspirators' den where, for some unexplained reason, homosexuals were plotting to subvert all efforts to contain AIDS. The author of the article implied that homosexuals should not be allowed to play a part in the AIDS struggle – totally forgetting that if homosexuals had not set up support agencies there probably still wouldn't be any.

The 'Is there a homosexual conspiracy?' feature bore a remarkable resemblance to the 'Jewish Conspiracy' theories that are popular with anti-Semites anxious to justify their prejudice and their sometimes murderous activities. But if *The Sunday Telegraph* had replaced the word 'Homosexual' with 'Jewish' in its feature, it could have been prosecuted under the Race Relations Act. It might be argued that because homosexuals are the last minority group to have no protection from this kind of vicious attack, there is a displacement of hatred on to them which would in other circumstances be directed at the other traditional targets – racial and religious minorities.

The following week, *The Sunday Telegraph* allowed Sir Ian McKellen a right of reply, in which the gay rights champion put forward a cogent and considered rebuttal. However, this 'conspiracy' angle had already gained some ground in other papers. George Gale in *The Daily Mail* wrote:

> Does the Government secretly believe that since AIDS chiefly affects homosexuals, the disease serves them right, so let them stew? Do the medical authorities secretly concur? Does the homosexual lobby want no serious measures taken, for fear of hurting the interests of homosexuals?[23]

The week after *The Sunday Telegraph*'s effort, *The Mail on Sunday* went on the attack with an article presented on the news pages under the banner 'Analysis' and entitled 'Scandal of the gay clergy'.[24] Journalist Iain Walker claimed that one in four of inner London's clergy was gay and that they were 'supported inside the wider church establishment by homosexuals in positions of the highest responsibility'. No names were mentioned to support this contention and, indeed, there was no evidence of any kind that would justify this piece of propaganda as 'investigative journalism'. In reality it was an attack on the Lesbian and Gay Christian Movement, which was at the time being evicted from its head-quarters at St Botolph's church after a campaign against it by conservative Anglicans. According to *The Mail on Sunday*, LGCM was selling 'obscenity . . . the kind of stuff you would expect to find in a San Francisco bath house'. The only evidence cited of this was a safer sex leaflet which, very cunningly, was reproduced only in part so as to obscure its real purpose – the prevention of the spread of AIDS – and make it appear to be simply a pornographic book. The leaflet was produced not by LGCM but by one of the AIDS agencies, and its inclusion in the article was a shameless attempt to confuse readers by not revealing the whole truth about it. Then *The Daily Express* joined in: 'The Government has not reckoned with the entrenched power of the homosexual community in medicine and the Civil Service when it is dealing with its advisory boards. It is high time it grasped the nettle.'[25]

The 'myth' of gay oppression

George Gale introduced another theme aimed at taking the wind out of the sails of the 'gay lobby' when he wrote in *The Daily Mail* that: 'The idea that homosexuals are an oppressed minority is nonsense. The idea that they are entitled to propagate their peculiar practices at the public expense is preposterous.' It was a theme that would turn up over and over again. Why, asked the columnists, are homosexuals demanding rights when they are not discriminated against in the first place? A prime example of this was provided by Keith Waterhouse in *The Daily Mail*: 'The Gay Rights movement is a sham and a fraud in that since 1967 gays have had rights coming out of their ears. Show me a gay who claims to be persecuted and I will show you a gay who is trying to screw a grant out of the local council.'[26]

John Akass also gave us a version of this in *The Daily Express*: 'What is lacking in the piercing protests of the Clause 28 agitators is any evidence that homosexuals are being persecuted . . . The British public find homosexuality oddly amusing. This may be irritating, but it is not the stuff of a pogrom.'[27] Ferdinand Mount said in *The Daily Telegraph*: 'Clause 28 or no Clause 28, there is no witch-hunt on against homosexuals or against anyone else. And if there is one thing which is almost as bad as a witch hunt, it is a witch hunt for a witch hunt.'[28] Garry Bushell, not to be left out of the pack, said in *The Sun*: 'Homosexuals already have equal rights before the law in all reasonable areas. Public intolerance towards them is stoked up by their own attitudes, behaviour and demands.'[29] On the knighthood of Ian McKellen, John Smith in *The People* commented: 'The suggestion that homosexuality is some kind of handicap when it comes to being honoured is yet another example of the gay community trying to prove prejudice where none exists.'

Peter McKay, a columnist on the London *Evening Standard* commented on – and tried desperately to discredit – the great March on Washington, a million-strong display of lesbian and gay solidarity, which occurred in the US capital in May 1993.[30] McKay was equally complacent about the oppression of lesbians and gay men:

> What did they want anyway? Gays . . . are not lynched, burned out of their homes or made to sit at the back of the bus . . . Discrimination on the grounds of sex and race is largely outlawed. Laws give them the same protection against violence as everyone else. The march was really about demanding complete acceptance for a way of life which, rightly or wrongly, many people found repugnant. Blacks weren't asking for special treatment. Just to be treated like everyone else.

Peter Tatchell wrote an angry letter in response to McKay's comments, which the *Evening Standard* published two days later. He said: 'Homosexuals *are* lynched. It's called queer bashing. In extreme cases, anti-gay violence has involved bombings, arson and shootings.' And even *The Independent* has given voice to this one, when it allowed space for Colin Welch to ride one of his favourite hobby horses:

> Does the homosexual community exist? If there is any prejudice, I am sure that it is not against homosexuals as such but against homosexuality organised, aggressive, imperialistic. It asserts 'rights' that are offensive to many . . . Homosexuals have described their sexuality to me as a grievous burden and a handicap, not to be eagerly or lightly transmitted onwards . . . They are not gay at all, but sad![31]

John Junor

One of the most extreme exponents of the anti-gay diatribe is John Junor, once editor of *The Sunday Express* and subsequently a columnist on that paper and *The Mail on Sunday*. His JJ column became famous for the unfettered expression of naked prejudice and bigotry. He is, perhaps, typical of the old-style Fleet Street commentator who still imagines that his readers will be cheering his repetitively toxic rantings. Needless to say, his detestation of homosexuals and the gay community is regularly, almost obsessively, expressed. Like so many of his contemporaries in the press, he jumped on AIDS as the perfect tool for constructing anti-gay arguments. In *The Sunday Express* he wrote about the Terrence Higgins Trust and one of its safer sex leaflets: 'It is probably the most filthy and crudely worded publication I have ever seen. Instead of preaching abstinence it gives illustrated advice to homosexuals on how to have perverted sex with less risk.'[32] He even went so far as to quote one of the offending passages, thus ensuring it reached a far wider audience than the original leaflet: 'Everyone is turned on by different things . . . as for Wanking . . . Go for It! Share the pleasure with a friend.' He fumed: 'Isn't it damnable that such a pamphlet should be available where children can pick it up?' The rather ludicrous 'fuming' and posturing which characterize his columns (as well as the question marks, which are another speciality of his) can be written off as the ranting of a bigot beyond redemption, but occasionally the offensiveness is breathtaking. When, in April 1994, a fire at a private porn cinema club in London resulted in nine men (some of them homosexual) dying in tragic and horrific circumstances, Junor wrote:

> One would have thought there would have been a national wave of sympathy for the dreadfully burned survivors and the relatives of the dead. Isn't it extraordinary that there has been none? One would have thought there would have been a wave of revulsion against whoever set the place on fire. There hasn't even been that . . . Coming just a few days after the unsuccessful attempt to lower the age for buggery to 16, the news of the fire in this sleazy cinema did not do the homosexual cause much good. How could it after the disclosure that a fire exit had been boarded up to stop homosexual patrons from using the unoccupied area for casual sex with complete strangers? . . . Are these really the sort of people whom Sir Ian McKellen and Mrs Edwina Currie want to hold up as men of respect?

(In connection with this same incident, Garry Bushell 'joked': 'Actress Teri Hatcher is hotter than a cinema full of Kentucky Fried Transvestites.')[34]

In September 1991, Junor took the Princess of Wales to task because she had spent more time than he thought was fitting at the hospital bedside of a friend who was dying from AIDS.

> One visit I could understand. But six hours in a single spell? Four visits in 48 hours? A further bizarre visit to the bedside even after he had died? And finally a dramatic starring role at the funeral? Isn't it all going over the top more than just a little? . . . Just what then do you suppose can explain her preoccupation with this disease? Could she really want to go down in history as the patron saint of sodomy?

This tasteless ranting was commented upon by another journalist, Lynne Barber:

JJ says it would be 'inconceivable' for Princess Diana to have behaved in the same way if her friend had died of syphilis. *Really*? Is there a pecking order of illness? Where would JJ stand on, say, cirrhosis of the liver? At any rate, when JJ is on his deathbed, I hope his friends, if such there be, will weigh these matters and think twice before visiting him.[35]

Lynne Barber's deep dislike of Junor seems to have sprung from an interview she did with him for *The Independent on Sunday* which was headlined 'There are no gays in Auchtermuchty'.[36] Ms Barber – well-known for her acerbic and probing technique – was trying to find out where the homophobic anger that pervades his column comes from:

> I saw the rage in action at lunch with him in Dorking, when I tried to argue with him that his view of AIDS as appropriate punishment for sodomy was wrong-headed and cruel. Immediately the eyes bulged and the skin marbled – it was as though someone had shot purple dye into his veins – the voice curdled into a snarl . . . But why did he hate homosexuals so much? 'Unhappily', he intoned, 'some men are born in a certain way and with those people I have great sympathy. It's the proselytisers I object to; the people who flaunt their homosexuality and try to convert and subvert other people to it. These are the people I have utter hatred for, because I think they are spreading filth.'
>
> By now the voice was booming round the walls of the genteel Dorking restaurant, the face was deep indigo and an unfortunate waiter who had come to collect our plates stood paralysed like a rabbit in a car's headlights. 'Filth, Miss Barber. I regard buggery' – he paused to savour the word – 'buggery as the putting of the penis into shit. Don't you, Miss Barber. Don't you?'

He claimed that 'homosexualism' is virtually unknown in Scotland and expressed shock that Lynne Barber had gay friends whom she invited to dinner at her home. 'I find that idea most . . . unusual. It does not happen in Auchtermuchty.' That interview was to come back to haunt him on several occasions, and *Punch* writer Mike Conway (describing himself as 'a wee man from Kirkcudbrightshire') made the pilgrimage to Auchtermuchty to find out whether Junor's assertion that there are no gays there was correct.

> 'Of course there are,' said the librarian Caroline John.
>
> 'I wrote to *The Independent on Sunday* complaining about the headline,' said the incomer (Caroline Fladmark). 'I've just been speaking to a gay man. He lives down the road with his boyfriend,' said the 67-year-old housewife.
>
> 'Oh he's so popular. He sometimes jokingly shouts 'Hello gorgeous' on the street' said the policeman.
>
> I was forced down the road to meet him. And very charming he was too.

Other residents didn't think much of Sir John, either. ' "Well, he can be funny, and he gives the town some publicity," said the librarian, "but . . . well . . . he's a ghastly old bigot and I think he's getting worse." '[37] Perhaps the best summing up of Junor the columnist and journalist was given by Julian Critchley, who wrote that JJ: 'owed less to Momus, the God of mockery, than a flair for vulgar and common abuse . . . His is the voice of the anonymous letter-writer, of the men and women with a taste for green ink, the senders of hate mail.'[38]

Ray Mills/Brian Hitchen

Many of the columnists could be similarly described, but some of them are so noxious that their insults cannot be allowed to pass. One such was Ray Mills, a man who began a column in *The Star* on 2 September 1986 under the heading 'The angry voice'. He began (writing in a bizarre third-person style): 'Mills will often find himself sharing a political bed of nails with . . . the National Front . . . "patriots" . . . and all those whose political philosophy is entirely encompassed by the four point plan: Hang 'em, flog 'em, castrate 'em and send 'em home.' He would, he said in this introductory column, also rail against: 'Wooftahs, pooftahs, nancy boys, queers, lezzies – the perverts whose moral sin is to so abuse the

delightful word "gay" as to render it unfit for human consumption.'
True to his word, the following week, on 9 September, under the
heading 'Get back in the closet', he said:

> Insidiously, almost imperceptibly, the perverts have got the
> heterosexual majority with their backs against the wall (the
> safest place actually) . . . The freaks proclaim their twisted
> morality almost nightly on TV . . . where will it ever end?
> Where it may end, of course, is by natural causes. The
> woofters have had a dreadful plague visited upon them,
> which we call AIDS, and which threatens to decimate their
> ranks. Since the perverts offend the laws of God and nature,
> is it fanciful to suppose that one or both is striking back? . . .
> Little queers or big queers, Mills has had enough of them all –
> the lesbians, bisexuals and transsexuals, the hermaphrodites
> and the catamites and the gender benders who brazenly
> flaunt their sexual failings to the disgust and grave offence of
> the silent majority. A blight on them all, says Mills.

Mills became a rallying point for the gay community, so
violent and abhorrent were his views. I made a complaint to the
National Union of Journalists Ethics Council, which was running a
'Campaign for Real People' in an attempt to curb the stereotyping
and misrepresentation of minorities in the press. Complaints were
made to the Press Council, too. The editor of *The Star* at the time,
Lloyd Turner, told Terry Murphy of the Wimbledon Area Gay
Society (during the course of his complaint about Mills):

> Mills is giving a point of view – a view that is given in any
> pub, any house, any street on any day of the year. His views
> reflect the views of people . . . views that may be they do not
> know how to make public . . . You do not agree with Mills.
> Fine. If you wish I will publish part of your response in The
> Star, But please do not ask me to ban a man who has a clear
> view. If you urge me to do that I also ban you.[39]

The Press Council excused itself with the reasoning that
although the Mills column was 'crude and abusive' it accepted *The*

Star's claim that 'the opinions expressed in it were those of a fictitious man whose thoughts resembled those of many readers based on thousands of letters received each week.' Mills boasted of this in his column, saying: 'Mills trusts that readers will not have overlooked the fact that the Press Council have rejected the latest whinge from woofter apologists. The score is thus Mills, 2. Woofters, 0.' (The Press Council eventually upheld a complaint against Mills after he referred to a man awaiting trial for murder as a 'black bastard'. The Council said it was a 'gross and deliberate breach' of the repeated ruling that a person's colour should not be mentioned unless it was directly relevant to the story.) Eventually, after months of these relentless attacks, the NUJ fined Mills £500 for racism and incitement to hatred against homosexuals. He reacted by saying that he would not pay the fine and awaited his expulsion from the union 'sadly but with head held high'. The Press Council, while rejecting a further complaint, described the column as 'outrageously racist, crude, offensive and inflammatory'. Mark Wadsworth, co-chair of the NUJ Ethics Committee, was quoted in *City Limits* as saying: 'It is our view that Mills has been guilty of a sustained campaign against black people, lesbians and gays, and we're seeking to stop that.'[40] He thought Mills's reaction to the fine was a matter of 'considerable concern for his NUJ colleagues on the paper's staff'. Eventually Mills was expelled from the union, but his rantings were as virulent as ever and continued to appear – at least until June 1988 when Brian Hitchen took over as editor. At the time I wrote: 'The Ray Mills column has disappeared from *The Star* only to be replaced by another by the editor Brian Hitchen. Although I don't agree with the man's politics or philosophy, his opinions are at least expressed with moderation.'

Little could I have known that, in fact, Hitchen and Mills would prove indistinguishable, and Hitchen went on to use *The Star* as a vehicle for some of the most vicious anti-gay campaigns undertaken by the British press. Typical of anti-gay angling of stories by *The Star* was the case of the 'gay weddings' which never were. On 25 May 1989, the paper reported – under the heading 'Poofters get right to wed' – that new licences granted 'all-men couples the same rights as other wedded folk in San Francisco'. Hitchen said:

San Francisco is one of the most beautiful cities in the world. In some ways it is also the ugliest . . . what is the reaction of the city of San Francisco to the plague launched on a sick wave of so-called free gay love (homosexual promiscuous sex). Horror? Shame? Not for a moment. Yesterday the city's law-makers voted to recognise homosexual weddings – the first time in history that such a travesty of marriage vows has been legalised . . . Anyone who thinks these 'marriages' are anything but a grotesque mockery of a solemn occasion is living in FAIRY-LAND.

Hitchen is also very keen to bolster the mythology which surrounds homosexuality. He promotes stereotyped and distorted images whenever possible. On 3 May 1989 he was commenting on child abuse – in particular the murder of a young boy by an alleged paedophile – and was anxious to lay this crime on the doorstep of the gay community:

How many child runaways who, for a variety of reasons, believe they cannot go home to face their parents . . . are easy pickings for the warped bastards who have carefully conditioned us into believing that there is nothing really wrong with homosexuality and that rent boys are a fact of life . . . Isn't it time for a massive crackdown on these sewer-dwellers in our midst? And if that doesn't work, how about flame-throwers?

Another example of the relentless nature of Hitchen's homophobia came when *The Daily Star* carried a huge front-page headline 'Poofters on parade' above a story about a recommendation (by the Parliamentary Armed Forces Bill Committee) that members of the services should not be prosecuted for homosexual acts that would be legal in civilian life.[41] *The Daily Star* reported this as 'homosexuality is to become legal in the Armed forces'. (This was untrue: even after the recommendation was implemented in 1994, homosexuality, even if not 'practised', was still grounds for dismissal and the same legal restrictions as in civilian life still applied.) An editorial in the same issue said:

The idea is repugnant to all decent people in this country. Our service men and women are the envy of the world. They have earned universal praise and respect for their courage, discipline and professionalism. Is this all to be destroyed by the poofters on parade? The House of Commons Armed Services Committee have allowed themselves to be shamefully manipulated by the gay brigade . . . So successful has gay propaganda been that most people are afraid to speak out for fear of being branded and vilified. There was genuine disgust when a Labour Government legalised homosexual acts between consenting adults. Since then Gay Lib has polluted our TV screens, even our schools.

The editorial labelled gay groups 'these strident, mincing preachers of filth'. The corruption of youth theory was once more invoked ('How sickening that young recruits will become open targets of filth') as well as indiscipline ('Just think of the effect on discipline of catfights among the queens on the front line'). In case there should be any doubt about the authorship of this piece, four days later Brian Hitchen was telling us in his weekly column to 'Shove your queer ideas in the closet'. In this diatribe he brought forward all the usual 'reasons' for readers to be outraged and fearful, including another outing for the 'powerful homosexual lobby':

> With a wink and a wiggle, homosexuals have managed to persuade MPs . . . to legalise poofs in uniform . . . Doesn't the Armed Forces Committee decision demonstrate the power of homosexual pressure groups? And doesn't it also show how deeply and dangerously those pressure groups must have tunnelled to persuade 11 otherwise sane MPs to their own perverted way of thinking? . . .
>
> Can you see our tank drivers welcoming a Pansy Division? And if a paratrooper was daft enough to indent for a candy-striped canopy, he might find that it didn't open too swiftly . . . And though the homosexual lobby will reach for their pens to complain or lisp falsetto abuse down my phone, I'll tell them this for free: people are sick and tired of your 'gay'

nonsense and the pretence that gays are normal and that it is heterosexuals who are out of step.

On the day before the recommendations of the Armed Services Committee were made public, *The Daily Star* ran on its front page the headline 'HMS Dyke'. It claimed that 'Lesbian Wrens face inquiry at top Navy base'.[42] This was a rather crude attempt to discredit and demean the reforms – the story itself amounted to nothing but the unproved accusations of one woman. Nothing further was heard of the supposed 'inquiry'. But Hitchen was right in one respect – the 'poofters' did reach for their pens, and over two hundred of them complained to the Press Complaints Commission about this disturbing outburst of almost pathological homophobia. The Gay London Policing Group (GALOP) and The Stonewall Group asked the Metropolitan Police to prosecute the newspaper under the Public Order Act for publishing material which was 'threatening, abusive and insulting'. They declined to do so. Eventually, however, the Press Complaints Commission upheld the complaint, saying that Hitchen 'rode roughshod over the sensitivities' of those of his fellow citizens who are gay. It said that *The Daily Star* had failed to 'make a distinction between the expression of strong opinions and their publication in terms which would encourage the persecution of a minority'. *The Daily Star* published the adjudication without comment, failing to explain to its readers that Hitchen was one of the leading members of the Press Complaints Commission when the complaint was made and that he had enthusiastically endorsed its code of practice when it had been produced. But far from curbing Hitchen's outpourings, the Press Complaints Commission was obliged to censure him again in 1994[43] for writing 'prejudicial and pejorative' remarks about identifiable homosexuals in an article on 24 May that year:

> Working at the BBC must be a poofter's idea of paradise. It's so wonderful that queer couples who 'marry' could, before yesterday, qualify for a £75 'wedding gift' voucher and a week's honeymoon . . . doesn't it make you want to vomit? . . . it's a good thing pansies can't get pregnant.

But Hitchen really came into his own when it was first mooted, in June 1992, that the gay age of consent might be lowered. It became apparent that one of the moving forces behind this proposed reform was the Conservative MP Edwina Currie. Hitchen raved in his column: 'With her latest outburst the pushy MP is demonstrating that it isn't only her jaw that's becoming unhinged . . . How can she possibly support such a hideously revolting idea which will contribute to the corruption of so many sick and weak-minded young kids?'[44] By the time the issue came before Parliament in February 1994, *The Star* went into a positive frenzy of hate. On the day of the vote, Hitchen wrote that it was a disgrace that MPs were even considering it. He claimed that the majority of Britons would be 'outraged' at any reform. 'If they win it will be a disgrace. MPs should stick to matters that affect us all, like jobs and wages. Not pander to a bunch of pansies and perverts.'

Hitchen has also 'spoken out vigorously' on the topic of AIDS. His opinion has been consistent – like so many of his contemporaries on other newspapers: AIDS is a plague visited upon poofters and junkies, a punishment which they richly deserve.

> Supporters of an AIDS centre in Bournemouth are miffed because Cliff Richard turned down a plea for help. Cliff is quite right. Why should anyone be obliged to help people who, mostly, have only themselves to blame for their predicament? Despite all the homosexual propaganda, AIDS is almost entirely a disease passed on by poofters and junkies. Only their promiscuity and stupidity has spread it like wildfire. Thank goodness that someone of Cliff's stature has stood out against the AIDS industry. Let's hope other showbiz stars follow his example.[45]

The Daily Star, like *The Sun*, has claimed on several occasions that it is not anti-gay. ('We believe that homosexuals have every right to do their own thing – in private. But to pretend their behaviour is normal – that's daft.')[46] Brian Hitchen has said of *The Daily Star*, in an interview with *Options* magazine: 'Where *The Sun* is brutal, we are mischievous and impertinent.'[47] But I suppose what constitutes 'brutality' is a matter of opinion – and perceptions will be influenced by whether you are on the receiving end. Mr Hitchen defined his political stance and its influence on *The Daily Star* in the same interview: 'Some people have described me as further right than Attila the Hun. My bootprint is stamped on this paper more than any other tabloid editor's on any other paper.' In August 1994, Brian Hitchen moved from the editorship of *The Daily Star* to take over *The Sunday Express*.

'The Sun *says*'

Another rich source of tabloid homophobia, expressed in hyperbolic terms, is *The Sun*'s editorial column (entitled '*The Sun* says'). Some of these leaders – often reading as though they have been reproduced directly from press releases issued by Conservative central office – have gained legendary status. They have been described as pithy and witty by fans, but often they are simply brutishly racist, sexist and, inevitably, deeply homophobic. They represent a concentration of all that is most disgusting about *The Sun*. During the 1980s many of these gems of bigotry were composed by a man called Ronald Spark, a Garnettesque rhetorician who even invented his own rules of grammar to express the near-illiterate pre-digested opinions of '*The Sun* says' column. An indication of Mr Spark's political persuasion can be gleaned from the fact that during the Falklands conflict he actually suggested that journalists who opposed Britain's activities in that war should be charged with treason.

Over the years literally hundreds of these '*The Sun* says' editorials have lambasted homosexuals and their supporters. (Ironically, a *Gay Times* survey of its readership showed that 36 per cent also read *The Sun*).[48] A very small selection is reproduced here to give a flavour of the extremity and consistency of *The Sun*'s detestation of homosexuals. On 28 September 1984, *The Sun* weighed in with its support for Rugby Council, which had declared that it would no longer promise not to discriminate against gays in job applications.

> Hooray for Rugby! The Tory council has scrapped a guarantee that it will not discriminate against homosexuals

seeking jobs. Farmer Gordon Collett declares robustly: 'We're not having men turning up for work in dresses and earrings.' Dead right! The Sun has nothing against homosexuals. What they do in private is their own affair. But they have no right to make *their* closet problems *our* problems. For years we have had to endure a campaign to cast homosexuals first as martyrs and then as heroes. Some employers have actually been bullied into giving them preference for jobs . . . The homosexuals have been led to believe that they are superior, healthy and normal while the rest of the community are out of step. A society which swallows that kind of sick nonsense is in danger of destroying itself. Let's ALL follow Rugby in fighting back!

Neil Barnett, writing in *Gay News* at the time, challenged Roy Greenslade, *The Sun*'s then assistant editor, to produce evidence to support Spark's contention that 'Some employers have actually been bullied into giving them preference for jobs'. He was unable to do so, but by way of justification he told Barnett:

Is it not the case that groups who are pushing from a point of gay liberation initially have now come full circle so that they believe that homosexuality is the norm, that it's a superior form of sexuality to heterosexuality? Their sense of themselves has changed, they're self-interested, self-absorbed, self-minded and practise separateness . . . All The Sun is saying is that we have to stop and take stock of how far the sexual revolution has gone. This liberal attitude . . . maybe the balance has swung too far the other way, and all The Sun is saying is perhaps Rugby has a point.

The implication of what was being said – that it is OK, even heroic, to hound gay people from their jobs – seemed to have completely passed him by. Obviously perturbed by the furore this editorial evoked, *The Sun* allowed Matthew Parris – at that time a Conservative MP, and obviously tentatively pushing at the closet door – a right of reply. This did not stop complaints to the Press Council about the editorial, one of which was upheld. The Council said that the paper had been 'improper and extremely offensive to advocate discrimination against homosexual people and encourage employers to discriminate'. Giving evidence at the Press Council's hearing into this complaint, Kelvin MacKenzie made the extraordinary claim that the gay community was harassing Fleet Street.

The disingenuous claim that *The Sun* is not hostile to homosexuals (perhaps made ironically) cannot cover up the contempt it repeatedly expresses. The paper once claimed: '*The Sun* has never been hostile to the gay community'.[49] This statement came immediately before an offer of a one-way ticket out of the country to any gay person who wished to go – as long as they didn't come back. Another example of the 'non-hostility' of *The Sun* came with this editorial:

> So-called progressives constantly argue that the mass of people are tolerant and even welcoming towards sexual deviants. An opinion poll gives lie to this poison. It shows that two thirds of the nation CONDEMN homosexual acts and lifestyle. This is reassuring news. A society which – like the ancient Greeks and Romans – approves a perversion is on the brink of disintegration. Britain is healthy and normal and the future is bright!

Every aspect of gay life has been severely criticized by *The Sun*. Here's its carefully reasoned argument, on 10 February 1988, for locking up members of the Campaign for Homosexual Equality (published under the heading 'Gay and wicked'):

> Homosexual organisations are sometimes seen as harmless, slightly comic eccentrics. In our view, they can be a force for destructive evil in the land. Just look at what is happening in Cambridge. There the Campaign for Homosexual Equality are urging sexual deviates not to take the AIDS test. Why? Because it could cause them unhappiness . . . It passes belief that any group of individuals should be deliberately setting out to sabotage what is being done. They deserve to be treated as pariahs. They deserve to be locked away where they can do no more harm.

Perhaps the nadir of Ronald Spark's gay-bashing was reached on 10 February 1988, when a full-page editorial, headed 'When the gays have to shut up' attempted to blame the whole gay community for the murder of a schoolboy, Stuart Gough. During the preceding days, the murder had been played for all it was worth. Both *The Sun* and *The Star* had put great emphasis on the fact that Victor Miller, the man accused of the crime, was gay. For several days they dwelt on Miller's background and implied that the way he lived and behaved was typical of gay men's lifestyles. Eventually came the editorial, which started by reasonably asserting that: 'No-one in reason can possibly blame the homosexual community for what happened to Stuart Gough, any more than a reasonable woman would blame all heterosexual men for an act of rape or murder . . .' Yet that is precisely what the paper tried to do. Having raised the emotional temperature by describing Stuart's funeral in great detail, *The Sun* went on to insinuate that it was 'homosexuals' who were responsible for the murder and not just an individual psychopath. According to Spark, homosexuals 'regard themselves as superior' and 'want preference for jobs' and, his favourite canard: 'they believe it is *they* who are normal and the rest of society which is perverse'. There then followed a whole shopping list of reasons why any decent *Sun* reader should detest homosexuals: they eat up the rates, they indulge in filthy sex practices, they spread AIDS, they're a threat to children, etc. In fact, the paper took the opportunity to regurgitate all its self-created myths about the gay community. I was so furious about the extremism of this editorial that I demanded a right-of-reply. To my astonishment it was granted and my unedited half-page piece was given a prominent position on page two on 12 February.

Francis Wheen in *The New Statesman* was equally flummoxed by *The Sun*'s sudden regard for fair play.[50] He had asked Spark why *The Sun* had broken with its tradition of shutting out opposing voices and had carried the right of reply. 'Basically,' Spark is reported to have said, 'we wish to be fair to all groups. We were very concerned not to give people the chance to say we were queer-bashing. We wish to be fair.'

The emptiness of these words were pointed up when, months later, Miller was convicted. In *The Sun*'s news section Miller's life was once more presented as that of a typical gay man. According to the report, his casual job as a gay stripper provided 'a clue to the twisted mind which led him to kill' and was also linked to 'his sordid relationship with a gay live-in lover'. '*The Sun* says' column commented: 'Those who preach that homosexuality is "normal" should remember Stuart. Those who try to corrupt children at school with gay propaganda should remember Stuart. Those who pour public money into gay and lesbian "action groups" should remember Stuart.'[51]

Broadsheet homophobia

Leaving aside the crudely abusive tabloid attacks, we move on to the broadsheets, the more 'thoughtful' and 'analytical' newspapers. It is in the 'serious' right-wing press that we are likely to find the same crazy logic, same naked aggression and same desire to halt gay progress, but expressed much more pompously. Perhaps the paper with the longest record of constructing anti-gay propaganda is *The Sunday Telegraph*. In the late 1980s it was under the editorship of Peregrine Worsthorne, a self-confessed 'feudal reactionary'. At that time, Mr Worsthorne was in the habit of contributing a weekly signed editorial to the paper and often he would meander on the subject of homosexuality and AIDS. On 31 January 1988 he was telling us that AIDS had brought a stark choice to homosexuals: 'Closet or coffin'. The gist of the piece was that if homosexuals didn't stop having sex they would inevitably succumb to AIDS. The following week he used Section 28 as the jumping-off point for another wander down the highways and byways of homophobia. But occasionally, the paper surprised everyone and allowed a columnist to put a point of view which contradicted the party line. One such was Celia Haddon who was filling in one week for Mary Kenny. Haddon took the opportunity to launch a thinly veiled attack on her journalistic colleagues – many of them working on *The Sunday Telegraph*:

> Almost all the middle-aged heterosexual men I know seem to have become unhealthily obsessed with and prejudiced

against homosexuality. They are intemperate, bigoted and hypocritical. Clearly their tolerance a few years back was only skin deep. AIDS has given them a chance to come out in their true colours. What really enrages me is the way they pretend sodomy (and therefore higher risk of passing on AIDS) is confined only to gay men. As many women know, it is something that quite a few completely heterosexual men like doing . . . You would think that straight men ought to be grateful that the AIDS epidemic started among gay men. Gay men are literally dying for all of us. The two or three people I have come across who are carrying the virus are an inspiration to me for their courage and humour.[52]

However, this was a brief respite in the paper's usual approach to gay matters and on 15 January 1989 it carried an editorial defending Mrs Thatcher and saying that her critics should not be dismissed because they are 'well-off sillies' but because they overstate their case. The campaign against Section 28 was cited as an example of this 'silliness'.

This was a measure which was supposed to enable local authorities to ban from municipally subsidised theatres and libraries any works by or about homosexuals. In fact it was introduced to stop teachers proselytising in the classroom on behalf of homosexuality and local authorities from subsidising 'Gay' events on the rates.

The writer of the editorial said that the 'arts lobby', which had argued against the Section, was 'hysterical' and subsequent history had shown that 'there have been no prosecutions under the clause, and any successful ones will be rare and have little to do with "the arts" '.

Perhaps the most overt statement of *The Sunday Telegraph*'s editorial attitude to gays was given by Roger Scruton, a conservative philosopher and right-wing polemicist. Writing in the 24 November 1989 issue, under the heading 'Why heterosexism is not a vice', the professor of aesthetics bizarrely claimed: 'Probably the comment pages of *The Sunday Telegraph* provide the last remaining place where you can criticise homosexuality in print – the last place where toleration will be extended to the heterosexist.' Scruton then went on to claim that there was no longer any 'moral shock' attached to homosexuality. He said that because it creates a 'languorous pacifism', homosexuality probably led to the rise of Hitler. The Second World War, it seems, was the fault of homosexuals! Scruton ended by saying: 'this lack of moral shock – or shamelessness – is far from fortunate for society, and may well contain the doom of us all'. A letter in the following week's correspondence column summed up the piece: 'The tabloid press is full of such stuff, but their scurrilous clap-trap is not dressed up as reasoned argument.' But at least one *Sunday Telegraph* reader had taken on board Scruton's ideas. On the same letters page, the Rev. Hugh Rom said 'homosexuality is no longer a private vice, but now is a many-headed movement, designed to make deviancy the norm by incestuous, underhand and dishonest propaganda'.

Other upmarket papers, too, constantly construct arguments which oppose anything the gay community does. Often these rest on the contention that not only is there no discrimination, but that because of their 'stridency' and 'flaunting', homosexuals actually create the problems they complain about. The message is clear: why don't you shut up? A classic example of this was written by William Oddie under the headline 'Gay pride may tempt a fall' in *The Sunday Times*:

> The present assumption of the gay lobby appears to be that all it has to do is to continue agitating in order to make further advances. But I suspect we have reached the point at which, as Quentin Crisp said, 'the more gay people now insist on their rights, the greater the distance becomes between the gay world and the straight world and that is a pity.'
>
> It is more than a pity, it is potentially a tragedy, and one that will make our society nastier and less tolerant than it was before.[53]

The point had been made many times previously that heterosexuals 'cannot help' being homophobic and that gays had better

better know their place if they value their safety. This example by Gerald Priestland is also from *The Sunday Times*:

> The gay cat is out of the bag and it will not be stuffed in again simply because most of us do not like thinking about it. At the same time, gays have to realise that – for whatever tangled reason – the majority cannot help reacting to them as though they were a new wave of immigrants, who need to settle down and show themselves good citizens.[54]

Mary Kenny in *The Sunday Telegraph* put it this way:

> Joan Bakewell in her TV programme about reducing the age of consent for teenage homosexuals . . . repeatedly alleged that the British were uniquely homophobic. This is simply not true. Until 1970, for example, the French had a regulation that someone who was openly homosexual could not be a school teacher or a civil servant while the Russians executed homosexual men. Why don't TV researchers ever do any proper research instead of just talking to propagandists?

Ms Kenny is incorrect. There has never been capital punishment for homosexuality in Russia, not even under the Tsars. And at least the French had seen the error of their ways and changed their law – twenty-five years previously.

Even *The Independent* has had a ride on this particular bandwagon and, in response to a public 'kiss-in' organized by OutRage!, the paper advised:

> Attempts by homosexuals to raise public awareness of the various forms of discrimination from which they believe they suffer tend to be counterproductive. Activism in any field is often one step from militancy and militant homosexuals are not generally good advertisements for their cause. Last night's gay 'kiss-in' . . . is unlikely to increase public support. Unless homosexuals wish to alienate the public, they should conduct themselves with restraint.[55]

When protests were made about the introduction of Section 25 of the Criminal Justice Bill 1991, which sought to make some crimes associated with gay men into 'serious' offences, Norman Stone wrote in the London *Evening Standard* (under the heading 'The gays do protest too much'):

> Now, what caused the Oscar Wilde disaster? Was it the persecution by law of homosexuals in England? Or was it just the nature of the beast that it would all end in tears? . . . We can do without any public statements to the effect that 'gay pride' needs statutory endorsement: public decency, the family, are part of civilisation, and we should support them.[56]

In that statement we have the 'gays bring it on themselves' argument, followed by the idea that if you give something to homosexuals, you have to take something away from heterosexuals (in this case, if gays get rights, straights lose their families). But, of course, sometimes even other commentators get fed up with reading the same old abuse over and over again and Simon Hoggart in *The Observer* was moved to write:

> Being a homosexual must often make for a difficult life, made worse by endless priggish preaching from some commentators. They were out in force last week after the argument on whether Ian McKellen should have accepted a knighthood. The gist seems to be that, in their infinite compassion, they didn't mind what homosexuals actually did, providing they retained a fitting sense of their own inferiority . . . They even trotted out the wearisome old saw that 'gay' was a serviceable little word before the homosexuals hijacked it. So it was, and so was 'queer' before the bigots got hold of that.[57]

Even Peregrine Worsthorne, one of the leading 'priggish preachers' of the age, was not unaware of the power his access to the press gave him or the temptation to misuse that power. In *The Sunday Telegraph* he wrote: 'How often is moral indignation simply the cloak under which journalists – and anybody else for that matter – hide their sadistic pleasure in putting the boot in?'

Mockery

Occasionally columnists will attempt to undermine the progress of gay rights with the use of mockery and ridicule. These attempts at satire require readers to accept the established 'funny' stereotypes of gay people – limp wrists, lisps, cross-dressing and supposed gender confusion. Take this from John Smith in *The People*:

> Bitch, bitch, bitch, the Gays are on the warpath. Peers in the House of Lords have received death threats over the controversial Clause 28 in the new laws governing the promotion of homosexuality in schools. They are thought to have come from the Gay Rights Action Movement. Time was when we thought Hell had no fury like a woman scorned. That's nothing compared to a poofter peeved[58]

Another favourite tabloid 'joke' is to pick on a story about a writer or composer who is being 'accused' of being gay and then making juvenile puns on the titles of his or her works. *The Sun* is particularly fond of this and has carried several rather stupid examples of its 'wit'. A classic came on 21 April 1989, when the paper claimed that Shakespeare had been gay, under the heading 'Friends, Romans and countrymen, lend me your rears':

> Schoolkids everywhere know that the bard's bawdy quotes do not include: Beware the AIDS of March; Once more into the britches, dearie friends; To be or not to be one, that is the question . . . Shakespeare did not title his plays Macbent, A Mince-Summer Nights Dream or King Queer.

Commenting on this, Bryony Coleman wrote in *The Guardian*:

> No doubt champions of Clause 28 will be greatly reassured by this sniggering new low in fourth form wit; yet another leg cocked against the 'promotion' of homosexuality, yet another thumbs up for homophobia. It's the sort of everyday drivel that gays have had to learn to live with.[59]

Sick of 'living with it', I complained about this piece to the then recently appointed 'independent' Ombudsman at *The Sun* who was to deal with complaints from readers. His name was Ken Donlan, and his 'independent' credentials were underscored by his being the paper's managing editor. His reply to my letter complaining of the cheap cracks about AIDS and the nasty stereotyping of gay people elicited the response that: 'The gay community invites the treatment which you rightly reject because of the antics of a minority'. And just to prove that they'd taken these complaints seriously, *The Sun* returned to the subject in February 1992, when a gay theatre company announced that it intended to reinterpret Shakespeare to point up the homosexual elements in the work. This time *The Sun*'s efforts were so feeble that *The Daily Star* felt the need to compete. *The Sun* came up with 'Romeo and Julian; The Fairy Wives of Windsor; A Mince Summer Night's Dream and Julius Teaser.' *The Star*'s efforts included 'Romeo and Julian, Julius Teaser, The Fairy Wives of Windsor; A Mince Summer Night's Dream'. (Incidentally, after being launched on a wave of self-congratulatory hype, the tabloid ombudsmen rapidly faded away.)

And so the stereotyping went on. In May 1991, the Metropolitan Police announced that it intended actively to recruit gay people into its ranks. This prompted Peter McKay of the London *Evening Standard* to write:

> Something will have to be done about that uniform. Gay friends of mine are notoriously fastidious about clothes. That domed hat will have to go. Perhaps a colonial-style cocked hat with egret feathers would sit well on top of an unstructured tunic; how about baggy blue trousers and a special 'run fast' trainers? The truncheon certainly needs looking at.[60]

John Pool in *The Hartlepool Mail* found the prospect of gay policemen irresistibly funny, too:

> Now I'm sure the boys in blue won't be sporting a pink uniform . . . but I dare say they could have one or two choice comments to deal with from the public . . . your average villain may have some reaction to the prospect of being

searched by a man with a limp wrist. I'm sure the boys and girls over at the local nick will be having a good chuckle at the story but it certainly adds a whole new meaning to what makes a bent copper.

The vast majority of the men and women chosen to write the columns in right-wing newspapers seem uniform in their authoritarian outlook on life. They are desperately conventional people, constantly harping on the conservative holy grails of 'tradition' (their own traditions, not other people's), the infinite superiority of a closely defined version of family life, the rigidity of sex differences, the protection of capitalism, the detestation of socialism. An excellent exploration of what motivates such demagogic individuals can be found in the book *The Authoritarian Personality*.[61] Reviewing it in *The Independent* Linda Joffee summed up the kind of person who harbours illogical and harmful prejudice – and in doing so she gave the perfect description of the average commentator and leader writer in the right-wing British press:

> The authoritarian personality . . . is a volatile mix of opposites. He possesses enlightened ideas and skills characteristic of a highly industrialised society, while retaining certain superstitions and irrational beliefs. He prides himself on being his own person, yet deep down fears being different. He slavishly subscribes to the dominant views of the social group with which he identifies, while staunchly insisting that he thinks for himself. Oblivious to these contradictions, he is fiercely protective of his rights and 'individuality', yet submits to authority with knee-jerk obedience.
>
> The studies are persuasively coherent in attempting to explain how prejudice and its associated political manifestations have everything to do with an individual's psychological needs, fears, fantasies and inadequacies – and virtually nothing to do with the reality of the people against whom prejudice is directed.[62]

A *new breed* of columnist

Fortunately the right-wingers don't have it all their own way. A new breed of more balanced and fair-minded columnists is emerging. Claudia Fitzherbert, Nigella Lawson, Jaci Stephen, Libby Purves, Frances Wheen and other writers working on traditionally reactionary journals have all produced copy that at least aims at seeing both sides of the story. These people seem much more willing to explore emotional complexities and sexual variety as social developments. Janet Daley in *The Independent* even went so far as to say that she was totally unable to 'get inside the heads of people who detest homosexuals'. In a stinging riposte to her fellow hacks' homophobia she wrote: 'I have honestly tried to understand this aversion (and I mean aversion, since the true homophobe manifests not so much disapproval as revulsion) but have never succeeded in getting so much as a glimmering of comprehension.'

Others have written supportively and sympathetically about the gay struggle. Jaci Stephen, for instance, in *The Daily Mail*, examined the reasons why gay men and straight women so often make the best of friends – and why heterosexual men find this so difficult to understand: 'Most heterosexual men only have to look at their own behaviour, or the behaviour of their friends to find out the answer. Even the briefest observation of their activities is enough to convince a woman that they are a species quite unlike anything else on the planet.'[63] Maureen Massent, a columnist in *The Birmingham Evening Mail* wrote in June 1992 about the proposed change to the homosexual age of consent:

> I'm disheartened that, in 1992, Britain is Hitleresque in its conviction that to be gay is evil. Please don't quote the Bible at me, either. There is nothing like the mention of homosexuality to bring out the bigots. I've always been troubled by the lip-smacking lubricity masked as modesty that emanates from the anti-gays. Homosexuals, after all, do not waste their time denouncing – as they have every reason to denounce – the sordid goings-on in the heterosexual community . . . Dozens of little children done to death annually are not

murdered by homosexuals, remember. They're mostly the victims of heterosexual parents.

Agony columns

Another area of newspapers which seems to have overcome homophobia is the agony column. Here a 'permissive' ideology and a willingness to confront diversity and the tangled nature of human relationships means that the 'sex beasts' and 'perverts' of the news pages are largely absent. Correspondents are treated as human beings with feelings that extend beyond their genitalia, and whose lives don't always operate according to the simplistic (not to mention cruel) moralistic dogma propounded in the paper's editorial stance. In the agony column there can be compassion and empathy for the suffering of fallible human beings. The same people who are abused and vilified in the news pages because of their 'aberrant sexuality', 'pervy' appetites and their 'weakness' in giving into temptation are accorded understanding and help from the aunties. Bad decisions and momentary lapses are seen here not as 'evil' and 'disgusting' but as everyday occurrences.

The 'agony aunts' or 'advisers' or 'counsellors' have been well-versed in the messes that people can make of their lives. They receive hundreds of letters a week from readers desperate for words of comfort, for fellow feeling, for information and support. It often seems that the agony aunt is left to clear up the feelings of guilt, shame and self-hate that are engendered by pseudo-moralistic and condemnatory sex stories in the news section. Having had some experience in this area myself (I worked on the 'Confidential Counselling Team' at *Woman's Own*) I know how seriously readers' problems are taken and what resources are put into the problem page. Newspaper editors may despise the philosophy of the agony aunt, but will also know that the advice column is an essential part of popular journalism. A high-profile agony aunt can bring the paper much prestige. Marje Proops, for instance, has been an enormous asset to the Mirror Group, representing its human and sympathetic face, while Claire Rayner has become a sort of mother to the nation – instantly recognized and trusted for her support and championing of those who would otherwise find little sympathy in the macho media.

None of the major problem page occupants would give a moralizing or disapproving reply to a gay person (unless, of course, that person was doing something reprehensible) and agony aunts have, in their time, provided that final encouragement to hundreds of gay people on the verge of coming out. Claire Rayner has appeared at gay charity events and is a vice-president of the Gay and Lesbian Humanist Association. She takes her commitment to the improvement of the gay lot very seriously – in her work as an agony aunt and in her life in general.

It was during the age of consent debate in 1994 that the Stonewall gay lobbying group asked agony aunts to demonstrate just *how* committed they were to the welfare of the nation's homosexual population. Marje Proops at first supported eighteen as the preferable age, but after a meeting with Ian McKellen changed her mind and joined the equality camp. At the behest of Stonewall, Claire Rayner initiated a letter to *The Times* supporting law reform. She persuaded twenty-two of the other leading advice columnists to sign the letter. It read:

> We would like to give our full support to Edwina Currie's amendment . . . to equalise the age of consent for gay men. In our work we receive many letters from young gay men who are frightened by the law, and are reluctant to speak openly to their teachers, doctors and even their parents about their sexuality. Yet how can we give these young men the advice they need when we are dealing with a criminal offence? How can the law be said to protect teenagers when it turns them into criminals and threatens to prosecute them for expressing love for another person? We know from our work as 'agony aunts' that it is absurd to suggest that people can be 'converted' into homosexuals, or that young men need more protection than young women. We believe that simple justice demands that the age of consent for sexual activity should be the same for both sexes, regardless of orientation.

Conspicuous by his absence from the list of signatories was Philip Hodson, who worked at the time on *The News of the World*. *The Independent*'s diarist was quick to spot that even those agony aunts who worked on other Murdoch newspapers, and who had signed the letter, had not included the names of the papers for which they worked:

> Hodson may well need some counselling himself following suggestions that a News International line on homosexuality – Rupert Murdoch, a born-again Christian, is believed to hold strong views on the issue – had influenced his decision to dissociate himself from his colleagues.[64]

The action of the agony aunts brought forth a torrent of abuse from the editorial pages of the right-wing press. *The Sunday Telegraph* managed to find several 'junior agony aunts' who did not support an equal age of consent (including Patricia Mansfield of *Take a Break*; Celia Taylor of *Me*; Lorna V of *Looks* and Carol Baker of *Living*).[65] *The Daily Mail* carried a vicious piece by Anne de Courcy which revealed information about the private lives of the counsellors themselves and asked: 'Is morality too important to leave to agony aunts?' Ms de Courcy wrote: 'What makes these women believe that they are specially gifted to offer moral guidelines?' One might, of course, ask the same of the endlessly moralizing columnists we have been looking at in this chapter. In *The Sunday Times,* William Oddie – himself no slouch in handing out ethical advice and opinion – said of the agony aunts:

> A repeated theme of agony-aunt advice is that inherited ideas of social morality, especially in the sexual sphere, have caused nothing but psychological 'hang-ups' and 'inhibitions' and need to be got rid of; most agony aunts in this sense are caught in a kind of 1960s time warp. If their advice has any consistent 'philosophy', here it is: let it all hang out, man, go with the flow, it is forbidden to forbid.[66]

Oddie's clinging to 'tradition' and 'inherited wisdom' is, in fact, the theme and overwhelming philosophy of the vast majority of columnists in the British press. The repeated cry is: 'Traditional morality has served us well until now, why change things?' The emphasis here is on 'us' - a very exclusive term in this context. 'Tradition' and 'the way things have always been' is a figment of the conservative imagination. Such spurious concepts have served the privileged by keeping their privilege intact, but their repeated invocation has oppressed and disadvantaged many other people. By rejecting this idea that old-fashioned values are inevitably best, agony aunts have released thousands of people – not only homosexuals – from debilitating guilt about their feelings and desires. Human sexuality is recognized in agony columns as multi-layered and complicated, and for this insight alone they should be applauded.

Of course, because of the human interest focus of agony columns, there is always the temptation to spice them up. Some of the tabloids now give more emphasis to sexual problems and play down the more mundane emotional problems which pack their postbag: depression, loneliness, financial difficulties and family conflicts. The agony column of a copy of *The Daily Star*, chosen at random, has the following headings: 'Little sister may be on the game'; 'Sir makes me weak at the knees'; 'I'm so starved of love'; 'New appetite for sex'. Another innovation is the photo story which renders the reader's problem into sometimes crude graphic terms. Most of these photo-strips concern sexual adventures – and misadventures – and seem to be little more than excuse to show scantily clad models engaged in simulated sex. It would be difficult to justify such photographs in other parts of the paper, but as long as it can be passed off as 'education' it seems to be considered acceptable.

In this context, homosexuality once again becomes a valuable vehicle for titillation. When gay problems (or, more frequently, perceived gay problems) feature in agony columns, the headline becomes all-important. The considered advice given is often undermined by the negative headline which stands over it. 'My mum's a lesbian – her new life wrecked our plans to wed' was an example from *The Sun*.[67] 'Dismay of being gay'[68] and 'Secret shame of Desert Rat buddy'[69] appeared in *The People* while *The News of the World* has given us 'Gay obsession with pal's son', 'Anguish of gay son's mum' and 'Secret gay grief'. Dear Deirdre in *The Sun* featured 'Gay gang rape ruined my life.' Notice the key words in all these examples: 'dismay', 'anguish', 'bored', 'shame', 'ruined', 'obsession' 'secret', 'grief'. After a crop of these misleading headlines, I wrote critically about agony aunts in *Mediawatch*. I was contacted by one prominent auntie – who asked me not to identify her – who told me that she is very pro-gay, but that often her copy is altered by sub-editors. She had no influence over the way in which her answers were presented in the paper. She considered herself one of the few people who was able to get gay-friendly copy into her particular paper.

Headlines apart, the advice given is often of a high quality. This example – completely at odds with the rest of the paper – comes from Sue Cook's teenage advice column in *The Sun*. A young man of seventeen wrote to her saying that he was having a sexual relationship with a man ten years older than himself. He was aware that the relationship was illegal, although his family and friends were supportive and accepting. He proclaimed himself happy. The problem was not the gay relationship but doubts about whether he was too young to make such a commitment. 'Am I too young to love?' he asked. Sue Cook replied:

> The legal age for gay male sex is 21 – until the new Act of Parliament lowering it to 18 goes through. That aside, you're not too young to love, but there are drawbacks to getting serious in your teens. You miss the experience of different relationships and you may want to revisit your teens later – which could be painful for a future partner.[70]

It's difficult to fault such advice – Ms Cook obviously does not regard this young man's worries any differently to those of a heterosexual teenager. The contrast between this approach and the treatment the same story would have received on the news pages could not be more stark.

As the battle for readers becomes more intense, it is possible that the position of the agony aunt in newspapers will be compromised, with orders for more sex and less support. In that scenario, homosexuality might once more become just another titillatory adjunct.

Notes

1.   28 May 1994.
2.   24 May 1994.

3.   2 January 1994.
4.   K. Wellings, J. Field, A. M. Johnson and J. Wadsworth, *Sexual Behaviour in Britain* (Penguin Books, 1994).
5.   21 January 1994.
6.   21 January 1994.
7.   21 January 1994.
8.   23 January 1994.
9.   14 July 1985.
10.   The Press Council, *The Press and the People* (1978 edition), p. 5.
11.   Quartet Books, 1983.
12.   12 April 1971.
13.   27 May 1994.
14.   27 May 1994.
15.   Reviewing one of Paul Johnson's collected works – *Wake up Britain!* – in *New Statesman and Society* (20 May 1994), Edward Pearce described it as 'a curate's egg – less bad than grotesque'. 'It speaks a strong personality, but a personality at war with the author's intelligence . . . This is the man in the pub – in the pub rather too long. The history is infantile, the opinions enraged and sometimes downright malignant, the work a certain hit with bad-tempered people over 65 in Reigate. It is unEnglish, a failure of imagination, a drought of sympathy, an annihilation of perspective and the profoundest imaginable disservice to Conservatism. The egg stinks.' This well describes many of Johnson's pieces mentioned in this book.
16.   20 May 1994.
17.   25 November 1992.
18.   3 September 1991.
19.   25 May 1993.
20.   8 August 1987.
21.   16 May 1990.
22.   5 June 1988.
23.   21 May 1988.
24.   10 June 1988.
25.   7 June 1988.
26.   28 January 1988.
27.   1 February 1988.
28.   29 January 1988.
29.   June 1990.
30.   29 May 1993.
31.   24 May 1993.
32.   2 August 1987.
33.   *The Mail on Sunday*, 6 March 1994.
34.   *The Sun*, 2 March 1994.

35. 1 September 1991.
36. 4 February 1990.
37. 10 August 1990.
38. *The Independent*, 9 February 1991.
39. Letter to Wimbledon Area Gay Society from Lloyd Turner, editor of *The Star*, 25 September 1986.
40. 6 August 1987.
41. 17 May 1991.
42. 15 May 1991.
43. Press Complaints Commission report for May/June/July 1994, No. 25.
44. 26 May 1992.
45. 18 December 1991.
46. 22 September 1987.
47. May 1994.
48. The results of this were published in January 1994 edition.
49. 6 May 1987.
50. February 1988.
51. 4 November 1988.
52. 24 July 1988.
53. 29 May 1994.
54. 5 February 1989.
55. September 1990.
56. 7 February 1991.
57. 20 January 1991.
58. 8 May 1988.
59. 23 April 1989.
60. 29 April 1991.
61. T. W. Adorno, Else Frenkel-Brunswik and Daniel J. Levonson, *The Authoritarian Personality* (W. W. Norton, 1984).
62. 28 May 1994.
63. 28 February 1991.
64. 2 February 1994.
65. 1 February 1994.
66. 6 February 1994.
67. 29 June 1989.
68. *The People*, 2 January 1990.
69. 18 November 1990.
70. 14 July 1994.

Chapter six
Sticks and Stones

DURING much of the 1980s the language used to express the tabloid obsession with homosexuality became increasingly abusive and contemptuous. Words such as 'poofter', 'woofter', 'queer', 'shirtlifter', 'dyke', 'lezzie' and 'lesbo' were employed by journalists and sub-editors in the never-ending effort to defame and dehumanize gay people. The loathing that was apparent in the way stories about homosexuals and homosexuality were presented was reinforced by the prominent use of insulting terms in headlines. The use of derogatory nouns has become an essential part of the distancing process. Gay people can be dehumanized by the use of words like 'poofter', 'queer', 'dyke' or even 'gay' when it becomes a noun. (I was once referred to in *The Sun* as 'a 41 year old gay who lives in London with another gay' - all of a sudden we weren't *people* any more but 'a gay' and 'another gay'.) This omission of gay humanity ensures that whatever else they are – however worthwhile – it's very simple to transform homosexual people into a subhuman species: 'the gay'; 'the poofter'; 'the queer'; 'the dyke'.

The clear implication of this demonization and dehumanization process is that the needs and feelings of homosexuals are of no consequence because they are, after all, only 'poofters', the lowest of the low, the bottom of the heap. Much of the language employed is an attempt to distance gay people from the rest of society.

Tabloid stories about gay people are also often decorated with an array of inflammatory adjectives, implying that anything homosexuals do is undesirable or outside the realms of the experiences of 'ordinary' people. This provides the reader with a comforting sense of their own 'normality' and a feeling of moral superiority. 'Sordid' is a favourite, as are 'sleazy', 'squalid', 'perverted', 'vile', 'kinky', 'bizarre', 'seedy', 'scandalous', 'disgraceful', 'abnormal' and 'disgusting'.

The word 'poofter' is, of course, widely used in Australian slang and it can be no coincidence that it first began to appear in the headlines of newspapers owned by Rupert Murdoch. *The Sun* pioneered its use – as well as many other derisive words ('nancy', 'Kharzi cruiser', 'fairy', 'pansy', 'bender' and 'iron hoof' are some of the other terms which turn up in pages of *The Sun* and *The Star*). 'Poofter' was enthusiastically taken up by some of the other papers causing gay individuals and groups to become alarmed at the level of almost triumphalist hatred that the word represented. Day after day ever more scornful headlines would accompany anti-gay stories and features.

The use of this language was, of course, another way of attempting to ridicule and diminish homosexuals. Not only were the stories constructed in a manner which intended to humiliate their victims, but the banner headlines above them made even more plain the thuggish intention in the stories. This was queer-bashing that both mirrored and encouraged the increasing amount of violence in the streets. It is difficult to prove a connection between anti-gay newspaper stories and the rise in criminal violence aimed at homosexuals, but some research from the USA seems to indicate that there may indeed be such a connection. The FBI was mandated by Congress to keep statistics on hate crimes in the USA and in 1992 it reported that there were at least 750 cases of assault and intimidation against homosexual men and women. The National Lesbian and Gay Task Force, however, reported 2,103 episodes from its own surveys in six cities alone – Boston, Chicago, Denver, Minneapolis–St Paul, New York and San Francisco. While cases in other cities declined very substantially in 1993, they rose by 12 per cent in Denver, because of an emotional debate over an anti-gay referendum on the 1992 Colorado ballot.[1] Some newspapers and TV channels enthusiastically carried and endorsed a great deal of anti-gay propaganda during that campaign, much of it unfair and inflammatory.

In 1985 in Britain, The National Union of Journalists attempted to challenge some of its members' more damaging habits

– such as the insidious stereotyping of minorities – with a 'Campaign for Real People'. In July 1985 the NUJ's Equality Council and Lesbian and Gay Group launched a poster and two booklets (*Guidelines for Reporting on Homosexuality* and *AIDS and the Media*) in the hope that it would encourage journalists 'to write more professionally about lesbian and gay lives'. At a press conference to launch the new material, Mick Power, a National Graphical Association member at *The Daily Mail*, said that 'although it was difficult to raise these issues in what was a very macho industry, more and more workers were becoming clear that their product "damages people's brains"'.[2] He thought there should be a 'right to report' as well as a 'right to reply' – which was prompted by the annual complaint that the Gay Pride festival had once more been ignored by the media. This initiative, like so many other challenges to media homophobia, was completely disregarded and quickly disappeared.

Gay people and groups began to see for themselves an urgent need to challenge this abuse. Direct challenges by letter and phone call to editors and journalists seemed to have no effect at all; if anything, they simply resulted in the journalists becoming more entrenched and constructing arguments to justify their behaviour. Only the Press Council seemed to offer a feasible line of attack.

Using the Press Council

The Press Council was the first self-regulatory body for the press. It was set up in 1953 after parliamentary rumblings indicated that, if the newspapers did not control themselves, the Government would do the job for them. This has become a familiar refrain from successive governments that have found themselves pressured by public opinion to 'do something' about the appalling behaviour of some newspapers. (As a result of this ongoing public repugnance there have been several royal commissions, public enquiries, Parliamentary committees and other investigations.) The Press Council's 'Four Principal Objects' were:

(a) To preserve the established freedom of the British press.

(b) To maintain the character of the British Press in accordance with the highest professional and commercial standards.

(c) To consider complaints about the conduct of the press or the conduct of persons or organisations towards the press; to deal with these complaints in whatever manner might seem practical and appropriate and record resultant action.

(d) To keep under review developments likely to restrict the supply of information of public interest and importance.

The Press Council's noble purpose, then, was to defend the press from legislation which could curb its freedom and dilute its function to protect democracy. Unfortunately, like so many self-regulating bodies, The Press Council proved an unsatisfactory watchdog and the limits of its power soon became very apparent. For instance, there was no mechanism for punishing recalcitrant newspapers other than by a public ticking-off, nor was there any sanction which could be applied to those papers which repeatedly flouted Press Council rulings. The Council was helpless in the face of a ruthless circulation war which was driving standards of tabloid journalism ever lower. Those who tried to avail themselves of the Council's complaints procedures soon discovered that they were complicated, time-consuming and took months to reach a conclusion. Anyone wishing to see a complaint through to completion needed to be determined and have a penchant – as well as the time – for seemingly limitless correspondence. The Council would not entertain phone calls from complainants or any other method which might have shortened the procedure. The newspapers had only a 'moral obligation' to print the Council's adjudications, and most of them did, but they were often buried in small type in an obscure part of the newspaper. Nor were they always presented with respect. One adjudication against *The Sunday Sport* which upheld a complaint about the paper's use of the word 'chinks' to describe Chinese people was printed under the large headline 'Bollocks to the Press Council'.[3]

Given that the adjudication was likely to be issued several months after the event (one of my own complaints took eighteen months to resolve), there was likely to be little sense of justice or satisfaction for those who had been traduced. Many complainants became cynical of and disillusioned by the Council's procedures; several told me that they had reached the conclusion that the bureaucracy (which also included short and rigidly enforced time limits for complainants) was not accidental but was a ploy to discourage complainants from pursuing their complaints. In March 1990, The Council announced that it had received 1,870 complaints, but only 142 of them had run the full convoluted course to adjudication. The rest had been withdrawn or simply faded away.

Few complaints about newspapers' desperately unfair and wicked treatment of homosexuals had been accepted for adjudication, let alone upheld. The reasons proffered were usually that newspapers 'are entitled to be partisan, to have strong opinions which it is permissible to express in strong language'. One such case occurred in 1983 when *The Portsmouth News* carried a 'One man's view' column by Wilfred Potter. Potter was commenting on a Channel 4 TV programme on homosexuality called 'One in five'. Headed 'A sick parade I'd rather miss', the column read, in part:

> Inmates of Britain's jails must have offered prayers that the Director of Public Prosecutions was not watching Channel 4's 'One in Five' because, if it is possible to importune the entire viewing public this programme did it; and no self-respecting mugger wants a homosexual for a cellmate.

Even though it was recognized that the article had been 'unbalanced, extravagant and intemperate and would be deeply offensive to many who read it', complaints to the Council were, because of the 'One man's view' heading, not upheld.

The poofter showdown

There had been previous unsuccessful attempts to get the Council to rule on the use of abusive terminology in newspapers, but it had refused to do so. However, the battle against 'poof' and 'poofter' began in earnest in 1988 when four separate complaints from gay men were lodged with the Council about a story in *The Sun* headlined 'Pulpit poofs can stay'. The story had been printed on 12 November 1987, the day after the Church of England's General Synod had voted against a witch hunt of gay clergy. The complainants had claimed that the headline contained 'an offensive expression likely to encourage hatred of homosexuals'. The Press Council did not agree: 'The headline was vulgar and intended to shock. Its coarseness would offend many readers and be found insulting to homosexuals, but the Press Council is unable to say that it was likely to encourage hatred of them.' This complaint was followed up soon after by another objecting to a *Sun* headline: 'Runcie backs ban on pulpit poofs'. After a great deal of deliberation and copious amounts of correspondence, the Council ruled:

> The words 'poof' and 'poofter' are commonly used, and their appearance in a newspaper story was not likely to encourage hatred of homosexuals, the Council said, rejecting a complaint over a report in *The Sun*.
>
> The report said that the Archbishop of Canterbury had revealed to *The Sun* that he was backing the battle against pulpit poofters. It added that ten bishops had by then spoken out in support of the Rt Rev David Young, Bishop of Ripon, who was refusing to ordain practising gays and that he had vowed not to train, ordain or employ gays unless they promised to restrain their sick desires.
>
> A complaint from [a gay man in] Warrington, Cheshire complained that *The Sun* published a misleading and inaccurate article under an offensive headline likely to encourage hatred of homosexuals.
>
> He said the article was offensive, inaccurate, used subliminal techniques and was inflammatory. He said for quite some time the newspaper had carried articles about homosexuals – a constant onslaught against gay people.
>
> He suspected the words 'sick desires' were those of the reporter, Allan Hall, and not the bishop's. The Rev David Hooper, domestic chaplain to the bishop, later confirmed that he did not use the words.

Mr Henry R. Douglas, legal manager, said the paper was entitled to take a view on homosexuality and had tried to give both sides of the question, while plainly stating its commitment to one side.

They would not construe either 'poof' or 'poofter' as necessarily implying effeminacy. They disclaimed subliminal intent. However, with hindsight, the paper regretted the use of the word 'sick' as a paraphrase of the bishop's outspoken censure.[4]

The Council also said that it did not find that references to 'poofs' and 'poofters' in this headline and story were likely to encourage hatred of homosexuals; the words were commonly used and their use here was 'within the editor's discretion'. Neither did they think the article had been substantially misleading or inaccurate. The complaint was, therefore, rejected.

However, the battle had just begun and this complaint was followed up by another from the Wimbledon Area Gay Society, which complained about three headlines from *The Star*: 'The poofter MPs', 'Runcie poofs ban' and 'Up, up and a gay / Council's free flying lessons for poofs'. The complainant said that the use of the words 'poof' and 'poofter' was derogatory and insulting to gay people. He said that newspapers would be roundly condemned by the Council if they used objectionable words like 'nigger' or 'yid' to describe black people or Jews and there was no reason why a similar approach should not apply to words which were insulting to gays. In response, Brian Hitchen, editor of *The Star*, predictably went on to the attack and said that the seventh edition of the *Oxford Dictionary* listed 'poof' as 'effeminate or homosexual man (origin unknown)'. 'Gay' was described as 'light-hearted, sporty, mirthful' and then, 'colloquially, homosexual'. He said it seemed that homosexuals had quite successfully hijacked the word 'gay' and made it their own. The Council's adjudication on this case was: 'The headlines' language was coarse and no doubt intended to be derogatory, and insulting to homosexuals. However, whether to publish it, using a word which though offensive is in common parlance, was within the discretion of the editor.'

In the meantime, in my role as media correspondent at *Gay Times*, I was encouraging readers to continue complaining, not only directly to newspapers but also to the Press Council and the National Union of Journalists' Ethics Committee. (The NUJ had withdrawn from membership of the Press Council in 1980 declaring it 'wholly ineffective' and 'incapable of reform', but unfortunately its own Ethics Committee also proved incapable of influencing press behaviour and cruelty.) Pressure on the Press Council was increasing as public disgust at the activities of tabloid newspapers increased. It was obvious that a heated debate was taking place within the Council over the treatment of gays. A letter to me dated 6 July 1989 from Raymond Swingler, then Assistant Director of the Council, gives some indication of this turmoil:

> You are quite correct in your view that the use of pejorative expressions for homosexuality are now commonplace in the tabloid press: personally I find such use wholly unacceptable and although many on the Council share this view it is, regrettably, not the common view of the body.

Around then, the Press Council's chairmanship was being taken over by the liberal lawyer Louis Blom-Cooper. The Council was formulating a new code of practice for journalists and, despite repeated requests, it became clear that it did not intend to include homosexuality in the clause dealing with 'discrimination'. A report in *Capital Gay* said that the Council's director, Kenneth Morgan, had 'considered the issue of homosexuality many times', but he stated that the Review Committee, which was considering amendments to the code of practice, decided to limit itself to race and colour in its discrimination clause. Morgan accepted that there was a widespread view that unnecessary references to race and colour should not be introduced into newspaper reports 'irrelevantly in any prejudicial context', but he said that there was 'not, or not yet, a sufficiently general view about such references to sex and sexuality to warrant these being prohibited by the code as well'.[5]

It became obvious that, unless the Press Council changed its mind about including sexuality in its code of practice, the press attacks would continue unabated. Recognizing that there was a real problem and widespread alarm within the gay community at the increasingly hysterical and hateful tone of newspaper coverage of homosexuality, Blom-Cooper agreed to meet a delegation from the Campaign for Homosexual Equality to discuss the issue and I was also invited to participate. The meeting took place at the Press Council's headquarters in Salisbury Square, London in January 1990. The delegation was received cordially and we were given ample opportunity to put our case. Blom-Cooper and his director Kenneth Morgan explained that although they sympathized with our alarm, the Press Council tended to rely on precedent in formulating policy and it seemed that, on this matter, there was no precedent for including sexuality in the code of conduct. On the subject of abusive anti-gay language, Blom-Cooper said that, although the Council had consistently ruled in the past that the use of such language was at the editor's discretion, it wasn't beyond the realms of possibility that it might change its mind. The message was clear – keep those complaints coming.

It wasn't difficult to find items to complain about; the abuse was constant. I waited until I found examples which I considered indefensible before launching my next complaint. Eventually I cited articles by Garry Bushell, *The Sun*'s 'TV critic', which had contained the words 'woofter' and 'poofter' used in a way that could only be described as gratuitously insulting.[6] I was pleased to be able to base the complaint on Garry Bushell's column as it had been a source of irritation for some considerable time. His constant insulting comments about gay people and his ruthless use of AIDS as a political battering ram was causing distress and fury throughout the gay community. In fact, at one point during an OutRage! demonstration he was burned in effigy – something which he subsequently professed made him very proud. As usual, a long exchange of correspondence began between myself, The Press Council and various people on *The Sun*. Garry Bushell maintained, rather unconvincingly, that:

My attacks have not been on homosexuals but on:
1) The use of TV programmes to promote homosexuality. I object to TV shows which are nothing more than

thinly disguised propaganda on behalf of the homosexual lobby.

2) The promotion of individual homosexuals on the basis of their sexual orientation rather than their talent. Many so-called 'gay' entertainers are so poor, I can think of no other reason for their success.

I make no apology for the language I use. It is the language of The Sun readers, and indeed, the majority of British people.

I responded by saying:

Mr Bushell says that his attacks 'have not been on homosexuals'. This is disingenuous when seen in the light of a comment he made in his column in *The Sun* dated 21 March 1990 which read: 'It must be true what they say about nobody being all bad . . . even STALIN banned poofs!'

Mr Bushell says that TV programmes are used to 'promote homosexuality'. It seems that any mention of the subject angers Mr Bushell and thus constitutes – in his opinion – 'promotion'.

He also says that individual homosexuals are promoted on the basis of their sexual orientation rather than their talent. He has made this comment in respect of one particular entertainer and part of his comment is contained in my complaint. I am not alone in considering the use of abusive language about homosexuals is on a par with racist abuse. Following Mr Bushell's comments about Simon Fanshawe (the entertainer in question), Ms Esther Rantzen, on whose TV show he appears, was moved to state (on *The Media Show* – LWT) that attacking a comedian on the basis of his sexuality rather than his comedic skills was akin to racism. Following a complaint from Ms Rantzen, *The Sun* was obliged to disassociate itself from some of Mr Bushell's comments and print an apology in the newspaper.

Mr Bushell says that he makes no apology for the language he uses as it is 'the language of *Sun* readers and, indeed, the majority of the British people.'

However, if every filthy and abusive comment that was made by 'the British people' were to be printed in newspapers, those same people would be up in arms about the degradation being heaped upon them. Mr Bushell should not ascribe his own opinions to others simply because it is convenient to do so.[7]

The Press Council issued its adjudication on this case on 14 May 1990. To my astonishment, the complaint had been upheld. Because the judgement had such wide-reaching implications and such a profound influence on the language used in newspapers to describe homosexuals, I will quote extensively from the reasoning that lead to the Council's *volte face*:

> Although the words 'poof' and 'poofter' are in common parlance they are so offensive to male homosexuals that publishing them is not a matter of taste or opinion within a newspaper editor's discretion.
>
> Upholding a complaint that *The Sun* had used words of unnecessary crude abuse in three articles about television, the Council said newspapers should publish offensive language only where it was necessary for proper understanding of an item. Nothing in the articles complained of made it necessary.
>
> When Mr Terry Sanderson complained at the words 'poof' and 'woofter', the managing editor, Mr William Newman, said they were in everyday use for homosexuals whose sexual activities were repellent to the vast majority of people including *Sun* writers and readers. Mr Sanderson said it was fallacious to say the words could appear just because readers used them. They created contempt and violence against innocent individuals.
>
> The Press Council's reasoned decision was:
>
> The sole question in the complaint is whether the words 'poof(s)' and 'poofter(s)' (or the variant 'woofter'), when used to describe male homosexuals, are permissible language in a newspaper. The specific complaint arises from the use of these words that appeared in *The Sun* in January and

February 1990. For the purposes of this adjudication it is wholly unnecessary to indicate the context in which these words were used, either in the headline or in the text.

Since the question focuses on the use (or misuse) of the English language it is helpful to trace the derivation of the word 'poof'. The shorter Oxford English Dictionary (3rd edition 1944 revised) notes that the word came into the language in the middle of the 19th century and was defined as a sound imitating a short puff of the breath, as in blowing out a candle. The editor goes on to say that the word 'poof' became an expression of contemptuous rejection. The dictionary entry for 'poofter' is said to be an Australian colloquialism meaning derogatorily 'effeminate man; male homosexual'. (It is not possible to say how 'poofter' became 'woofter' which appeared only in the item of 10 February 1990). The words, therefore, are not slang although the editor of the Collins English Dictionary (2nd edition 1986) does regard the word as derogatory slang. If, however, the word is to be treated as part of the ordinary English language, presumptively it could not be taken objection to. When, however, the word or words are used as offensive and opprobrious descriptions of a definable class of people, the question arises whether in 1990 such use can be tolerated in a civilised society, always bearing in mind that to condemn its use is to restrict (however minimally and inconsequentially) freedom of expression. The newspaper in this case defends its use of the words on the grounds that they constitute 'the language of Sun readers, and indeed, the majority of British people'. Whether that assertion can be made good or not, the Press Council is merely setting the standards of journalistic conduct and not in any way seeking to circumscribe people's speech, in public or private . . .

In the Press Council's view newspapers may publish partisan views on contentious issues, even intemperately and intolerantly. What is in issue is whether the author and publisher may use offensive and opprobrious language. As the complainant in the instant case pithily wrote to the Press

Council: 'Surely he can make his views known without recourse to insulting language?' . . .

The Press Council is not a court or tribunal applying a body of legal rules, but is setting and maintaining standards of journalistic ethics. Ethical standards, whether they be in journalism, in the legal or medical profession, or other regulated occupation, change over time. Whereas it might be judged that a word was permissible yesterday, its use today or tomorrow may become impermissible. For example, a few years ago the Press Council ruled that the use of a four-letter word constituted a breach of journalistic ethics. Nowadays the word is permissible so long as its use is necessary – not merely justifiable – for the proper understanding of the item in which the impugned word appears. So here. So long as the word 'poof' or 'poofter' is used necessarily for the proper understanding of the item about sexual orientation or homosexuality, the Press Council will not condemn its use.

But when (as here) the words are used with evident offence and intended to wound homosexuals the Press Council believes that such use is no longer acceptable. The Press Council is convinced that the public – and not just that part of the public whose sexual orientation is being attacked – now regards the application of proper English words to an exclusively opprobrious use directed at homosexuals as socially unacceptable.

The Press Council adduces in support of this view of public opinion the evidence it received on that part of its recently published Code of Practice which dealt with discrimination on the grounds of race and colour. The Council received a volume of letters from a variety of sources (not all from homosexuals) advocating the inclusion of sexual orientation as one of the grounds of discriminatory treatment. While rejecting for the time being any reference in the code to sexual orientation, the Press Council was made aware of the intense feeling that the homosexual community is often unfairly treated in the kind of language used in hostile opposition to its pattern of life.

Conclusion

Words describing an identifiable class of people, which are not merely coarse or intended to be derogatory but are plainly insulting, should not generally appear in a newspaper.

The words 'poof' and 'poofter' which appear in the headlines and text of three items in *The Sun* in January and February 1990, while no doubt used in common parlance, were so offensive to male homosexuals as not to be a matter of taste or opinion within the editor's discretion.

Newspapers should publish offensive language only where its use is necessary for the purpose of proper understanding of the item in which the offensive words appear. There was nothing in any of the three items in *The Sun* which made the use of the words 'poof' or 'poofter' necessary. The complaint against *The Sun* is upheld.

The publication of this adjudication caused a furore in Fleet Street which claimed that 'free speech' was being curtailed and that political correctness had overwhelmed common sense. It is understandable that newspapers should react with alarm at the idea that what they say and how they say it should be in any way 'controlled'. Outside the rarefied atmosphere of Fleet Street, however, it was widely felt that the 'free speech' touted by the tabloids had turned into a freedom to abuse innocent people. There was rejoicing in the gay community that at last someone with influence had had the courage to say that the popular press was treating homosexuals in an uncivilized and unacceptable manner – if only as far as the language was concerned. *The Sun* responded with an editorial 'You can't call 'em poofters' which read:

> In Alice in Wonderland, the Queen of Hearts ordained that words meant what SHE SAID they meant. The Press Council has the same lordly manner over language. In their judgement today they seek to tell us which words we may or may not use. Our offence was that we spoke of homosexuals as poofs and poofters. The Press Council researched in the Shorter Oxford Dictionary before reaching its conclusion. The Council's Chairman, Louis Blom-Cooper, QC, knows a

lot about the law. But we know a great deal more about how ordinary people think, act and speak. What is good enough for them is good enough for us.

Incidentally, our dictionary defines gay as carefree, merry, brilliant. Does the Press Council approve of homosexuals appropriating such a fine old word?[8]

Bushell himself was furious, and wrote in a letter to *Journalist's Week*:

The Press Council's ruling . . . is quite frankly daft . . . The Sun is accused of fostering intolerance. But in reality the homosexual lobby and their pet liberals are responsible for stirring up intolerance by trampling contemptuously and persistently on the popular sense of what is right and wrong. Not content with removing anti-homosexual laws, they now demand that we *approve* of their activities, too.

Writing in the Spectator, Paul Johnson has said that our basic freedoms are under threat from the forces of 'liberal fascism'. He is talking about the way well-organised and increasingly aggressive pressure groups seek to actually stop people from voicing opinions that they disagree with. Will *The Sun* be alone in standing up to them?[9]

The reaction of *Sun* readers to the ruling did seem to indicate that what Bushell said about their attitudes to homosexuality was true. In a 'Letters Special' we were advised that 'You back Bushell In great "poofter" row'. The paper said it had received 'bags of mail' and that 99 per cent backed Bushell. One reader wrote:

Congratulations! You expressed exactly the opinion we all hear in the office, the factory, the pub. Let these people get on with it, so long as they keep out of my way. But once they start parading their preferences as if they are right and the rest of us are peculiar then it's time they were shown their proper place in society.

This was an amazing echo of Bushell's own view, and expressed in language which he could almost have written himself. So was the next letter: 'When I see how gays behave, even on television, it makes me sick.' Another correspondent thought that Bushell was 'far too easy on poofs' saying that most people call them queers and secondly 'what they do helps to spread AIDS'. A Mrs Watson wrote: 'The amount of evil that arises from these perverts who ruin children and desecrate Christian beliefs scares me.' There were four other letters in similar vein – all coincidentally making points previously well rehearsed by Bushell in his 'TV column'. One letter came to the defence of 'the gays'.

Anxious to align himself with the lynch mob was George Gale in *The Daily Mail*, who opined:

> You can no longer describe queers as poofters. Come to that we probably can't call them queer either . . . There is another word not dissimilar to words like poofs and poofters which well describes members of the Press Council. It begins with a 'w' – but I fear to use it for the repercussions.[10]

Richard Ingrams in *The Observer* thought it all a part of 'a campaign by militant homosexuals to dictate the vocabulary. On the whole their campaign has been very successful.'[11] (This brought a stinging response in the following issue by a woman reader who said: 'This sort of arrogant, militant, intolerant and boorish behaviour is just what gives heterosexuals a bad name.') John Junor in *The Mail on Sunday*, too, thought the whole thing ridiculous: 'The utter idiocy of the solemn decision to ban newspapers from using the words . . . when this is what they are called by 90 per cent of the adult population.'[12] Paul Johnson didn't agree, though, and in *The Spectator* he wrote:

> 'Poof' and 'poofter' I have often seen written, but I have never heard them used in speech. My impression is that [manual workers] never refer to homosexuality at all if they can help it. They find it embarrassing, a middle and upper class thing which has nothing to do with them . . . What they find unacceptable is pure guesswork. The only reliable judges are readers. If they object they will make their views plain. The rest should keep their middle-class traps shut.[13]

The Sun's sister paper, *The News of the World*, tried to settle the argument once and for all by inviting its heterosexual readers and its homosexual readers to ring separate telephone numbers in order to nominate their preferred terms.[14] Voters could choose from 'poofter', 'pansy', 'fairy' 'queer', 'gay' and 'homosexual'. The result, published the following week, was that heterosexual *and* homosexual readers both plumped for 'gay'.

The Independent, tried to widen the debate and saw the Press Council's ruling as simply highlighting one of many examples of the prejudice against gay people. In the same issue the paper had carried a well-researched feature on the increasing incidence of anti-gay violence in Britain. In an editorial it said:

> The persecution of homosexuals is spiritually akin to anti-Semitism, Hitler proved the point by despatching homosexuals as well as Jews and gypsies to his concentration camps. It is intolerable that people should be persecuted for not belonging to the same race as the majority. It is no less excusable that they should be vilified and assaulted because their sexual orientation differs from the norm. A report on our news pages, and a Press Council ruling which breaks new ground, come as a reminder today that in this particular form of aggressive intolerance the British are amongst the worst offenders.[15]

The Sun's immediate reaction to the Press Council's ruling was predictably petulant and nasty and it featured a spate of homophobic stories and comments. But once it had calmed down, the offending words disappeared from its pages. This is not to say that other journalists, feeling miffed at having one of their favourite weapons taken from them, didn't try to undermine the Press Council's ruling. By 3 June that year John Smith, the so-called 'Man of *The People*', appeared to be issuing a direct challenge to the ruling when writing about the Gay Pride carnival: 'The highlight will be a procession. With all those poofs on parade, I bet it's going to be a real bitch choosing a Carnival Queen.' I made a further complaint about this to the Press Council, hoping that it would reinforce the original decision and make clear that it meant what it said. The editor of *The People*, Richard Stott, then wrote to me saying that he had considered John Smith's article before publication, and anticipating that I would complain about it, he had allowed it to be published. He wrote: 'I do not suggest that our use of the word "poofs" was anything other than derogatory – indeed it was meant to be.' He then claimed that Smith was irritated by the fact 'that something known as the "Lesbian Strength and Gay Pride Festival" was taking place' and his intention had been to ridicule that, not individual homosexuals. In further letters his arguments became even more desperate. 'I ask: would homosexuals not be offended or angered by a "Straight Sex Pride Festival"? Would they not consider it unnecessary; aimed at embarrassing homosexuals.' However, he did say that he would not use the words 'poof' in his newspaper as a 'standard description for homosexual people' but only when he thought it appropriate.

By September, the Press Council had bewilderingly decided that I had not made a 'sufficiently substantial case to warrant adjudication' and my complaint against *The People* was disallowed. But others were keeping up the pressure. Veteran press-watcher and campaigner for newspaper ethics Bob Borzello (who made a record 220 complaints to the Press Council on all kinds of issues) had made follow-up complaints about Garry Bushell's use of the term 'pulpit poofs'. This complaint, too, was rejected with the reasoning:

> In this case in a critical opinion article about television, the writer identified a programme on homosexuality and the clergy as a special on 'pulpit poofs', words published in quotation marks which had appeared on screen in the programme. It was entitled to do so even though the phrase had originally been coined, unfortunately, by *The Sun* itself. The Press Council cannot say that the words were published on this occasion gratuitously. The complaint against *The Sun* is rejected.

However, Borzello already had another complaint pending pertaining to John Smith of *The People* who had commented on a claim that one in seven Church of England clergymen was gay. He said he did not believe that there were so many 'poofs in the pulpit'.

In correspondence with the editor of *The People*, the Press Council discovered that Stott had been on holiday at the time of the publication of this piece. If he had been in the office, he said, he would have asked John Smith not to use the phrase. This did not mean, though, that he thought the writer was necessarily wrong. This time the Press Council upheld the complaint, saying that the words had been used: 'gratuitously without the possible justification that the word was necessary for proper understanding of the item or the opinion expressed'. Of course, not all gay people considered that tabloid abuse was a bad thing. Matthew Parris told *The Sunday Times*, in an interview:

> The homophobic kind of tabloid story has actually helped the gay cause more than any other phenomenon in the past 20 or 30 years. The worse thing for gays is the kind of courteous way in which the subject used to be treated in the press. There was always some sensitively designed euphemism. But what screaming words like 'poof' do is get people used to the idea that homosexuality is around.[16]

While all this had been going on, the Government had commissioned a report on press self-regulation from Sir David Calcutt.[17] He concluded that 'the press should be given one final chance to prove that voluntary self-regulation can be made to work' although he was doubtful that it would do so. He recommended the creation of a Press Complaints Commission to replace the Press Council, although it was clear from what Sir David said that he was not optimistic about the ability of such a body to exert any control over the press's disgusting behaviour without statutory backing. He also recommended that there should be a review of the new Commission's performance within two years.

Having recognized that the Government might mean business this time, the newspaper industry created its second 'self-regulating body', the Press Complaints Commission. This, we were told, would be much more effective than the Press Council in protecting privacy and preventing unwarranted intrusion into private lives. The main difference would be that it would not entertain third party complaints – it would look into complaints only from those directly affected by a story. This rang alarm bells with some activists who tried, before the Commission's terms of reference were finalized, to have this modified. Keith Wood wrote in *Capital Gay*:

> The Commission has said it will not accept complaints from those 'not directly affected' by a story. If for example, there is an offensive piece about 'poofs' they could try to avoid accepting it by claiming that no individual complainant is *directly* affected. Some individuals, especially after invasion by the press of their privacy, may not be able to face starting a complaint, or perhaps haven't the knowledge, facilities or stamina to do it. Without third party complaints, no-one else could complain on their behalf and the newspaper would get off scot-free.[18]

Despite this pressure the refusal to accept third party complaints remained (although this would be 'interpreted liberally', according to one of the architects of the Commission, Andreas Whittam Smith). The Commission's membership would include 'lay and industry members' – which meant that newspaper editors themselves would be required to judge each other. Each editor was required to serve on the Commission for a period of three months, although 'those who are editors do not participate in the adjudication of complaints against their publication'. The PCC's code of practice was a modified version of that recommended by Calcutt, and it included 'sexual orientation' in its clause covering discrimination. Clause 15 reads:

(i) The press should avoid prejudicial or pejorative reference to a person's race, colour, religion, sex or sexual orientation or to any physical or mental illness or handicap.

(ii) It should avoid publishing details of a person's race, colour, religion, sex or sexual orientation, unless these are directly relevant to the story.

This seemed hopeful – at least it was recognized that the privacy of gay people did need to be protected. But it would take some time before it became clear whether the PCC would be any better than the Press Council in protecting the gay community from such unfair treatment.

The Press Complaints Commission replaced the Press Council on 1 January 1991. According to David Mellor, the then Secretary of State for National Heritage (the Government department which oversees the media), the Press were 'drinking in the last chance saloon'. It was a fateful comment; within weeks Mellor had fallen victim himself to the very abuses he was warning about. He was exposed in several newspapers to be having an affair with an actress – a story which was played for all it was worth for several weeks. The papers were relentless in embroidering the tale until eventually the pressure on Mellor became irresistible and he was forced to resign from the Government.

The first test of the PCC came with *The Daily Star*'s infamous 'Poofters on Parade' headline (the details of which can be found in the Chapter 5). In October 1991 the Commission adjudicated on a complaint from the Stonewall lobbying group, which had been named in the story on the front page of *The Daily Star*. The Commission found that *The Daily Star* had 'no excuse' for being inaccurate and failing to 'distinguish comment, conjecture and fact'.

> The Commission strongly upholds the right of editors to criticise and attack public policies, even in the most vigorous language. Nevertheless, they should not ride roughshod over the sensitivities of their fellow citizens, in this case, the minority who are homosexuals who, as far as the law is concerned, are behaving blamelessly. The newspaper failed to make a clear distinction between its legitimate expression of strong opinions and their publication in terms which could encourage the persecution of a minority.

In 1994 Brian Hitchen was again censured by the Press Complaints Commission (see Chapter 5) for the use of 'prejudicial and pejorative references' to homosexuals. In that adjudication the Commission revealed that it was 'unwilling to compile a list of proscribed words or phrases' and would 'judge the whole passage that gave rise to the complaint'.[19] It seemed we were back to square one.

What price gay privacy?

Meanwhile, another spate of press 'outings' had begun and it seemed appropriate that the Press Complaints Commission's commitment to its code of practice should be tested. A suitable case was not long in coming. In July 1993, Norfolk social services department turned down an application for adoption from a local couple, Jim Lawrence and his Asian wife Roma. The Lawrences had wanted to adopt a black child, but a selection committee had decided, on the recommendation of – among others – one of their social workers, Terence Dunning, to turn the application down on the grounds that the couple were 'racially naïve' and did not 'have enough experience of racial abuse'. The Lawrences felt aggrieved by the decision and decided to go public with it. The story caused a great furore among the right-wing papers who were outraged at this latest example of what they considered to be 'political correctness gone mad'. So intense was the fuss that the Government set up an inquiry. Before it could be published, however, the tabloids got wind that Terence Dunning was gay. On 30 August 1993 *The Daily Express* revealed that Dunning had a gay lover. From that moment on he became the centre of a familiar tabloid scramble. Despite the fact that Dunning's part in the adoption saga was a very minor one, he was singled out as the villain of the piece. He had become the perfect scapegoat for the tabloids' 'family values' agenda. Here was a gay man making decisions which (as far as they were concerned) disadvantaged 'real' people and not only that, he also qualified as that other gay stereotype, the home-wrecker. However unfairly, Dunning could now be portrayed as a symbol of 'what is wrong with this country' – a favourite theme of the middle-market tabloids.

He told me later in an interview that he was unable to leave his house because reporters had both front and back door covered. 'I did not make the decision in that case,' he says. 'It was taken by a panel, but I was set up as the bad guy, which was unfair and wrong. I was hounded for ten days by the press. They went to amazing lengths to dig out my private life – speaking to neighbours, going to the church I attend and pestering my son and my ex-wife.' Somehow – and he does not know how – they obtained copies of his wedding photographs and used these to illustrate articles about him.

This seemed a perfect case to test Clause 15 of the Press Complaints Commission's code of practice. Dunning's sexuality, as far as I could see, had been drawn into this story quite gratuitously and bore no relevance to it. However, the Commission rejected the complaint, reasoning that Dunning's sexuality *was* relevant to the story because 'the prospective adoptive parents had spoken to the press about their concern that one of the social workers who took part in the decision to refuse them as adoptive parents did not himself maintain a traditional family unit'.

Meanwhile, both *The Daily Mail* and *The Daily Express* revealed that Dunning had once been married and had left his family to live with his male lover. From there the story grew until the lover decided to tell his story to *The Daily Mail*, which splashed it over two pages under the headline 'My years with the gay social worker'. In the story Dunning was presented as a fickle man who had thoughtlessly abandoned his wife and children in order to live an unnatural and promiscuous life. It began:

> For six years they lived 'like any other couple' sharing the chores in their rented flat, enjoying the occasional trip to the theatre or disco. But social worker Terry Dunning and his gay lover had achieved their happiness at the expense of the family Mr Dunning walked out on. They were no longer living together by May of this year, when Mr Dunning, 55, hit the headlines . . . Mr Dunning had moved on to a new relationship with another man.
>
> The relationship got off to a less than romantic start – the pair met in a public lavatory in Norwich in 1979. Each had gone there in search of a sexual partner . . .[20]

Norfolk County Council called a press conference to try and stem the mounting hysteria. Mr Dunning told reporters that his professional judgement was in no way affected by his sexual orientation. His employers, Norfolk Social Services, backed him up.

'We don't want to make any judgement about his private life,' they said. 'There is no doubt about his ability as a social worker. The Director of Social Services is appalled at the way the two things are being linked.' Unfortunately, the press conference simply provided more fodder for another attack the following day. *The Sun* said in an editorial:

> So what are his qualifications for acting like a little tin god? He ABANDONED his wife after 20 years because of his love for another man. He ADMITTED his homosexuality on a TV programme. It didn't stop him getting promotion and a pay rise. He's still sitting in judgement on ordinary couples. Terence Dunning's bedtime habits are his own affair. A pity he can't show the same tolerance to others that he expects for himself.

This new and nasty development caused me to write once more to the Commission:

> Mr Dunning is now being pilloried because of his homosexuality. There are numerous examples of the way the press has used his sexual orientation quite irrelevantly to try and smear his professional judgement. There are examples in today's *Sun* newspaper, *Daily Express* and *The Daily Mail*, as well as last Saturday's *Daily Mail*. Mr Dunning felt that, after the speculation and comment about him reached fever pitch, he needed to call a press conference to put his side of the story. The newspapers used this to launch a further fusillade against him. This is despite the fact that his employers do not consider his sexuality to be in any way a factor in his professional judgement, and specifically not in this case.
>
> As gay people we, too, feel outraged on Mr Dunning's behalf, and on behalf of all gay people who, the press are implying, are incapable of making properly reasoned judgements in their professional life – simply because of their sexuality. In Mr Dunning's case, his sexuality was irrelevant and should not have been raised as an issue by the press. It is contrary to Section 15 of your code of practice.

The Commission threw out this complaint too, saying:

> The Commissioners took the view that it is in the public
> interest for readers to know that someone who is involved in
> family matters and relationships as part of his work, and
> whose recommendations have been criticised in some
> quarters, has had two broken relationships. His ex-lover was
> seemingly not averse to giving the story. The emphasis in the
> article was on those broken relationships (one heterosexual
> and one homosexual). It was not prejudicial against the
> homosexual relationship.[21]

The Government inquiry completely exonerated the decision which
Norfolk Social Services department had taken over the adoption
application, saying it had not been a case based on individual
'political dogma' but on social services' 'onerous duty to see the best
interests and welfare of a child to be adopted are paramount'.

Dunning, however, felt traumatized by his treatment by the
press. Fortunately he reports that his colleagues, friends and family
were all as supportive as his employers had been. Other victims of
press harassment have not been so lucky.

When Discrimination is not Discrimination

Also during 1993 a series of stories concerning the neglect of
children were originated by the tabloids. However worthy and 'in
the public interest' such stories might be, they were not treated
seriously. They were given prominence only because they fitted the
common tabloid technique of linking events to a film which was
proving popular at the time (in this instance *Home Alone* starring
Macauley Caulkin). The stories concerned very small children
'abandoned' by parents who had allegedly gone off on holiday or
out to the pub leaving them unattended. There was, quite rightly,
much outrage that parents should behave in this manner and several
cases were prominently featured in a short period. But on 26 August,

the papers ran another example which concerned two women who had allegedly gone on holiday leaving seven young children to fend for themselves. This story was different from the others in that the women concerned were discovered to be lesbians. '2 gay mums dump 7 kids to go on holiday' was the front page headline the of *The Daily Star*, the story continuing inside under the heading 'Dumped by gays'. This was despite the fact that the paper knew that the children had been left with sixteen-year-old baby-sitters. But what exactly did the women's sexuality have to do with it? The papers had not found it necessary to mention in preceding cases that the parents involved had been heterosexual.

The reason that these women's sexuality had become the central focus of the story soon became apparent. Over the next few days the story changed from being about alleged child neglect into one that implied lesbians are not fit to be mothers – even though a police investigation concluded that the women had done nothing criminal. Fortunately, because of the involvement of children, the women could not be named, but their location would not have been difficult to find – particularly as the London *Evening Standard* had run a particularly unpleasant piece about the housing estate where the women lived (reporting on the resentment of neighbours at the existence of the 'lezzy house'). One woman was quoted in this story as saying: 'I feel that lesbians and gays shouldn't have children. They live their lives as they want, but they don't stop to think of the little ones.'[22]

This was a sentiment with which the papers obviously agreed and the story ran for several days. I complained to the Press Complaints Commission that the women's sexuality had nothing whatever to do with the incident. They replied that they:

did not find that the substance of your complaint suggested that the Code had been breached. The Commissioners did not consider that the newspaper made any misleading link between the women's sexuality and their suitability for parenthood, but reported the facts of the case which was in the public interest.

On 22 August that year, apropos of nothing, *The News of the World* carried a story headed 'AIDS kills lover of gay Take That boss'. The story began: 'The manager of heart throb band Take That is gay and had a male lover who has died from AIDS.' Although the story went on for another twenty-three paragraphs, that first sentence is the sum total of the 'news' which it conveys. The man in question – who was named and pictured – was quoted at the end of the article as saying that he did not want to talk about his private life or his sexual orientation. He obviously considered himself a private business person; he had not sought any 'limelight' or personal publicity. This surely represented a quite gratuitous outing and a perfect example of the invasion of privacy that Clause 15 is supposed to protect against. Off went a complaint to the Press Complaints Commission and back came the reply. The Commission decreed that the man's association with a pop group qualified him as a 'public figure' and therefore made him fair game.

On 20 October 1993, *The Sun* carried a story, stretched over two pages, headed 'The homo Provo'. Its sub-heading was '25 years for IRA bomber who cruised loos for men'. The story began: 'An IRA terrorist jailed yesterday for plotting Britain's biggest bomb attack is a gay pervert who cruised public toilets for sex with strangers.' It was difficult to see what relevance this man's sexuality had on his trial for terrorism. The article also made several 'pejorative' remarks about the man's homosexuality, which, it seems, even the IRA 'won't touch with a barge pole'. It was difficult to tell which crime *The Sun* considered most heinous: attempted mass murder or cottaging. Once again, The Commission did not agree with my contention that 'irrelevant reference' had been made to this man's sexuality.

> The Commissioners took the view that the story focused on how strange it was that the IRA, given their strong prejudice against homosexuals, had recruited this particular man who was not only known to have been a practising homosexual for most of his life but also to have convictions for gross indecency and sexual soliciting of men. The piece quoted a senior detective as saying 'The IRA are normally very conservative about sexual matters and prejudiced against

homosexuals.' The reference to the man's sexuality was therefore not unfair as it was central to the story.[23]

Casual observers might be forgiven for imagining that the centre of the story had been the man's attempt to plant the largest bomb ever on the British mainland. Then came *The Sunday Express*[24] and *The Daily Star*'s outing of a solicitor representing a man accused of multiple murder. There was no other purpose to the story than to reveal the solicitor's – and his boyfriend's – sexuality. He was involved in no crime and had specifically stated that he did not want his homosexuality to be made public. The Commission, however, once more threw the complaint out, saying: 'As someone who is involved in a highly publicised case which is in the public eye, the Commission considered that the reporting of the man's personal life did not raise a breach of Clause 15 of the Code.'

The question remains: just what *would* raise a breach of Clause 15? We have yet to see the Press Complaints Commission place any value upon the privacy of gay people. As a result of this, and its many other shortcomings, the Commission is held in even lower esteem than was the Press Council. A second Government-commissioned report on press self-regulation, again from Sir David Calcutt, published in 1993 after two full years of the Commission's operation, said:

> The Press Complaints Commission is not, in my view, an effective regulator of the press. It has not been set up in a way, and is not operating a code of practice, which enables it to command not only press but public confidence. It does not, in my view, hold the balance fairly between the press and the individual. It is not the truly independent body that it should be. As constituted it is, in essence, a body set up by the industry, financed by the industry, dominated by the industry, and operating a code of practice devised by the industry and which is over-favourable to the industry.[25]

The second Calcutt report recommended sweeping reforms to protect privacy including the creation of a Press Complaints Tribunal, which would have statutory powers. Meanwhile, in the 1988–89 Parliamentary Session two Private Members' Bills relating to the press had been introduced – one concerned with the protection of privacy and the other with the right of reply. They had been introduced by MPs who had detected a growing public unease at newspapers' arrogant disregard of the privacy and feelings of ordinary people. The press was creating more and more offence with its unending parade of crude stories – especially about the royal family and other public figures. These two Bills – like previous attempts to curb the press through legislation – were destined to fail, but not before they had received second readings and reached committee stage. Both Bills received widespread cross-party support, particularly Clive Soley's Freedom and Responsibility of the Press Bill, which had called for a statutory right of reply for those who were aggrieved by untrue or inaccurate press coverage of their activities.

The House of Commons National Heritage Committee then conducted an inquiry which resulted in a report on *Privacy and Media Intrusion*. In 1993 a consultation paper from the Lord Chancellor's Department and the Scottish Office entitled *Infringement of Privacy* was published. The Lord Chancellor's main proposal was the creation of a new civil wrong of infringement of privacy.

The Government at that time was preparing its own White Paper taking into account the recommendations of the Calcutt reports and the National Heritage report. There were widespread fears in Fleet Street that the White Paper would recommend some kind of legal restraint, and the press reacted violently at this prospect. Many articles were published warning about the threats to democracy such legislation would pose, how the newspapers' all-important right of free speech would be taken away. They warned that the press's sacred duty to expose the wrong-doings of the mighty would be endangered. The Association of British Editors, even issued 'an alternative white paper' to pre-empt the official one. In it they argued that: 'a privacy law or any statutory regulation of the media on the lines proposed would be seriously detrimental to freedom of speech and freedom to publish, without which a democratic society cannot operate properly'. In an annexe they included 'summaries of articles, programmes or documentaries that would have been difficult to research, record or film under the kind of regime proposed by the consultation paper *Infringement of Privacy*. In consequence they would probably not have been published or broadcast.' However, it would be difficult to see how any of the proposals which had been made (all of which had a 'public interest' over-ride clause) would have interfered with *genuine* investigative journalism rather than simple intrusion. Naturally it would be preferable if the only restraint on the press was self-restraint, but, as far as the lower end of the market is concerned, this seems impossible. The serious newspapers also cry out at the injustice of having legal checks on *their* activities even though they have behaved responsibly. Unfortunately – and I am not the first to make this point – the broadsheets have stood by saying little while the tabloids have tainted the reputation of the press. The intelligent press should speak out more clearly in condemning the activities of the tabloids, particularly when remaining silent could have a wholly regrettable effect.

In the event, the official White Paper was postponed several times before eventually being quietly sidelined. John Major's Government was aware of the strength of feeling among newspaper proprietors and within the industry generally and judged that it was better to have the press as an ally than an enemy. Meanwhile, homosexuals have no protection from the attacks, which continue as before (if not as frequently or expressed in quite such violent language). The privacy of homosexual people, it seems, is not as precious as that of other citizens and although 'discrimination' against homosexuals is expressly forbidden in the Press Complaints Commission's code of practice, there is little sign – on current performance – of the principle being enforced.

Notes

1. *Time* magazine, 27 June 1994.
2. *Capital Gay,* 19 July 1985.
3. 18 November 1990.
4. Press Council annual report, 35th edition, 1988.
5. *Capital Gay,* 19 January 1990.
6. *The Sun,* 31 January, 10 February and 13 February 1990.
7. Letter to Press Council, 8 April 1990.
8. 14 May 1990.
9. 25 May 1990.

10. 18 May 1990.
11. 3 June 1990.
12. 27 May 1990.
13. 26 May 1990.
14. 20 May 1990.
15. 14 May 1990.
16. 6 May 1990.
17. *Report of the Committee on Privacy and Related Matters* (Cmnd 1102), 1990.
18. 14 December 1990.
19. Press Complaints Commission Report No. 25.
20. 13 September 1993.
21. Letter from Press Complaints Commission Ref: 931297, 14 October 1993.
22. 27 August 1993.
23. Letter from Press Complaints Commission Ref: 931418, 5 November 1993.
24. 10 April 1994.
25. *Review of Press Self-Regulation* (HMSO 1993).

Chapter seven
Evolving Gay Coverage

THIS new era of gay confidence and energy has been disconcerting for the popular press, which had assumed – and frequently announced – that AIDS spelled the end of what they considered 'proselytizing', 'flaunting' queers. They were convinced that HIV would ensure that those fairies that weren't dead would return to the closet where they belonged. Or, as 'morals campaigner' Mrs Victoria Gillick put it, in The London *Evening Standard*: 'I regard most things gays do as a swansong, because there is not going to be enough of them left in twenty years' time. There will not be enough of them left to squeak.'[1] But, rather than silencing homosexuals, the AIDS crisis gave them a new determination and drew in people who might otherwise have remained uninvolved. As homosexuality has risen on the social agenda, and gay demands have emerged in just about every area of life, the nature of press coverage has gradually evolved. In this chapter we will examine some of the milestones in that process.

AIDS hysteria

The wave of anti-gay revulsion which AIDS released during the 1980s was frightening and depressing. The emergence and development of the 'AIDS epidemic', and the medical profession's apparent helplessness in the face of it, convinced many gay people that HIV would not only severely deplete the emerging gay community, it would significantly weaken the attendant political movement. Right from the beginning, the newspapers had grabbed the opportunity to express the unbridled homophobia that AIDS provided. They harped constantly upon the idea that AIDS was 'self-inflicted' and that it was 'punishment' for gay men's immorality. *The Times* summarized this in an editorial in December 1984:

> The infection's origins and means of propagation excites repugnance, moral and physical, at promiscuous male homo-sexuality. Conduct, which tolerable in private circumstances, has, with the advent of 'gay liberation', become advertised, even glorified as acceptable public conduct, even a proud badge for public men to wear. Many members of the public are tempted to see in AIDS some sort of retribution for a questionable style of life.

The Spectator, was even less restrained in its editorial comment:

> Given an inch, the homosexuals demand all. Granted legal-ity, they have advanced boldly, noisily, immodestly, without shame, flaunting and organising themselves, proselytising vigorously, demanding ever-fresh 'rights', privileges, hand-outs, immunities, special representation and public respect . . . perhaps all glamour, licit and illicit alike, may fade from what may once again be thought an unnatural vice.

Popular journalists created categories of blame – the innocent (haemophiliacs, children, those who had caught the virus through blood transfusions) and the guilty (homosexuals, drug abusers, prostitutes). Brian Hitchen in *The Daily Star* epitomized this attitude when he wrote about Princess Diana's concern for those with AIDS:

> Whoever plans her schedules should cut out the endless handshaking with unstable dope addicts and the time spent listening to tales of woe from homosexuals whose promiscu-ity has made them HIV-positive. There is nothing exotic about sticking hypodermic needles in yourself and there's no romance in buggery. I feel desperately, achingly sorry for

haemophiliacs, many of them children – who have con-
tracted AIDS through infected blood. Of course Princess
Diana should continue to visit and comfort them. But as to
the rest of them – forget it!

Those infected were demonized, and panic was created where there
need have been none. Instead of using their immense power to
disseminate life-saving information, the newspapers used it to
purvey fear and to indulge in crude moralizing. As *The Sun* put it in a
November 1984 editorial: 'In the streets of Britain there are an
unknown number of men who are walking time bombs. They are
homosexuals with the killer disease AIDS. When they volunteer as
blood donors they become a menace to society.'

By the mid-1980s, the AIDS-inspired homo-hatred had
reached epic proportions. But, instead of trying to calm the
situation, the tabloids (and some broadsheets) actively inflamed it.
One example – of the many that could be cited – of newspaper
attempts to attack gay people using AIDS as a weapon began on 11
December 1986, when James Anderton, the deeply religious Chief
Constable of Greater Manchester made a speech to representatives
of the emergency services in the city. He said:

Why do homosexuals continue sleeping with each other?
Why do they still engage in sodomy and other obnoxious
sexual practices knowing the dangers involved? We should
ask them head on and challenge them to answer it. People at
risk [of AIDS] are swirling around in a cesspit of their own
making.

The following day, the newspapers picked this up with a relish
quite out of proportion to the importance of the speech, or the man
who had made it. The explanation for this prominence was, of
course, that Anderton had articulated the same line that the papers
had been preaching for years – that AIDS was a moral come-
uppance. Anderton's speech gave *The Sun* the opportunity to run a
headline – 'Perverts to blame for the killer plague' – which
encapsulated everything that the paper had been saying over the past
four years:

> Three cheers for James Anderton . . . For the first time a
> major public figure says what the ordinary person is thinking
> about AIDS . . . Their [homosexuals'] defiling of the act of
> love is not only unnatural. In today's AIDS-hit world it is
> LETHAL . . . The Sun hopes that Mr Anderton will treat
> these perverts with the contempt they deserve. What Britain
> needs is more men like James Anderton – and fewer gay
> terrorists holding the decent members of society to ransom.

The London *Evening Standard*'s editorial said: 'In leading a moral
crusade against the decadent sexual attitudes of society that
condones homosexuality and prostitution and thereby fosters the
spread of AIDS, Mr Anderton is articulating a deep-rooted feeling in
Britain.'[2] This seemed to be confirmed by a telephone poll on LBC
radio which showed 74 per cent in favour of Mr Anderton's views.[3]
The Manchester police claimed 99 per cent support for their chief's
views from the 'hundreds of calls' they said they had received.

Epidemic or no epidemic: gays are to blame

When it eventually became apparent that the doom-laden
scenario which had been predicted was not going to come to pass,
and that no widespread AIDS epidemic was apparently taking place
among heterosexuals in the Western world, the papers managed to
turn even that against homosexuals. A conspiracy theory arose that
gay activists had been manipulating the Government into 'mass-
aging' the statistics and deliberately feeding the public 'disinformation' that AIDS was an equal threat to the whole community when,
indeed, it really was a 'gay plague'. ('It is *wrong* to whitewash
Freddie Mercury's life, *wrong* to spread the myth of heterosexual
AIDS and criminal to divert funds from less trendy but more
pressing concerns like cancer research,' wrote Garry Bushell in *The
Sun*.)

William Oddie – in an attack on The Terrence Higgins Trust,
one of the main support and education groups dealing with HIV and

AIDS, wrote in *The Daily Telegraph* that AIDS statistics issued by the Department of Health revealed that only 5 per cent of the total cases were women, while 82 per cent were gay men: 'Such facts cannot simply be abolished: but there has been a massive attempt to smother them under a blanket of obfuscation, for reasons which have little to do with public health.'[4] He went on to say that the THT had 'a hidden agenda', which was to protect gay people's 'newly-won respectability'. Another of the many examples claiming that homosexuals were manipulating information about AIDS was voiced in an editorial in *The Sunday Telegraph*. It criticized:

> the self-righteousness of homosexuals whose spokesmen have effectively intimidated the media and officialdom into censoring a grim truth: though AIDS is not a 'gay plague', it is nevertheless the gay community's promiscuity which created the principal vector for the spread of AIDS into Western society. Though many victims showed great dignity in the face of death, some in the gay community did not. One of these quite deliberately made it his business to spread the illness, coupling with gay men in one city after another, then flaunting his Kaposi's sarcoma and saying 'This means I'm going to die. And so are you.'[5]

The assertion that HIV was 'self-inflicted' – constantly reiterated by journalists – gave some kind of justification to the idea that gay men's lives (and those of drug abusers and prostitutes) were distinctly less valuable than anyone else's. The homophobia underlying this kind of thinking was almost unbelievably callous. At last the anti-gay brigade had the opportunity to say what they had been longing to say: homosexuals deserved to die prematurely.

It was also unfair to blame gay-inaugurated AIDS education and support groups for 'exaggerating' the threat to heterosexuals. Throughout the 1980s, respected organizations including the British Medical Association and the World Health Organization had done their best to predict the direction of the epidemic based on the best information available at the time. Those predications subsequently proved to be inaccurate, in the West at least. The immense potential danger surely justified the advocating of simple precautions. Journalists, however (many of them triumphant that their own interpretation of events had proved correct), poured scorn on 'homosexual propagandists' and their supposedly compliant allies in Government.

A long campaign was launched among educators and other interested parties to try to 'educate' journalists about HIV and AIDS and to encourage them to behave more responsibly when writing about them. The NUJ's Equality Council issued a leaflet asking journalists to be more careful about the terminology they employed and how they interpreted figures: 'There is no excuse for describing AIDS as a "gay disease". It didn't start among gay men, it is transmitted by heterosexuals as well as homosexual contact and through blood, and the term is comparable to "black crime" in the way it stirs prejudice.' All attempts at calming the (predominantly tabloid) hysteria failed. AIDS was proving far too useful for the promotion of ultra-conservative agendas for it to be spoiled with compassion. The broadsheets, however, took their duties more responsibly and many journalists – particularly specialist medical correspondents – took it upon themselves to attempt to correct some of the damage done by their populist counterparts. Several won awards for their efforts. The more liberal and serious end of the press begin to see that AIDS was not a matter for simple moralizing or political manipulation and began to pay it serious attention. Not only the medical developments, but the social implications were addressed. An editorial in *The Independent* berated its tabloid brethren:

> Heterosexual smugness will be the real killer. [We must] rid ourselves of the idea that AIDS is a 'price' to be paid, that some victims . . . are 'innocent' while others are 'guilty'. But we need to be rid of the idea now. It cannot be said too often that AIDS is a disease and it is possible to get it from a single unprotected encounter. Apportioning guilt to people with potentially fatal infections is not just morally repugnant, it is also foolish.[6]

Despite the attempts by the sensible papers to bring balance to the debate, AIDS was still providing endless, dark copy for the bottom end of Fleet Street. This was dramatically illustrated when the pop singer Freddie Mercury died from AIDS in November 1991. Once more a homophobic torrent poured from the tabloids: 'Freddie's life was consumed with sodomy. He died from it,' wrote Peter McKay by way of obituary.[7] This was a theme that journalists enthusiastically embellished. Freddie Mercury became, for a few days, the quintessential homosexual: he represented every dire warning that the popular press had been issuing over the years, he was the personification of that tabloid demon 'the promiscuous homosexual'. When they wrote about Freddie Mercury, they were writing not about an individual but about every homosexual in the land. Joe Haines in *The Daily Mirror* put it this way:

> He was sheer poison, a man bent – an apt word in the circumstances – on abnormal sexual pleasures, corrupt, corrupting and a drug taker . . . Mercury died from a disease whose main victims in the Western world are homosexuals. For his kind, AIDS is a form of suicide . . . his private life is a revolting tale of depravity, lust and downright wickedness.[8]

The Mirror revealed that hundreds of readers had written and rung the paper, appalled at what Haines had said, but twice as many had contacted them to support him. (Strangely, at this time both *The Daily Mirror* and *The People* were owned by Robert Maxwell who said at an AIDS seminar in Canada: 'AIDS hysteria, added to public ignorance, self-serving politicians and tunnel-visioned guardians of law and order will affect not only those inevitably likely to be infected with the virus but its erosion of civil liberties will touch us all'.[9] Appeals to him to control the behaviour of his papers' own 'AIDS hysteria' went unanswered.)

Heterosexuals 'not at risk'

Now that it is taken for granted that AIDS 'no longer poses a major threat to the heterosexual population', the subject has fallen largely from the tabloid pages. Occasionally it will recur when some commentator wishes to make a point about the 'public money' being wasted on AIDS prevention and research. After all, goes the argument, it is 'only' a threat to homosexuals and drug addicts (and 'sub-Saharan Africans' as Garry Bushell likes to point out) so why are 'we' subsidizing research into it? *The Sun* was so anxious that its 'normal' readers should not fall for the 'big lie' that it even managed to run the headline 'Straight sex cannot give you AIDS – official!' In an editorial, the paper said:

> The killer disease AIDS can only be caught by homosexuals, bisexuals, junkies and anyone who has received a tainted blood transfusion . . . the risk of catching AIDS if you are straight is 'statistically invisible'. In other words impossible. So now we know – anything else is just homosexual propaganda.[10]

Meanwhile, *The Sun*'s medical correspondent, Dr Vernon Coleman, called AIDS 'the hoax of the century' and explained 'why it paid prudes, gays and business to scare us all'. Its columnist Richard Littlejohn wrote:

> After all, it is hardly a disease which affects the vast majority of the population, despite the misleading propaganda being peddled by the gay lobby. If you steer clear of sleeping with woofters and drug-users you should be safe . . . The Government seems more concerned with a handful of homosexuals than with millions of women. Perhaps if more lesbians got cervical cancer, the Government would consider doing something.[11]

AIDS expert Michael Adler was given space in *The Observer* to put the other side of this particular coin: 'If reinventing myths and delighting in fantasies is all that happens, then silence is better, so that we can get on unimpeded with the battle.'[12]

AIDS and health workers

Another manifestation of AIDS hysteria is the occasional 'scandal' over HIV-positive health workers. A glut of these occurred in 1992 after *The News of the World* broke the story of 'a £90,000 a year eye surgeon' who had, apparently, conducted 140 operations after his status had become known. The paper said: 'He has already made funeral arrangements. And he has started writing his own obituary . . . But he still carries out several operations a week. Many of his patients are children.'[13]

The Royal College of Surgeons made it quite clear that there was absolutely no risk to any of the people involved and a spokesperson said 'Mr Curran would have had virtually no hands-on contact with patients in the operating theatre because of the hi-tech nature of micro instruments and lasers used in eye surgery'. It was pointed out also that doctors are far more 'at risk' from patients than patients are from doctors. There is no proven case, anywhere in the world, of HIV passing from a doctor to a patient during treatment, but these facts were carefully ignored by the press who realized that they were on to a story that would provide many dramatic headlines. With an abandon that would not be tolerated in any other sphere of life, the demonizing of the eye surgeon began. He turned from being a saver of sight and a giver of life into being a monster of depravity. 'Secret life of AIDS surgeon' said the front page of *The Daily Express*.[14] 'Eye specialist vows to work on as gay lover speaks out.' And once more we had the cruel spectacle of a private life being pruriently pored over for public scrutiny and derision. *The Sun* 'urged that all AIDS victims should be named', although its reasoning for this was unclear. Several other health workers were similarly exposed in the years that followed. All were vilified, although not one shred of evidence was produced to show that they had behaved irresponsibly.

Despite a lessening of interest in AIDS in the tabloids, the serious press continues to keep its readers informed of developments, with the occasional renegade. For a while *The Sunday Times* maintained that HIV does not cause AIDS and that, in fact, AIDS is much more likely to derive from 'lifestyle factors' (such as promiscuous gay sex and the use of poppers). The paper has contended that there is no AIDS epidemic in Africa and has said that the World Health Organization's predictions about it were 'clearly false'. It has also said that the validity of the HIV test is in doubt. These ideas were propounded by Neville Hodgkinson, who was, at the time, *The Sunday Times*'s medical correspondent and were given prominence by Andrew Neil, the paper's editor. Many commentators thought that Neil had embraced these outlandish ideas in the hope that, if proved correct, they would restore the prestige that *The Sunday Times* had enjoyed in its pre-Murdoch days. This AIDS 'revolution' or 'dissent' was, many thought, Neil's shot at immortality. Just as his paper had once led a successful and public-spirited campaign against the drug Thalidomide, so this 'discovery' about AIDS would prove that *The Sunday Times* had been right all along and every other mainstream scientist had been wrong.

Hodgkinson was furiously attacked for his stance by the editor of the respected science magazine *Nature*. *The Sunday Times* was also angrily criticized by other newspapers for promoting 'the worst kind of anti-science'.[15] Writing about it, James Fenton said in *The Independent*: 'Now this particular argument over AIDS has been taken beyond its origins in a distaste for homosexuals and developed into a weapon against the "scientific establishment" which is depicted as conservative and intolerant of dissent.' But this criticism appears to be having the effect of making *The Sunday Times* even more convinced of its position. It now presents itself as a lone voice against an enormous conspiracy it calls 'the AIDS establishment'.

As AIDS continues to claim the lives of thousands of people, with many thousands more still to come, it is more important than ever that newspapers behave responsibly in their approach to the virus and the syndrome. All theories are worth looking at but, as James Fenton said in his *Independent* article, newspapers shouldn't 'play hobby-horse while people die'.

Gays and children: the ace up their sleeve

The tabloid press have opposed every one of the advances that the gay community has achieved over the past few years, using arguments that seem ever more desperate. There remains only one area where they feel confident that their opposition will be effective: that of children. Indeed, the only major setback in the gay struggle over the past few years has been the enactment of Clause 28 – which came about after a direct appeal to the nation's fears about the subversion of its children's supposed universal heterosexuality. As Maureen Freely wrote in *The Guardian*: 'There is a strong link in the public mind between homosexuality and paedophilia. A few years ago, I had a long argument with a very nice priest who insisted that the words were synonymous. When children enter the picture, the metaphors of fear go lurid.'[16] This stubbornly resistant opinion that homosexuals must be kept away from children at all costs is being deployed by journalists as their last line of attack. It is used in several ways: to suggest that, given the opportunity, all homosexuals are child-molesters; that homosexuals make inappropriate role models for 'impressionable' young minds; and that homosexuals are 'proselytizing' and 'recruiting' in order to replenish their ranks. A huge front-page headline in *The Sun* read: 'Martina turns girls into gays' and contained a quote from ex-Wimbledon champion Margaret Court saying: 'Martina [Navratilova] is a great player, but I'd like someone at the top who the younger players could look up to. It's very sad for children to be exposed to homosexuality.'[17]

This same argument is used also to prevent gay people from contributing their parenting skills in the arena of adoption and fostering. Those gay men and women who want to give expression to their parental instincts take the full brunt of the 'we must protect the children' gambit. *The Mail on Sunday* conducted an opinion poll and said (my italics): 'Another surprising finding of the survey was that *only* 74 per cent of the public disapprove of a lesbian or gay couple caring for a child, and 14 per cent of 25- to 34-year olds would approve of such an arrangement.'[18] *The Sunday Express* carried out an investigation into local authority policies on adoption by gay couples: 'Stop This Outrage' was their front page.[19] The paper had contacted 133 local authorities in the UK and found that 91 had said that they would not rule out placing children with homosexual couples. Only eight admitted that they had already done so. In what was supposed to be a balanced investigation, the paper gave 'the case for' and 'the case against'. There was also a 'case history' attacking the Albert Kennedy Trust, an organization set up to help teenagers made homeless on grounds of their homosexuality. As usual, it gave only one side of a very complex story. *The Sun* reproduced this story (omitting the case 'for' and any other positive statement which might have appeared in the

Sunday Express original). However, it did later try to balance the matter by publishing an interview with a woman who had actually been brought up by lesbian parents and survived into happy adulthood ('I'm proud of my gay mum').[20] The problem was that the case for lesbian mums was almost as insulting as the case against. 'I didn't grow up learning to be a lesbian. I grew up a proper woman,' said the young woman in question. Her husband found the idea of having two mothers-in-law 'Hilarious'.

Then a lesbian couple in Newcastle were allowed to adopt a two-year-old boy with a severe handicap. *The Daily Star* was first off with the story:[21]

> Labour-controlled Newcastle council has taken him from his loving foster mother. And allowed him to be adopted by two LESBIANS. Since six weeks old, the boy has been looked after by foster Mum Helen Grant . . . But for some incredible reason the council has now handed the poor little mite into the care of two sexually maladjusted deviants.[22]

The Sun followed up by calling on 'child expert' Lynette Burrows, who also happens to be a 'committed Christian' and frequent contributor to *The Sunday Telegraph,* to tell readers that she could 'hardly believe her ears' when she had been told the story. Under the heading 'Lesbian parents will ruin tragic tot's life', Ms Burrows, like the clever propagandist that she is, wheeled out all the mythology which clings to the idea of gay fostering and adoption:

> Well-adjusted people tend to come from families which have both a loving mum AND dad . . . Other children pick on them . . . Child experts agree that a person's sexual behaviour is partly influenced by the tendencies they are born with – and partly what they see going on in their family . . . these two women will colour his sexual attitudes and behaviour . . . it could ruin his life.[23]

In this instance, what the original heterosexual foster mother was offering could hardly have been called a 'traditional family' – she had been divorced for twelve years. Only by careful reading of some of the newspaper stories did it become apparent that, in fact, 'she had not been in a position to adopt' the child when he had been offered to the lesbian couple. There was also a suggestion that her ex-husband was exerting influence on her not to adopt. These complications were totally disregarded by the tabloids, which presented the case as one of 'preferential treatment' for homosexuals over the wishes of a 'normal' woman ('Foster mother loses baby to lesbians' – as *The Daily Star* succinctly put it).[24]

Pretend family relationships

From time to time, individuals are discovered who are living in 'pretend family relationships' and their stories are told in the tabloids because of the 'human interest' angle. But, whatever the facts of the cases and the evidence before the journalists, they are almost always presented with the mythology intact. An example of this was carried in *The News of the World*. It concerned 'gay telly actor Jim McManus' who 'revealed how for 18 years he has led a bizarre secret life – as a secret DAD'. Reading on, it soon becomes apparent that there was nothing 'bizarre' about Jim's life; he simply helped raise boyfriend Terry's child, who came to live with the couple when he was three years old. Jim is quoted as saying: 'Terry split up from his wife not long after his son's birth, but later she asked us to take care of the boy . . . we were by no means well off, but we had a happy life. And I can assure everyone that he has grown up as a perfectly "straight" heterosexual young man.'[25] This seems a perfect example of successful gay parenting, but in case *News of the World* readers should be disturbed by having their prejudices challenged, the story goes on to claim that Jim McManus is 'AGAINST gay and lesbian couples being allowed to adopt children.' McManus contacted me after this was printed, anxious that *Gay Times* readers should know that he certainly was not against gay fostering and adoption and he never said he was. *The News of the World* reporter had heard what he wanted to hear and told his readers what he imagined they wanted to know.

Soon after this came the 'scandalous' discovery by *The Sunday Mirror* that Southwark Council in London had fostered a fifteen-year-old youth with two gay men. As the newspaper prepared to harass and vilify the people involved, the Council obtained a court order stopping *The Sunday Mirror*. The paper challenged the order in court and managed to get it modified. It could carry the story, but the people involved could not be named or approached. 'A victory for free speech' the paper announced in an editorial:

> *The Sunday Mirror* has won a great victory . . . Southwark Council, voted in by local people and funded by every tax payer in the country, did not want YOU to know what was going on in YOUR name and with YOUR money. In short they did not want you to know the full story.[26]

This might sound noble, but it rings rather hollow when inside the same issue the 'freedom of speech' championed by *The Sunday Mirror* turns once more into a licence to persecute innocent people. The paper had managed to track down the boy's mother and, in a double-page spread, headlined 'How could they hand over my mixed-up boy to a couple of gay men?', it proceeded to twist and distort the situation. The story began by claiming that the mother was 'outraged' and 'shocked' at the decision of social workers to place her son with the gay couple. 'I'm saddened and disturbed by what is going on, but I'm powerless. It's like he doesn't belong to me any more.' However, all was not as straightforward as it seemed. Much further into the article it was revealed that the boy had been physically and mentally abused by his father. The mother admitted that her son had been a rent boy but said she was convinced that he wasn't really a homosexual. The young man himself insisted that he *was* gay. The implication that this youth's mother was concerned about the 'danger' her son was in from his foster parents was not borne out by the story. Near the end she is quoted as saying that she is not anti-homosexual and respects the men caring for her son:

> He has introduced me to his foster parents and I like them. He seems happy and stable. I'm not trying to say that there is anything wrong with their home life. It's just that this whole thing was rushed through while I was looking the other way. I should have been consulted.

This does not sit very easily with *The Sunday Mirror*'s shock-horror presentation of the story. The two men involved in this episode contacted me to ask how they should deal with the press which was 'monstering' them. They lived on a particularly rough council estate and although journalists were forbidden to approach them directly, they were questioning neighbours and anyone else connected with them. Quite soon the pressure from unfriendly people on the estate became so bad that they were forced to move out. When I spoke to them a couple of years after this incident they were still extremely anxious and fearful that one day their act of public-spirited kindness would once more cause the press to hound them from their new home.

Their case caused much comment in the press. 'Outrage grows over gay foster parents,' announced *The Daily Mail*, ensuring that its readers knew that Southwark Council was 'Labour-controlled'.[27] The London *Evening Standard* said in an editorial that the Council's decision was 'absurd and perverse': 'What sort of values allow them to discriminate against heterosexual foster parents? And how many children are going to be betrayed by the folly and laxity of Southwark social workers before they are brought to book?'[28] Then it was the turn of *The Sunday Express* to reveal that two gay men had adopted a fourteen-year-old girl with Down's Syndrome from – of course – a Labour council (which they were prevented from naming) in what the paper said was 'the first case of its kind'.[29] The paper then brought on a right-wing MP to reinforce the disapproving tone of the story. 'I do not believe any child should be fostered or adopted by lesbian or homosexual couples. It makes no difference whether they are handicapped or not – it does not give them a fair start in life,' said Rhodes Boyson. The two men in this case met while working in a centre for people with learning disabilities, so it could hardly be claimed that they weren't suitable for the job. Indeed, an article in *The Guardian* by Meg Henderson said: 'Advertising campaigns to recruit fosterers of children in care produce ever fewer replies. It seems that in bad economic times, children come off worst, and as the extended family is largely a nostalgic dream, social workers have to pick up the pieces.'[30] None of this has any effect whatsoever in convincing those who are opposed to gay people contributing to the care of disadvantaged children that their stubborn prejudices might be standing in the way of children having a life away from an institution.

The issue was raised again when the Government launched an 'Adoption Charter' which was ambiguous on its stance towards gay parents. *Today* reported that 'New charter bans gay couples from adopting',[31] while *The Daily Mail* claimed ' "Gay" adoptions go on'. This latest flare-up caused *The Daily Telegraph* to carry an editorial which seemed to go right against the prevailing tide: 'To declare that all homosexual couples regardless of their circumstances are totally incapable of providing such care and must therefore be ruled out would not be sensible.' *The Observer* added its voice of support by carrying an interview with two women, Judith Weeks and Pat Roman, who had fostered fifty-two children and adopted one during their twenty-eight-year relationship. The Government's instruction that local authorities must make strenuous efforts always to place children with heterosexual foster parents and only excepted 'older, profoundly handicapped children who may have sought adoption by a married couple without success' was roundly condemned by Judith Weeks: 'This is saying to the carer: "You are so fourth-rate you can only have a fourth-rate child". It's saying to the child: "As you haven't any sense or feelings, you can go off with anybody." There is a double insult.'[32]

A small change

By 1994 there was evidence of a small amount of change. Although the decision by a Manchester court to award a lesbian couple joint legal rights over the upbringing of their twenty-two-month-old son caused *The Daily Mail* to fulminate that Britain existed in a 'moral vacuum', the supportive comment far outweighed the disapproval. Carol Sarler in *The People* said that there were no 'qualifications' for parenthood other than a desire to love your children.[33] She cited the case of two little girls aged two and six in Newcastle-upon-Tyne who, a court was told, 'had to eat out of dogs' bowls; who growled in place of speech; whose flesh was ingrained with dirt and whose bodies were riddled with worms'. For the first time, I believe, in a tabloid newspaper, Ms Sarler made a point of indicating that their mother was *heterosexual*. 'She is married – and the children do have a father.' Suzanne Moore in *The Guardian* said that:

> Lesbian friends of mine who were having difficulty with a teacher who had never before encountered a gay couple with a child finally went into school to explain whey their daughter had two people she called mum. The teacher's hostility soon vanished. 'Oh, so she's got two parents, then? Well, that puts her one up on most kids in the class'.[34]

Apropos of this case, MP Emma Nicholson had remarked that she was 'immensely unhappy when adult sexual behaviour inflicts a distorted lifestyle on children'. This had been widely reported, and brought a retort from Libby Purves in *The Times*:

> If you are looking for distortion caused by adult sexual behaviour, however, we live in a positive Hall of Mirrors. The children of MPs, royalty, journalists and other moral prodnoses do not need to read underclass horror stories to find out about the lifestyle problems which adult sexuality inflicts on children. They are familiar with it all: access arrangements, vendettas, embarrassment, law-suits, confusion, hypocrisy . . . As for the . . . 'perversion' of the women's lives, if normal parental sex-life is anything to go by, it will probably be pretty underwhelming . . . Most children grow up with a heterosexual relationship in the background and barely notice. Frankly, the incidence of sizzling sexual energy in the average family household is depressingly low.[35]

Dillie Keane in *The Mail on Sunday* also came to the women's defence: 'Children need to see true loving kindness demonstrated day after mundane day. Security gives kids a fighting chance of survival as adults. And if those two parents are women, so be it.' However, she finished by saying:

Moral battles aren't won by High Court rulings. They are won by sheer hard slog. The battle that homosexuals and lesbians are fighting won't be won for 20, 30, 40 years when and if the children they rear turn out to be happy, balanced adults who tell us that having two parents of the same sex is just fine. Until then I reserve my judgement.[36]

Like so many other people, Ms Keane seems oblivious to the fact that gay fostering and adoption has been going on for decades. It is unnecessary to wait forty years to find out whether they are successful. *The Guardian* revealed that there have been:

four big controlled studies – one in the UK and three in America – comparing children being brought up in lesbian homes with the children of heterosexual mothers. The studies have found no difference in the children's social functioning, self-esteem or ability to express themselves. The psychologists said they appeared able to put their parents' lifestyle 'in a broader cultural context'. The last study, not yet published, followed the children they interviewed in the seventies through their adolescence in the eighties, to adulthood. They found that it is a myth to believe that children brought up in lesbian homes will automatically be homosexual.[37]

And anecdotal evidence was supplied by *The Sunday Times* when a thirty-four-year old man told of his own experience in being raised by two women in a lesbian relationship. 'Don't knock lesbian mothers . . . Any court that obstructs access to a child, or refuses a residence order, because a parent is gay is wrong. As a teenager I looked among the parents of friends and could not see one happy marriage. I was raised in a house of love.'[38] However, the children-must-be-protected brigade continue to sow the seeds of doubt, to disregard and obscure the evidence that is all around them and to insult those gay people who wish to have the fundamental experience of parenthood. 'The needs of children must be paramount,' they say. But they don't say what needs are served by keeping children in local authority care when they could be living – as the last quoted man said – in a house of love.

Reform resisted

At the time of the 1967 Sexual Offences Act, newspapers had, on the whole, supported reform. They did so reluctantly, but they recognized not only the injustice and cruelty of the law as it stood but the practical need for change; blackmailers were making a fat living from the law, innocent men – some of them admired and important to the Establishment – were being destroyed for no good purpose. Only *The Daily Express* remained intractably hostile. Although the newspapers saw the pragmatic benefits of changing the law in 1967, they were still far from enamoured of homosexuality and continued to refer to it in scathingly moralistic or pitying terms.

Prompted by law reform once more coming on to the agenda in 1994, *The Independent* commissioned an opinion poll on 'moral attitudes' in Britain. It showed that 25 per cent of the survey thought sexual relations between two adults of the same sex 'are not all wrong' – in 1983 the figure had been 17 per cent – whereas 'homosexuality is always wrong' according to 35 per cent (as opposed to 50 per cent in 1983). Disapproval was greatest among the over-fifty-fives, Conservative voters and those in the lower income groups. This indicated that there had been a small softening of attitudes in some areas. But most disappointing was the question about the age of consent. Only 12 per cent of the survey thought it should be sixteen. Those who thought it should remain at twenty-one totalled 56 per cent.[39] *The Daily Telegraph* reported that the International Social Attitudes poll had found that 'easier going sexual attitudes do not extend to homosexuals', with only 12 per cent of men and 14 per cent of women agreeing that homosexual couples should have the right to marry.[40] Although vigorous support came from the expected sources (*The Independent, The Guardian, The Observer*), a great deal of hysterical opposition emanated from some of the other papers. The tabloids' claim to speak for 'the vast majority of people in this country' seemed to justify their implacable opposition to lowering the age of consent.

Then the debate began in earnest. Joan Bakewell devoted one of her 'Heart of the Matter' TV programmes to looking at the topic, and then the deluge began. The 'we must protect the children' argument was played for all it was worth. *The News of the World* carried an exposé of a 'kiddie porn ring' and promptly linked it with the age of consent controversy:

> Any MP tempted to lower the homosexual age of consent to include schoolboys will benefit from reading today's News of the World. What chance does a 16-year old boy stand against a confident adult paedophile set on corrupting him? . . . Nobody knows for certain what the causes of homosexuality are. But physical introduction to homosexual behaviour must be among them . . . The lobby for reducing the age of consent to 16 argue that parity with girls is fair. They forget that women are protected by a law imposing a possible life sentence for the dangerous practice of anal sex. No such law protects boys who are much more likely to be the target for that particular perversion.[41]

Powerful support for lowering the age of consent came from the British Medical Association, but this was distorted by *The Daily Express* into a headline 'Teenage AIDS scourge'.[42] The paper rightly reported that the BMA had found that 'those aged 15 to 24 account for nearly a fifth of HIV cases', but the point of the BMA's action in calling for law reform – that it would be easier to educate younger people about the dangers of AIDS if they were not deemed criminals – was difficult to ascertain from the *Express*'s report. Amid the obfuscation, however, the paper managed to find room for Tory MP David Shaw to compound the confusion by saying: 'The move would only encourage homosexuals to approach children outside schools'.

    The Sunday Telegraph published a piece by Lynette Burrows entitled 'A licence to deprave'.[43] The article was illustrated by a cartoon of a pair of lock gates imprinted with the word 'consent' being opened ready to engulf the unsuspecting people below. Meanwhile, Richard Littlejohn in *The Sun* said that: 'the only argument for keeping the age of consent at 21 would be that it would upset professional sodomites such as the odious Peter Tatchell – who holds recruiting drives outside schools.'[44]

    A mini shock-wave greeted the London *Evening Standard*'s

decision to come out in favour of equality. This paper had previously been the originator of many crude anti-gay stories, but in an editorial it said:

> Sexuality is private. It is our own business – not that of the Crown Prosecution Service. And as long as it remains consenting and does not cause offence to anyone else, it should remain our business. But the current differential between ages of consent is a legal inconsistency which criminalises perfectly honest members of the community – while leaving others to lead their private lives with impunity.[45]

The Standard reiterated its stance during the week the issue came before Parliament. But *The Sunday Telegraph* remained implacable and its columnist Mary Kenny – a devout Catholic – having exhausted all other avenues, tried the 'unnatural' argument. She said that although there is evidence of homosexuality in the animal world ('pygmy chimpanzees have lots of same-sex orgasms') there is no evidence of exclusive homosexuality in any other species except man ('the chimpanzees don't stop being heterosexual at the same time'). She said that biologists are always drawn back to the evidence of 'Natural law' to conclude that exclusive homosexuality is not 'natural'. She then scuppered her premise by quoting Pope: 'The only proper study of mankind is man.' Indeed. When was the last time you saw a chimpanzee reading the Bible?

Janet Daley in *The Times* objected to equality from a different perspective. She said that children are at 'psychological risk' from 'the more strident activist voices' who are 'turning homosexuality into a commitment which might have been a transitory stage of their emotional development. A commitment, which it happens, cuts them off from parenthood – one of the major satisfactions of adult life.' She says that to be gay is now 'to be part of a movement' and that gay activism 'takes away the freedom to move away from the gay community' if that is what your feelings dictate. She says that 'gay activists' want young people to believe that 'what you do in bed is what you are: that your sex life is not an incidental fact about you, but your essence'.[46] Ms Daley overlooked the fact that homosexuality cannot be 'incidental' – because straight society will not let it be.

In February 1994, after several postponements, the date was set for the Parliamentary debate. Literally thousands of column inches were devoted to the campaign and its aftermath. *The Independent* even designed a special logo which it used, in the weeks leading up to the vote, over a daily feature describing developments. Paul Johnson wrote in *The Spectator* about a familiar bugbear of his – that gay people have a stranglehold on the media. During the age of consent debate, he asserted, the opposition never got a look in. Every time an editor speaks out, he said, he is inundated with angry letters and his offices are invaded:

> As a result of this campaign of intimidation, this putsch to reduce the age of consent for male homosexuality to 16 has met virtually no resistance from the media. I have counted a dozen articles in the national papers written by members of the homosexual lobby, putting their case. I have not seen a single forthright statement against, though some editorials have made caveats and one or two readers have managed to get letters of protest published. There is no question, of course, of broadcasting anything critical of homosexuality on radio or television. Quite the reverse.[47]

Johnson, as usual when on the topic of homosexuality, lost all sense of proportion – either that, or he did not read as widely as he would have us believe. Or perhaps he meant that the criticism which did appear wasn't vituperative enough, that there wasn't enough *loathing* for his liking. My reading of the press at that time revealed enough hatred to stoke the fires of hell. In *The Jewish Chronicle*, Chaim Bermant wrote on 18 February:

> The homosexual lifestyle is inherently sterile and the very promiscuity that goes with homosexuality is an attempt to stifle the void at the core of the homosexuals' existence. Momentary gratification, frequently repeated, can, in its crude way, add up to a form of satisfaction, but the constant search for physical gratification is in itself proof of unhappiness.

Under the heading 'Don't let gays make us lower our standards' Phillipa Kennedy in *The Daily Express* wrote on 24 February:

> What I hate to see, and what reinforces prejudice against gays, is the kind of performance we witnessed outside the House of Commons on Monday night, of painted transvestites, weeping men of all ages, strident intolerance and surging anger bordering on violence. At a time when reasonably-minded people are genuinely willing at least to be persuaded to drop the age of consent to 16, they behaved like a bunch of stereotyped screaming queens which only served to underline that MPs made the right decision.

Simon Heffer in *The Daily Express* wrote on 20 February: 'If liberal opinion – and this Government – worried a bit more about the freedom of families to get on with their lives . . . and a bit less about legalising sodomy with schoolboys, it might achieve something useful.'

In *The Sun*, Richard Littlejohn delivered a diatribe that began with his usual caveat: 'My view of homosexuality has always been that I couldn't care less, provided I don't have to watch, participate or pay for it through my taxes', but then he went on to say: 'Homosexual activists say [the vote] was a cop out and there should be equality . . . That depends on whether you believe normal sex is the same as your sixteen-year old son being buggered by some wheezing moustachioed leather boy two or three times his age.'[48] He claimed that a sizeable number of those supporting equality were actually 'solely interested in increasing the supply of fresh "chickens" on the sordid gay meat rack' and described Edwina Currie – who had sponsored the Bill – as 'the most vociferous MP in favour of . . . schoolboys barely past puberty legally to have anal sex – even though it is the quickest and surest way of spreading AIDS'. He concluded by saying: 'I think my views on this issue are a fair representation of what most reasonable people in Britain think.'

The newspapers also heaped personal abuse on those who had been involved in the campaign. Of Edwina Currie, Peregrine Worsthorne in *The Sunday Telegraph* said: 'She is such a dreadfully vulgar woman. I would have been against reducing the age of consent for homosexuals anyhow. But with her brazen hussy hectoring added to their camp and insensitive clamour, the cause, as far as I was concerned, never had a chance.'[49] Simon Heffer, in *The Daily Mail*:

> Now that she is associated with the screaming deviants who besieged the House of Commons on Monday night, Edwina Currie is in trouble. Her chances of winning the Bedfordshire Euro-seat were never strong. Now she is regarded mainly as a fag-hag, they are receding. So what do you think she should do next? Learn to write? Become an Anglican woman priest? Edit a new edition of Baden-Powell's Scouting for Boys? Run ChildLine?[50]

In the event, the age of consent was reduced to eighteen. The papers made much capital from the 'riot', 'siege' or 'rampage' outside the House of Commons which followed the outcome of the vote. *The Daily Express* even allowed MP Peter Bottomley space to say that the 'riot' – which he said had been instigated by a 'bunch of screamers' – had swung the vote against equality (even though it occurred after the vote had been taken). The opposition was feeble, irrational and, as we have seen, hysterically abusive.

Where gay people were allowed to put their own case – which was, it has to be said, in most papers at some point – they won the argument hands down. But the small concession that was made was made grudgingly and with bad grace. Despite the ground-breaking campaign – a skilful and efficiently orchestrated lobby from a highly-motivated community – middle England was unimpressed.

Notes

1. 12 June 1991.
2. 12 December 1986.
3. 12 December 1986.
4. 7 May 1991.
5. 28 June 1992.
6. 17 November 1992.
7. London *Evening Standard*, 28 November 1991.
8. 28 November 1991.

9.   July 1987.
10.   17 November 1990.
11.   4 December 1990.
12.   10 December 1990.
13.   5 July 1992.
14.   9 July 1992.
15.   Anthony Lewis, *The Guardian*, 7 July 1994.
16.   11 August 1994.
17.   12 July 1990.
18.   5 March 1989.
19.   30 September 1990.
20.   4 October 1990.
21.   9 October 1990.
22.   A *Gay Times* reader wrote to *The Daily Star* to protest at the use of the term 'maladjusted deviants' to describe the lesbian couple. He received a reply from Peter Hill, Associate Editor: 'I think it is perfectly justified by any standards of decency. The idea of lesbians bringing up children is a cruel mockery of family values. And, by the way, it is ILLEGAL for lesbians to adopt children. They have to lie that they are single parents.'
23.   13 October 1990.
24.   9 October 1990.
25.   31 March 1991.
26.   30 June 1991.
27.   1 July 1991.
28.   2 July 1991.
29.   5 April 1992.
30.   8 April 1992.
31.   20 October 1992.
32.   25 October 1992.
33.   3 June 1994.
34.   1 July 1994.
35.   1 July 1994.
36.   3 July 1994.
37.   2 July 1994.
38.   3 July 1994.
39.   December 1993.
40.   2 December 1993.
41.   16 January 1994.
42.   14 January 1994.
43.   2 January 1994.
44.   13 January 1994.
45.   24 Januay 1994.
46.   27 January 1994.

47.   12 February 1994.
48.   24 January 1994.
49.   27 February 1994.
50.   24 February 1994.

Epilogue

UNTIL the early 1980s, the terms of the debate on homosexual rights were almost entirely controlled by those in power – and their media mouthpieces. Activists trying to effect change were frustrated to see their efforts consistently misrepresented, ridiculed or completely ignored. Since then, the gay community has become much more effective in making its voice heard; it is beginning to dictate more of the agenda as well as the terms in which gay topics are discussed. Gay lobbyists and pressure groups have learned the lessons of media manipulation and have employed them effectively to ensure journalists are properly briefed; to originate stories from a gay point of view; to provide the media with articulate and informed spokespeople and with 'stunts' that are imaginative, witty and photogenic. Leading exponents of the public relations game for gay rights have been Stonewall and OutRage!, the former primarily a Parliamentary lobbying group which has gained respect in media circles and whose voice is trusted by journalists; the latter a 'direct action group' which has scored some significant media coups. It is a sign of the maturity of the community that each regards the other as complementary, sometimes even undertaking joint ventures.

Stonewall's critics say it is undemocratic and has no right to claim that it represents the gay community, while OutRage!'s approach dismays many people who see it as an aggravating challenge to straight perceptions which, they say, need to be nurtured and changed by the slow process of persuasion rather than confrontation. But both have the attention of the media.

As if we were from the moon

The question then becomes: who can possibly speak for such a diverse collection of individuals as those that comprise the gay community? The community seems split between those who feel that 'extreme' images of lesbian and gay life – usually drag-queens and shaven-headed dykes – do the cause no good – and those who insist on 'telling it like it is' – take it or leave it. But how is it for the majority of gay people? The annual Gay Pride event is surely the testing ground for this. The largest gathering of lesbians and gay men in Europe occurs each June in London, a huge representation of the many and varied styles of life that gay men and lesbians have adopted. Most of the time it is completely ignored by the media. For some gay people this seems a blessing – they cringe at seeing yet another drag-queen 'flaunting' on the *Nine O'Clock News* while the 'real' issues are ignored. For others it is a source of frustration in that this vast positive statement about the gay community is rendered invisible outside of central London. Surely the march could be considered a 'newsworthy' event – if only because of its size – yet, with a few exceptions, it has been systematically ignored by the mainstream press. One of those exceptions was 1993, when Pride had the extra bonus of a 'gay serial killer' on the loose to attract the tabloids. As a result, the festival received a much higher profile than usual, giving us pause to consider what images of lesbians and gays were being projected by the straight media. At the time, I ruminated on this in *Mediawatch*:[1]

> Right-wingers in America are claiming that representation of April's 'March on Washington' which attracted a million gay men and lesbians, were 'whitewashed'. A group called 'Accuracy in the Media' and the right-wing *Washington Times* say that the nation's newspapers and network television 'bleached' the event. Where were the bare-breasted lesbians 'some with rings through their nipples' and men in leather trousers and studded harnesses? Excised from the reporting also were the self-styled 'fierce dykes' who screamed that they wanted to make love to the first lady. Nowhere to be seen were the T-shirts proclaiming 'Every

tenth Jesus is Queer'. Only the most 'reasoned' spokespersons were allowed air-time and only 'normal' looking
participants were shown marching down the Mall towards
the White House. ('Gap-wearing middle-managers having a
day out' as *The Economist* described them). Lesbian and gay
groups in the states dispute that this is what actually happened, but we could expect no such restraint (or censorship,
depending on your point of view) from our own tabloid
press. Thanks to the activities of a murdering maniac this
year saw unprecedented coverage of Pride. The link between
the serial killer and Pride once more gave the tabloids the
opportunity to present the gay community in London as a
'seedy' den of vice peopled entirely by pathetic night-crea-
tures. 'Police hunting the serial killer of five homosexuals are
working in London's bizarre gay pubs and clubs,' said *The
News of the World*[2] and within four paragraphs had
included all its favourite canards: 'the kinky twilight world',
'the macabre, seedy pubs and clubs where gays into sado-
masochism hang out', 'the dark sinister world' and 'weird
lifestyle' of 'people living on the edge of real danger'. *The Sun*
treated us to a mangled version of 'Gays' hanky panky code',
while *The Daily Mirror* said that 'Regulars at the Coleherne
pub . . . stand in the bar, where photos of male buttocks and
leather-clad bikers adorn the walls' and quotes a rentboy as
saying: 'It won't stop me. I'll just be a bit more wary.'[3]

Christopher Howse in *The Sunday Telegraph* wanted to
know 'Why are so many murders done by one homosexual
upon another?'[4] One has to say: are they? The numbers seem
to pale into insignificance when set against the number of
men who murder their wives, girlfriends and mistresses. But
we mustn't let pesky old statistics get in the way of point-
scoring must we? 'Who is the most famous serial killer in
Britain?' he also asks. And before you can say Yorkshire
Ripper (a heterosexual woman-killer), Mr Howse nominates
Dennis Nilsen, whom he describes as 'a rootless, promiscuous homosexual'. *The Daily Express* did the business on
the West End pub Brief Encounter: 'It's a lonely place and a
place for the lonely – a place where men seek love with one

another. Or, indeed, a brief encounter. There are many such meeting points for gays in London and other parts of Britain. They do not attempt to disguise their purpose'. The reporter, Michael O'Flaherty says: 'Of course, gays have to be careful in choosing a partner, whether or not it is a one-night stand. They declare: but so do you heterosexuals (as if we were from the moon)'.

Ah, now we are getting to the nub of the issue: 'As if we were from the moon'. Isn't that what gay people could claim after reading the coverage of their lives in the British press? That we don't inhabit the same planet as everyone else and that we aren't, in fact, members of the human race? In tabloid terms we seem to represent all things alien; we become, in their fantasy, bizarre, unknowable, frighteningly different.

The 'woman editor' of *The Sun* certainly seems to think so. Amanda Cable described her experience of being caught up in the Pride parade: 'I've never had anything against gays and lesbians,' she began, but rapidly changed her mind when she found herself 'wedged in a tube carriage full of lesbians and gays on their way to join the rally.' According to her account, she was then subjected to a display of groping, swearing and general anti-social behaviour from a group of 'shaven-headed lesbians' with 'hoarse, low voices'. These women were, she says, drunk, loud and intimidating and 'the most sordid bunch I have ever met'. She describes how a mother needed to put her hands over the ears of her child as a 'lesbian boasted loudly about the sexual conquests she was setting out to make.' Ms Cable concludes that 'Their sexuality wasn't merely being flaunted – it was flung in our faces. Perhaps they thought being gay gives them the right. But the rest of us have rights as well. A right not to be gay and not have gayness thrust upon us. A right to say not loud but firmly and with dignity: We're straight and we're proud and we don't want to be part of any trendy crowd'.[5]

Notice it again? That nice little exclusive 'we' which seems to indicate that no-one but heterosexuals will be reading the article. Once more gay people are 'the other', something apart. And, according to *The Sunday Telegraph* it's the end of life as 'we' know it. Mary Kenny said that the visibility of homosexuals represented 'signs of Weimar in England today' while Ambrose Evans Pritchard thought the Los Angeles Pride parade was being hijacked by radical queers for whom 'tolerance is not enough. They want to force themselves on to society, finding new recruits by exposing the maximum number to their way of life.' He concludes: 'Perhaps I was really witnessing the exotic rites of a dying civilisation'. Or what about Frank Johnson in *The Daily Telegraph* who said, apropos 'the twilight world' of newspaper fantasy: 'Some homosexuals explain this kind of thing [cruising] by reference to centuries of persecution that have made them behave oddly. But it is unclear what the politically correct line is, because there are others who deny that they do behave oddly. Suggestions that there is anything odd about anything that homosexuals do is greeted with pious outrage by their various spokespersons. We are concerned, they tend to say, about tabloid stereotyping which says that there is something inherently abnormal about gay pubs and clubs with a dress code requiring steel-capped boots and leather cod-pieces.'

Even *The Independent* was at it. Columnist Margaret Maxwell was questioning what Gay Pride was all about. Having witnessed men wearing 'dog-collars and leads' as well as 'cross-dressing, make-up, small leather jackets over bare, hairy chests, and padded crotches' she suddenly felt she had 'seen too much'. She was horrified at the dehumanisation involved in much of the S&M imagery ('Why should a pet shop purchase, an article used to restrain dogs, be used on a human being?') and asks why gays insist on making themselves into 'figures of fun' by behaving in this way. She is of the opinion that we should court the approval of the heterosexual majority by refusing to flaunt activities at them which would 'make them gasp'. She concludes by saying: 'My instinctive reaction to mass gay marches, if I am honest, is to be thankful that I am straight and do not need to buy dog-collars with studs to please my partner.'

The question arises from all this: just how do we want to be represented in the media? And how much control do we have over that representation anyway? As *The Independent on Sunday* put it: 'After a week of headlines following the trail of a serial killer in London, the unknowing heterosexual could be forgiven for thinking that homosexuality equals seedy night-clubs equals sado-masochism equals AIDS equals murder. Prejudice and voyeurism are no doubt mainly to blame, but some of the wilder strands of the gay movement, which is part social and part political, are not entirely innocent either. Sometimes they seem to define gayness with the subtlety of a *Sun* leader describing attributes of Britishness'.[6]

There is no doubt that most of what the papers reported about Pride was true – there were lots of leather-clad clones, drag queens, bull-dykes and shaven-headed lesbians – but there were other things too. The issues which concern gay people, like the age of consent, exclusion from the military, adoption and fostering and a thousand others were totally ignored by the tabloids. They were interested only in the fancy dress, the mud-wrestling, the nudity and the apparent decadence of it all. So do we want to win friends and influence people or do we want to scream defiance in their faces? We are told constantly by the Tory Press that our openness and our 'bizarreness' will inevitably lead to a backlash. If we want equal rights, they say, then we had better integrate. Indeed, a book which reached number one in the American best-selling charts[7] warns that we had 'better stop fanning the fires of bigotry' if we want to stop being victimised by it. 'Gay Pride marches for self-affirmation tend to degenerate before the TV cameras into ghastly freak shows, courtesy of newsmen seeking "human interest" material and gender benders who think the mental health of uptight straight viewers is improved by visual shock therapy.' The authors of the book are firmly of the opinion that we should tone down and start playing the game by straight rules if we want to attain equality. The whole book is geared towards promoting positive propaganda that will get the population at large on our side; and that means conventional, non-frightening imagery.

This would be heresy to the activists of OutRage, Queer Nation, the Sisters of Perpetual Indulgence and so on. But it is a question which becomes more pressing as the media embargo on our activities is lifted and our lives are scrutinised as never before. It could be argued, of course, that the tabloids are incorrigible and however nobly we behave they would make a scandal out of it. But the broadsheets and TV companies are, on the whole, prepared to give us a fair hearing. We can't escape the fact that Mr and Mrs Ordinary out there depend on the media for their information about and images of lesbians and gay men. Like it or not, we need them on our side if we are to get the legal and social reforms that are rightly ours. Do we go the American way and pragmatically tone it down while in public, or do we continue on our unfettered way and bugger the PR?

The lack of interest in Gay Pride resumed the following year when there was no shadow to cast over it. One reader of *Gay Times* was so frustrated by this calculated neglect that he wrote to the editors of the Sunday broadsheets asking why they had decided to downplay the event. Only one editor, Ian Jack of *The Independent on Sunday*, replied:

> Perhaps we should have carried a report on the Lesbian and Gay Pride march and perhaps newspapers need to think about what their definition of news is. In the conventional definition of news – the surprising, the unexpected – the Gay Pride march is no more or less interesting than Trooping the Colour.

Public perceptions

So, what about public perceptions? Has this changing view of gay people in the media had any effect upon the way a generally homophobic society regards its gay citizens? Maureen Freely, a straight woman, gave her opinion in *The Guardian* in August 1994:

A decade on we can see a shift in attitude that could be mistaken for progress. In the still very mistrustful public eye, gays and lesbians are no longer just deviants and eccentrics, but also political activists. Despite all the sound-bytes about their pathological way of life, they have been seen to look after their own. This grudging respect can be measured in silences. The tabloids might get maximum mileage out of a gay serial killer, but you do not often open up a paper and see the Terrence Higgins Trust accused of behaving irresponsibly . . . Outside, over there on the fringes of medialand, muscular gays are joining hands with chic lesbians to march from strength to strength. Meanwhile, on the other side of the television screen, they live in urban ghettos. And they keep a low profile at work. And learn to lie on a need-not-to-know basis – even if this means smirking appreciatively when their own parents dismiss the case of Torch Song Trilogy as a bunch of nancies.[8]

Progress has certainly been seen in broadsheet newspapers and on television, but it has been less evident elsewhere. The US magazine *Time* reported on the state of play after twenty-five years of gay liberation. An opinion poll it conducted showed that 65 per cent of Americans thought gay rights were 'paid too much attention'. It also worryingly found that the 53 per cent who described homosexuality as morally wrong made up the same proportion as in a poll in 1978. The magazine concluded:

If the view over the past quarter century suggests that gay progress is inevitable, the picture today suggests that gays may be, as their opponents argue, a unique case rather than just another minority group. Far from continuing towards inclusion, gays may already be bumping up against the limits of tolerance.[9]

Responses to TV portrayal

From the very first mentions of homosexuality on radio and TV there has been a consistent hostility to its portrayal in broadcast media. In 1992 the Broadcasting Standards Council commissioned a report[10] to find out what the public 'really' thought about the presentation of sex in TV programmes. The survey asked 1049 adults a series of questions about the portrayal of homosexuality. To the statement 'I would find it embarrassing to watch homosexual sex scenes with some of the people with whom I watch TV', 71 per cent agreed. To the question 'Programmes and films about gays and lesbians should be banned' 39 per cent agreed, while 61 per cent disagreed. Similarly, 38 per cent thought 'Gay characters should not be shown on television at all' while 62 per cent disagreed. Two-thirds of the sample thought that children should not see programmes with gay characters, while 79 per cent thought that 'Homosexual scenes should only be shown after 10pm'.

The Broadcasting Standards Council also consulted gay people about how *they* thought homosexuality should be shown on television. The people chosen for this research were those whose opinions were not usually canvassed (e.g. 'non-activists'). The Council found:

> The homosexual respondents were more interested in the way in which sexuality was 'packaged' by television rather than by the way in which sexual acts were portrayed. They felt it was important that homosexuality was presented in the same way as was heterosexuality and that the characters who were homosexuals were not seen in stereotypical roles (as in comedy). They stressed that television programming should show that homosexuals were people who had a particular sexual preference. Through such characterisations, they felt they could remove their defensive stance in society and be more honest in their feelings and sexuality.

Lesbians felt particularly hard done by and complained that they were treated less well in TV than gay men. Their sexual preferences were, they said, either ignored or included for titillation. Gay people felt that TV has a dual responsibility: to change the perceptions of ignorant and hostile heterosexuals and also to provide entertainment and information targeted specifically at its gay viewers.

In January 1994 the Broadcasting Standards Council published another report analysing two weeks' television viewing in May and September 1993. It found that 'homosexual characters are far less evident on television than in the general population' with only 0.03 per cent of characters in TV drama shown during that period being 'obviously lesbian or homosexual with male homosexuals far outnumbering lesbians'.[11] Even so, there are very few editions of the Broadcasting Standards Council monthly bulletin that don't contain several complaints about gay images on TV. It seems that even the mildest and least offensive references upset some people to the extent that they feel the need to oppose them actively. To the Council's credit, these complaints are very rarely upheld.

There is no doubt that as the struggle for gay rights continues and attains an ever-higher profile, opposition will grow accordingly. But active opposition – rather than indifference – seems to be coming from well-defined sources: fundamentalist religions, authoritarian parliamentarians and tabloid newspapers. (Even in 1994, Garry Bushell was still trying to get positive images of lesbians banned from *EastEnders*. 'Ditch the dykes and let us have an EastEnders knees-up!' he wrote,[12] implying that the lesbian story line was proof that the soap opera was depressing and pessimistic and unrepresentative of 'real life'.)

Away from the way-out churches, the Tory back benches, Fortress Wapping and a few neo-Nazi groups, organized opposition seems to have given way to tolerance and a reluctance to discriminate. The gay struggle as portrayed by the media may have changed some minds in the past decade, but I am not sure how many hearts have been won. Significantly, the hearts of many popular journalists – who consider themselves to be the only true spokespeople of the country at large – remain stony and cold.

Notes

1.   *Gay Times*, August 1993.
2.   20 June 1993.
3.   17 June 1993.

4.   20 June 1993.
5.   24 June 1993.
6.   20 June 1993.
7.   M. Kirk and H. Madsen, *After the Ball – How America will conquer its fear and hatred of gays in the 90s* (Plume, 1992).
8.   11 August 1994.
9.   27 June 1994.
10.   A. M. Hargrave, *Sex and Sexuality in Broadcasting* (BSC/John Libbey, 1992).
11.   As reported in *The Daily Telegraph*, 27 January 1994.
12.   30 August 1994.

Index